Full Preterism—
Ignored but Fulfilled

Full Preterism—
Ignored but Fulfilled

How the Church Missed the End of the World

WILLIAM JOHN RANKINE TAYLOR

WIPF & STOCK · Eugene, Oregon

FULL PRETERISM—IGNORED BUT FULFILLED
How the Church Missed the End of the World

Copyright © 2025 William John Rankine Taylor. All rights reserved. Except for brief quotations in critical publications or reviews, no part of this book may be reproduced in any manner without prior written permission from the publisher. Write: Permissions, Wipf and Stock Publishers, 199 W. 8th Ave., Suite 3, Eugene, OR 97401.

Wipf & Stock
An Imprint of Wipf and Stock Publishers
199 W. 8th Ave., Suite 3
Eugene, OR 97401

www.wipfandstock.com

PAPERBACK ISBN: 979-8-3852-4335-8
HARDCOVER ISBN: 979-8-3852-4336-5
EBOOK ISBN: 979-8-3852-4337-2

VERSION NUMBER 05/20/25

Unless otherwise indicated, Scripture quotations are from the King James Version of the Bible, which is in the public domain.

Quotations from the Septuagint (LXX) are from Alfred Rahlfs, ed., *Septuaginta: Id est Vetus Testamentum Graece iuxta LXX interpretes*, 2 vols. (Stuttgart: Deutsche Bibelgesellschaft, 1935).

For my mother, whose love preserves me through every tribulation

Contents

Acknowledgments | ix
Abbreviations | xi
Introduction | xiii

Section 1: Historical and Theological Foundations | 1

1. The Hellenization of the Early Church | 3
2. The Early Church Fathers: Humanity, Nuance, and Eschatological Expectations | 14
3. The Errors and Evils of the Church: A Lukewarm Legacy | 24
4. Rationalism and the Decline of the Mystical | 30
5. Addressing the Critique of Over-Spiritualizing | 43

Section 2: Key Full Preterist Interpretations of Prophecies | 47

6. Mystery Babylon Was Old-Covenant Israel | 49
7. The End of the Age (*Olam haZeh*) | 55
8. The Mark of the Beast and 666 | 67
9. The Sun, Moon, and Stars | 75
10. The Identity of Beasts: Sea, Scarlet, and Land | 79
11. The Two Witnesses of Revelation 11 | 88
12. Every Eye Will See Him | 94
13. Wipe Away Every Tear | 99
14. No More Sea, New Heaven and New Earth | 106
15. The Millennial Reign Explained | 110

16 The Martyrs in Revelation | 117
17 Feast Fulfillment | 123
18 The Age of Harvest | 128
19 The Great White Throne Judgment | 133
20 The Timing and Nature of the Resurrection | 138
21 The Return of Our Lord Jesus Christ with His Kingdom | 145
22 The Dating of Revelation | 151
23 Yes, But... | 162

Section 3: Implications and "What's Next" for Full Preterism | 167
24 The Void and Reorientation | 169
25 God's Will in a New Era | 173
26 Spiritual Rebirth and Nicodemus | 178
27 Sin and Evil in Society | 185
28 The Christian Worldview vs. Ideology | 195
29 A Critique of Israel-Only Theology | 199
30 Our Eternal Story | 209

Appendix A: 101 Statements of Imminency | 223
Appendix B: The Lukewarm Legacy | 229
References | 237

Acknowledgments

To MY LATE FATHER and brother, whose memories guide me every day and inspire me to pursue truth with conviction and humility.

I would like to extend heartfelt gratitude to Don K. Preston, whose scholarship and passion for eschatology have been a source of both knowledge and inspiration. His work has challenged me to think deeply and approach these topics with intellectual rigor and integrity.

To my YouTube subscribers and online community—your questions, encouragement, and engagement have shaped this journey in ways I could never have imagined. You remind me daily that theology is not just a pursuit of the mind but a dialogue of the heart.

Finally, to all who dare to ask difficult questions and to those brave enough to seek answers—this book is for you.

Abbreviations

AGJU	Arbeiten zur Geschichte des antiken Judentums und des Urchristentums
APOT	*The Apocrypha and Pseudepigrapha of the Old Testament.* Edited by Robert H. Charles. 2 vols. Oxford: Clarendon, 1913 [Note: This originally had listed only vol. 2]
BECNT	Baker Exegetical Commentary on the New Testament
BETL	Bibliotheca Ephemeridum Theologicarum Lovaniensium
Bib	*Biblica*
BSac	*Bibliotheca Sacra*
ConcC	Concordia Commentary
CNT	Commentaire du Nouveau Testament
HTR	*Harvard Theological Review*
IO	Israel only
LCL	Loeb Classical Library
NDE	Near-death experience
Neot	*Neotestamentica*
NIBCNT	New International Biblical Commentary on the New Testament
NICNT	New International Commentary on the New Testament
NIGTC	New International Greek Testament Commentary
NovT	*Novum Testamentum*
NTS	*New Testament Studies*
SPCK	Society for Promoting Christian Knowledge

Abbreviations

VCSup	Vigiliae Christianae Supplements
WBC	Word Biblical Commentary
WTJ	*Westminster Theological Journal*

Introduction

ESCHATOLOGY IS THE FINAL frontier of theology—the place where our deepest beliefs about the end of history collide with our daily lives. It's not merely an abstract theological concept tucked away in scholarly debates. No, eschatology reaches into every corner of our existence, dictating everything from the way we structure our households to the shape of our societies, even influencing global foreign policies. In many ways, it's the fault line running beneath our worldviews, subtly shifting our understanding of life's meaning, purpose, and ultimate destiny.

At its core, eschatology is about how we interpret the future—what's next for humanity and the cosmos. But it's more than that. It's the lens through which we filter hope, fear, and the very purpose of existence. From political leaders to religious communities, the apocalyptic question—"What will happen at the end of all things?"—can shape not just personal devotion but the course of entire nations. Like a slow-burning fire at the world's edge, eschatology ignites passions and anxieties, casting long shadows across history, philosophy, and culture. Whether we realize it or not, we are all participants in this drama, living under the weight of a future that many believe has already been written.

One of the most iconic scenes of eschatological significance comes from the fall of Jerusalem in AD 70. The destruction of Herod's Temple, the epicenter of Jewish worship and national identity, marked more than just the fall of a city; it signaled the dissolution of an entire world order. As the temple's stones crumbled under the weight of the Roman siege, some early Christians saw in it the fulfillment of prophecy. The symbolic and literal toppling of Herod's grand architectural marvel sent ripples through the theological landscape, challenging those believers to reconsider their understanding of divine judgment, the resurrection, and the second coming of Christ. However, the institutional church that developed post–AD 70 largely overlooked this perspective, instead fostering ongoing anticipation of these eschatological events in the future.

To understand the profound implications of full preterism, we must ground our exploration in key historical and theological moments. The Second Temple, enhanced under Herod's reign, represented more than national pride; it was a focal point of Jewish hopes for redemption. Yet, its destruction in AD 70 marked a pivotal shift—not merely a historical tragedy but a cornerstone in Christian eschatological thought. In the full preterist view, this event, among others, aligns with the fulfillment of biblical prophecies concerning judgment, renewal, and divine presence. Here, the anticipated second coming of Christ, often envisioned as a future apocalyptic event, is reinterpreted as a divine intervention already realized in the first century, transforming the resurrection into a present reality within this new framework.

THE THREE SECTIONS

This book is divided into three key sections, each designed to confront the most urgent questions surrounding eschatology and, specifically, full preterism.

Historical and Theological Foundations

The first section dives headfirst into the origins of full preterism, asking a critical question: Why wasn't this view embraced immediately by the early church? Was it buried under the weight of Hellenistic thought, or was it sidelined by other pressing theological concerns? This section will shed light on the complex interplay between early Christian eschatology and the philosophical currents of the time, inviting you to reconsider what might have shaped the trajectory of our beliefs. We will confront the unsettling reality of how theological shifts impacted the understanding of prophecy, particularly through the lens of Second Temple Judaism, and why recovering this view matters.

Introduction

Key Preterist Interpretations of Prophecies

Moving beyond the past, the second section takes us into the heart of prophetic literature. This is where full preterism cuts through the noise of future speculation, offering clarity to what many believe are still-looming events. But are they? This section will challenge you to see prophecy as something not meant for a far-off future but for a past already fulfilled. Why does this matter? Because the implications are seismic. By reexamining prophecies through the lens of full preterism, we will address how shedding light on these texts could reshape everything you thought you knew about the end times, eternity, and the divine plan.

Implications and "What's Next?" for Full Preterism

Finally, we turn to the present and future. What does full preterism mean for us today? What's the practical relevance of accepting that all prophecies have already been fulfilled? This is where the stakes become personal. If we are no longer waiting for a future apocalypse, how does that change the way we live, worship, and engage with the world? The third section will explore the transformative power of living post-apocalypse, and why understanding this might just alter your spiritual journey forever. The "what's next" isn't about awaiting some cosmic event but about finding profound significance in the here and now, in the light of a fulfilled prophecy.

ESCHATOLOGICAL PERSPECTIVES

To help frame these discussions, this book presents a list of key eschatological perspectives, representing the major lenses through which people interpret biblical prophecy. These perspectives range from the widely popular to the historically sidelined, and by the end, you may find yourself seeing these timelines in a new light:

Futurism

The belief that most biblical prophecies, including the second coming and final judgment, are yet to be fulfilled.

Introduction

Full Preterism

This view holds that all biblical prophecies, including the second coming, were fulfilled by AD 70, particularly with the destruction of Jerusalem.

Partial Preterism

The belief that some prophecies were fulfilled in the first century, but others, such as the second coming, remain in the future.

Historicism

The interpretation that biblical prophecies are fulfilled progressively throughout history, linking specific historical events to prophetic texts.

Idealism

The belief that prophecies are symbolic, revealing timeless spiritual truths rather than specific historical events.

Amillennialism

The view that the "millennium" in Revelation is symbolic of Christ's present reign from heaven through the Church.

Postmillennialism

The belief that Christ's return will follow a "golden age" of Christian prosperity and righteousness on earth.

Premillennialism

The view that Christ will return before a literal thousand-year reign on earth, during which he will establish his kingdom.

Introduction

THE TONE

This book is written with a pop theology approach, ensuring accessibility while maintaining scholarly referencing for academic rigor. All references are included in a references section at the back of the book, allowing you to further explore the scholarly sources behind these insights. While the book invites deep reflection, it remains grounded in a conversational style, making the complex comprehensible.

A bit about myself: I am both a teacher and a counselor specializing in addiction and stress-related mental health. My academic journey includes a PGDE, PGCert in alcohol and drugs studies, an honors degree in sociology with a thesis on religious mobility in Scotland, and a master's degree in psychology, which I completed with distinction. These credentials, along with my experience in counseling, shape my approach to theology, spirituality, and the human experience.

While I argue strongly for full preterism in this book, I want to make two things clear: this is not a theology test, and I am not an inquisitor. I do not condemn those who see things differently, and I urge us to resist the temptation to be cruel to others for holding different views. This book is an invitation—a challenge perhaps—to consider a perspective that offers profound explanatory power for the interpretation of prophecy and Scripture.

My choice not to capitalize "full preterism" reflects a deeply held conviction: theology, while important, is not the ultimate measure of our worth. We are judged by our actions, our character, and how we live out our beliefs—not by the precision of our eschatological timelines.

SECTION 1

Historical and Theological Foundations

OUR JOURNEY BEGINS IN the deep vaults of history, a place where ideas are preserved but often buried beneath layers of time, theology, and tradition. Venturing here is like stepping into an ancient tomb where each corner hides relics of belief—treasures guarded by doctrines long defended yet fraught with the dangers of challenging orthodoxy. To critique the early church's eschatology is to trigger booby traps of reactionary critique, where even a glimmer of revision is enough to summon cries of heresy. But within this labyrinth lies a rich tapestry: the resurrection hope that sustained early believers, the transmission of ideas through generations, and the cultural confluence that shaped Christian theology. We will uncover the influences of Greek thought, early Jewish apocalyptic visions, and later Enlightenment rationalism, all of which melded to form an intricate eschatological landscape. As we dig deeper, we also expose the limitations of the church as a human institution, often constrained by bureaucracy, social currents, and political forces. This excavation reveals why the early church might have missed the full significance of Christ's return, setting the stage for a full preterist perspective that reinterprets these ancient and formidable foundations. It is a journey both daring and necessary, revealing how a faith built upon historical moments has evolved and, at times, obscured its own origins.

1

The Hellenization of the Early Church

Christianity was born inside the womb of Hellenism.
—RICARDO DUCHESNE, HISTORICAL SOCIOLOGIST

THE AFTERMATH OF AD 70: SCATTERED FRAGMENTS OF FAITH

As THE FINAL CINDERS of Herodian ash dissolved into the air in AD 70, Roman forces under General Titus caught their breath in the thick air of a world remade—a world heavy with the scent of stone and scorched earth, tinged with the blood and fire of judgment. It was clear then that the spiritual landscape—and its boundaries—had shifted as profoundly as the physical.

During the chaos of Jerusalem's fall, believers were urged to flee to the mountains and hide in caves (Luke 21:21). It was a desperate escape from the physical destruction, but it also marked the beginning of a spiritual retreat. In many ways, some of us have remained in those metaphorical caves ever since, shrouded in the darkness of incomplete or distorted interpretations, afraid to step into the light of the Spirit that reveals the true, undivided message of Christ.

The aftermath of AD 70 scattered not only people but also ideas. The early church, fragmented and dispersed, found itself surrounded by the towering intellectual peaks of Greek philosophy. Gentile converts, influenced by these towering ideas, reshaped the teachings they received, filling in gaps with their own cultural understandings. This was not the fault of the gentiles alone; the times were turbulent, and the church, like a ship without a compass, drifted wherever the cultural currents pulled it. But as they rebuilt, they often used stone and mortar foreign to the foundation Christ had laid.

DISPELLING THE MYTH OF A PURE, ORIGINAL CHURCH

Before delving deeper, we must dispel the myth of an unblemished, pure church at the start. There was never a golden age of perfect unity and clarity. This is evident throughout the New Testament, where the apostles themselves are portrayed as struggling to grasp Jesus's teachings (e.g., Mark 9:32). Scholars like Jevons (2011) and Martens (2015) have shown that the early Christian communities were a melting pot of beliefs and practices, much like today's diverse theological landscape—ranging from creationist museums in the USA to the pope's endorsement of evolutionary theory in Vatican City; from Calvinism to Wesleyanism, and from various end-times perspectives like amillennialism, postmillennialism, and preterism. The first-century church was no different—a bewildering swirl of doctrines and interpretations, each vying for dominance, like voices shouting over one another in a busy market square.

This diversity isn't a flaw but rather a feature of the faith, reflecting the dynamic nature of its context. Early Christianity felt like riding through New York City with your head out of a cab window, each neighborhood—Chinese, Italian, Jewish, Irish—blasting its own unique sounds and scents. Just as the city's cacophony is overwhelming yet vibrant, so too was the spiritual atmosphere in which the early church was born: a tumultuous fusion of Jewish tradition, Greek philosophy, and Roman pragmatism, all intermingling in the bustling urban centers of the ancient world.

THE APOSTOLIC STRUGGLE AND HUMAN ERROR

It should come as no surprise then, that Jesus himself did not have a flawless discipleship. His followers often misunderstood his teachings, as seen in their confusion over the resurrection (Luke 24:25–27) or their disputes over status (Mark 9:34). They fell asleep in Gethsemane, quarreled over who would be the greatest, and Peter even openly rebuked Jesus, earning a sharp rebuke in return. Despite their profound transformations, they were never able to completely shed their humanity or the cultural baggage they carried. Paul, for example, grappled with the desire to depart this world but understood that his work lay in this hellenized context, reaching people where they were—in their time, in their place (Phil 1:23–24).

PAUL AND THE GREEK WORLD: STYLIZING THE MESSAGE

In Athens, Paul's strategy was masterful. By quoting Aratus's poem "Phaenomena"—"For we are his offspring" (Acts 17:28)—Paul repurposed a line originally about Zeus to speak of humanity's connection to the Christian God. It was a deft move, acknowledging and reinterpreting the philosophical currents of his day to build bridges between Greek thought and Christian revelation (Beyer 2024, 453, 460–61). Aratus, a Stoic favorite, resonated with themes of a rational, orderly cosmos governed by divine law—concepts that the Stoics cherished and that Paul could use to communicate his message in a familiar language (Sider 2005, 40–42). His fields of harvest were thick with gnostics, Stoics, Platonists, hedonists, and cultists—Greek ideas were not merely in the air; they were the nutrients in the soil of his mission.

We might bristle at the idea of inserting pagan verbiage into the sacred text, but Paul understood that the seeds of faith would take root more easily if the soil was tilled with concepts familiar to his audience. The harvester must make contact with the earth, after all. In the same way, Paul used his humanity to relate to the people; he used the cultural touchstones of his time to connect with them. So, let's put the plow to the ground and dig deeper into these Greek ideas—ideas that have left an indelible mark on the tapestry of early Christianity.

Now, let's traverse this bustling theological metropolis. Imagine driving through the ancient world like a New York City cab, head out the window, the cultural chaos of the first century swirling around you: Greek temples on one corner, Roman statues on another, and, just a few blocks away, the synagogue with its stern-faced scholars debating Torah. It was in this dizzying mix that the early church tried to find its voice. We're here to uncover how these diverse and often conflicting philosophies shaped the faith we know today.

Section 1: Historical and Theological Foundations

HELLENISTIC INFLUENCES ON CHRISTIAN THEOLOGY

Despite its Hebrew roots, the early Christian movement was significantly shaped by Hellenistic thought. Alexander the Great's conquests spread Greek culture and language across the Near East, including Judea, where Hellenistic influence persisted even under Roman rule. This influence was not merely superficial; it penetrated the very fabric of Jewish religious thought and practice. The earliest Christians, being primarily Jewish, operated within this hellenized context, but as the faith spread to gentile regions, the integration of Greek cultural and philosophical ideas became even more pronounced (Fisher 2024, 248–61).

With the influx of gentile converts came a corresponding infusion of Greek theological concerns. The early church fathers, eager to communicate their faith to a Greek-speaking audience, often found themselves adopting and adapting Hellenistic frameworks to express Christian doctrines. This process was not merely a passive adoption but a strategic engagement, as seen in the works of thinkers like Philo of Alexandria (20 BC—AD 50), who synthesized Greek philosophy and Jewish theology. For example, Philo reinterpreted the Jewish Scriptures through a Platonic lens, portraying God as an abstract, transcendent being whose nature could not be grasped by human reason—a concept that was foreign to the relational God depicted in the Hebrew Bible (Fisher 2024, 256).

This hellenization process is perhaps most vividly illustrated in the Letter of Aristeas, a second-century BCE document that aimed to legitimize Judaism in the eyes of the Hellenistic world. The letter recounts the translation of the Hebrew Scriptures into Greek—the Septuagint—under the auspices of the Egyptian king, and it portrays this translation as an effort to bridge the cultural divide between Jews and Greeks. In this text, the God of Israel is equated with Zeus, demonstrating an attempt to make Jewish religion more palatable to Greek sensibilities: "They worship the same God—the Lord and Creator of the Universe, as all other men, as we ourselves, O king, though we call him by different names, such as Zeus or Dis" (*APOT* 2:26). This strategic alignment laid the groundwork for the later assimilation of Christian theology into Hellenistic philosophical systems.

THE SHIFT AFTER AD 70: FROM JEWISH TO GENTILE CHRISTIANITY

The destruction of Jerusalem in AD 70, which led to the demise of the Jewish Christian leadership, further accelerated the shift towards a gentile-dominated Christianity. As the movement's center of gravity moved away from Judea, it became increasingly shaped by Greek philosophical ideas. The integration of these ideas into Christian theology was not merely incidental; it was a deliberate effort to make the faith comprehensible and attractive to a Hellenistic audience. This effort is evident in the works of early Christian apologists and theologians who often claimed that Greek philosophers had borrowed their ideas from Moses. For instance, Eusebius, in his *Preparation for the Gospel*, cites the philosopher Numenius of Apamea's assertion that "What else is Plato than Moses speaking Attic Greek?" (Eusebius of Caesarea 1903, 533), suggesting that Greek philosophy was, in essence, a derivative of earlier Jewish thought (Van Kooten et al. 2015, 239–40, 247).

PLATONIC, NEOPLATONIC, AND STOIC INFLUENCES

Platonic Thought: The Influence of the Forms

Plato's philosophy, particularly his theory of Forms, posited that the material world is merely a shadow of a higher, perfect reality. This perspective had a profound impact on early Christian thought, but rather than fostering a focus on the true spiritual essence of faith, it led to a distortion. By categorizing the material world as inherently inferior, Platonic thought encouraged early theologians to view physical existence not just as a lesser reality but as something to be transcended through intellectual and philosophical pursuit.

This led to a form of Christianity that, instead of emphasizing the spiritual presence and transformation described in the New Testament, became fixated on the soul's separation from the body and its journey to a nonmaterial realm. For instance, Plato's allegory of the cave, which illustrates the soul's ascent from darkness (ignorance) to light (truth), was adopted by early Christians to depict the journey of the believer (Lane 2012, 77). However, this allegory also introduced a dualistic mindset that prioritized abstract understanding over the relational, dynamic faith seen in the teachings of Jesus.

The focus on escaping the material realm to achieve a higher spiritual state inadvertently laid the groundwork for a hierarchical view of salvation. This view often clashed with the New Testament's emphasis on the immediacy of the kingdom of God and the accessibility of divine truth to all believers, regardless of their intellectual prowess or philosophical training. Consequently, Platonic thought, rather than enriching Christian spirituality, diverted it into a complex web of philosophical distinctions that overshadowed the simplicity and directness of the original Christian message (Fisher 2024, 102; Van Kooten et al. 2015, 240).

Neoplatonic Thought: The Hierarchical Cosmos

Neoplatonism, while emphasizing the ascent of the soul and the immaterial nature of the divine, paradoxically contributed to a theological model that obscured the early Christian emphasis on spiritual realities. By positing a hierarchical cosmos where the material world was a distant emanation from the divine source, Neoplatonism reinforced the notion that physical reality was inferior but still significant as a means to understand spiritual truths. This led to an overemphasis on metaphysical constructs and a complex hierarchy of being, which often drew attention away from the New Testament's focus on the unseen, inner transformation and the mystical nature of the kingdom of God (Fisher 2024, 88; Van Kooten et al. 2015, 242).

In Neoplatonic thought, the concept of the *Great Chain of Being* became prominent, describing a hierarchical structure of all entities from the lowest forms of matter to the highest divine principle, the One. This system encouraged theologians to speculate on the exact nature and ordering of spiritual and material entities, such as angels, demons, and the soul's progression through various metaphysical stages. Such speculation often drew focus away from the New Testament's emphasis on the immediate, transformative experience of faith and the inward renewal of the believer.

For instance, the intricate discussions on the nature and levels of the soul in Neoplatonism shifted attention towards understanding one's place in a cosmic hierarchy rather than focusing on personal, spiritual transformation and communion with God in the present. This shift in focus can be seen in the early Christian theological debates over the precise nature of Christ's divinity and the metaphysical distinctions between the persons of the Trinity, which, while important, often overshadowed the simpler, yet profound, teachings of Jesus on living in the Spirit and the mystical aspects of the kingdom of God (e.g., "the Kingdom of God is within you" [Luke 17:21]).

Stoic Thought: Logos and the Order of the Cosmos

Stoicism, with its emphasis on rational order and the unity of all things, also left a significant mark on early Christian theology. The Stoic concept of Logos as the rational principle that governs the universe found a natural resonance with the Johannine depiction of Christ as the Logos incarnate. Additionally, Paul's use of Stoic metaphysical language, particularly his deployment of prepositions like "from," "through," and "into" to describe God's relationship with creation, reflects his engagement with Stoic cosmology. Gregory Sterling notes Paul's use of a Greek prepositional metaphysics to articulate the fate of the cosmos and individuals within the providential plan of God, framing the entire universe's destiny as rooted in God's creative and redemptive action (Van Kooten et al. 2015, 241).

Paul's adaptation of Hellenistic rhetorical and philosophical techniques is also evident in his reinterpretation of Jewish Scriptures for a Greek audience. For instance, in his Letters to the Corinthians, Paul reinterprets Hosea's depiction of Hades and death—not as instruments of God's wrath but as conquered foes, illustrating Christ's triumph over the grave. This reimagining aligns Christ with heroic figures from Greek mythology, such as Hercules, who descended into the underworld to rescue the dead. Such parallels would have been compelling to a hellenized audience, highlighting the cosmic victory of Christ in terms familiar to them (Van Kooten et al. 2015, 243).

GREEK INFLUENCE ON NEW TESTAMENT ESCHATOLOGY

Early Christian eschatology, as found in the writings of Matthew, Luke, Peter, and Paul, reveals a remarkable synthesis of Greek philosophical concepts with Jewish apocalyptic thought (Van Kooten et al. 2015, 239–40). This fusion of ideas was once dynamic, complex, and deeply reflective of the Hellenistic world in which Christianity emerged. However, as these concepts became foundational to Christian eschatological doctrine, their Greek origins were gradually obscured, and what was once a vibrant, multifaceted approach became more rigidly codified in later Christian tradition. Here, we explore the Greek influence on key New Testament eschatological ideas, examining how these concepts—initially foreign to Jewish thought—were adapted by early Christian writers and later solidified into the structures we recognize today.

The Gospel of Matthew incorporates Greek eschatological terminology, notably in its reference to the "rebirth" or *palingenesia* (παλιγγενεσία). In Matt 19:28, Jesus speaks of the rebirth of the world when the Son of Man will sit on his glorious throne. The term *palingenesia*, rooted in Greek Stoic and Platonic philosophy, was used to describe a cyclical renewal of the cosmos after its destruction. For instance, Stoics envisioned the universe undergoing periodic cycles of destruction by fire (the *ekpyrosis*) and subsequent regeneration, a process that repeated eternally (Long 2002, 44). This idea of cosmic renewal was not native to Jewish eschatology, which typically focused on linear time and the ultimate fulfillment of God's promises at the end of history (Collins 1998, 53).

Matthew's use of *palingenesia* reflects a Hellenistic influence in which cosmic renewal, once a Greek philosophical concept, is reimagined within a Jewish apocalyptic framework. The incorporation of this term highlights the syncretic nature of early Christian eschatology, blending Greek and Jewish elements to articulate the eschatological transformation of the world.

Similarly, Luke employs the term ἀποκατάστασις (*apokatastasis*), another Stoic concept that implies the restoration of all things. In Acts 3:21, Peter declares that heaven must receive Christ until the time comes for God to restore everything (ἀποκατάστασις), a term laden with Greek philosophical meaning. For the Stoics, *apokatastasis* referred to the cosmic restoration that occurred after the universe's periodic destruction by fire (Lapidge 1978, 183–84). This cyclical cosmology contrasted with Jewish eschatology, where the focus was often on the restoration of Israel and the final consummation of history.

Luke's eschatological vision, while grounded in Jewish prophecy, reflects a broader cosmic scope, one more at home in Greek philosophical traditions. By adopting the term ἀποκατάστασις, Luke introduces a universal element into Christian eschatology, suggesting a restoration not only of Israel but of the entire cosmos. This Greek influence was later taken up by Origen of Alexandria, who used the concept of *apokatastasis* to develop his doctrine of universal restoration, where all creation, including the damned, would eventually be restored to communion with God (Daley 2002, 48).

The Hellenization of the Early Church

In 2 Pet 3:10–12, the apostle describes the destruction of the heavens and the elements by fire: "But the day of the Lord will come like a thief... the elements will be destroyed by fire, and the earth and everything done in it will be laid bare." This apocalyptic imagery bears a striking resemblance to the Stoic doctrine of *ekpyrosis*, where the universe undergoes a purifying conflagration before being reborn (Reydams-Schils 2003, 135). While Jewish apocalyptic literature, such as Daniel and 1 Enoch, often depicted divine judgment through cataclysmic events, the idea of cosmic fire dissolving the elements and preparing them for renewal is distinctively Stoic.

Peter's eschatology reflects an early Christian engagement with Greek philosophical concepts, showing how the Hellenistic worldview was integrated into Christian thought. The Stoic vision of the universe's cyclical destruction and renewal provided a schema that helped Christian writers articulate the final transformation of creation.

The apostle Paul's eschatology provides perhaps the clearest example of Greek philosophical influence. In 1 Cor 7:31, Paul states that "the form of this world is passing away" (παράγει γὰρ τὸ σχῆμα τοῦ κόσμου τούτου), a phrase that mirrors the Stoic concept of the form of the cosmos undergoing cyclical change (Engberg-Pedersen 2000, 155). Paul's eschatology envisions a cosmic transformation akin to Stoic cosmology, where the universe is periodically regenerated.

Moreover, Paul's discussion of the spiritual body (σῶμα πνευματικόν) in the resurrection (1 Cor 15:44) reflects Greek notions of the body and soul. While Jewish resurrection theology often emphasized the physical resurrection of the body (as seen in 2 Maccabees), Paul's description of the resurrected body as spiritual suggests a synthesis of Jewish eschatology and Greek spiritualism. According to Stoic thought, after the final conflagration, the body becomes fully spiritualized, identical with the divine Reason (Lapidge 1978, 183–84). Paul's eschatology, while rooted in Jewish traditions, clearly incorporates these Greek elements to describe the transformation of the cosmos and the resurrected body.

Additionally, Paul's use of the term *parousia* (παρουσία), meaning "arrival" or "presence," echoes Hellenistic political and religious language. In Greek culture, "parousia" was used to describe the arrival of a king or deity, particularly Caesar (Wright 2013, 1415–20). Paul redefines this term in Phil 2:10–11, applying it to the second coming of Christ: "At the name of Jesus, every knee will bow, in heaven and on earth and under the earth, and every tongue confess that Jesus Christ is Lord." By adapting this Greek political concept, Paul subverts the imperial imagery and reaffirms Christ as the cosmic ruler, emphasizing that Jesus, not Caesar, is the true Lord. This use of Greek political terminology highlights Paul's ability to merge Jewish and Greek ideas to express Christian eschatological hopes.

The eschatological elements found in Matthew, Luke, Peter, and Paul reveal a remarkable fusion of Greek and Jewish thought. Concepts such as *palingenesia, apokatastasis,* and the conflagration—while foreign to Jewish apocalyptic traditions—were seamlessly integrated into the early Christian understanding of the end-time. These Greek ideas provided early Christian writers with a cosmological framework through which they could articulate their eschatological vision, combining the linear expectations of Jewish thought with the cyclical cosmology of Greek philosophy.

As these ideas became more embedded in Christian doctrine, they were codified and often stripped of their Greek origins. What was once an exotic blend of Jewish and Greek thought became the foundation for Christian eschatology, with little recognition of the Hellenistic influence. Today's mainstream Christian eschatology presents these concepts as purely Christian or Judeo-Christian, but a closer examination reveals their Greek roots and the fluidity with which early Christian writers borrowed from Hellenistic philosophy to express their eschatological beliefs.

THE SHIFT TO A MORE MATERIAL THEOLOGY

While rejecting certain Platonic ideas, early Christian thinkers retained Hellenistic cosmology and metaphysics. While Christianity denied the inherent immortality of the soul without divine intervention, it nonetheless accepted the idea that matter could be sanctified. This concept, which sought to strike a balance between Platonic dualism and the radical gnostic rejection of the material world, proposed that matter, though created, could participate in the divine if renewed or resurrected. This theological position laid the groundwork for a more literal expectation of a physical resurrection and a material eschatology, where the renewed creation would reflect God's ultimate purposes (Wright 2008, 154).

The early church fathers' struggle to articulate the relationship between the spiritual and material worlds also shaped their views on the resurrection. Their emphasis on bodily resurrection, though a departure from Platonic dualism, reflected deeper Hellenistic influences. By asserting that the material world, though fallen, could be redeemed and sanctified, they sought to counter both Platonic and gnostic extremes. However, this position inadvertently led to a more materialistic interpretation of eschatological hope, focusing on the restoration of the physical body and the created order, rather than a purely spiritual fulfillment (Scroggs 1968, 276).

While Hellenism provided a philosophical framework that facilitated the spread of Christianity among gentiles, it also introduced elements that fundamentally altered the nature of Christian theology. The metaphysical hierarchies of Neoplatonism and the cosmic order of Stoicism contributed to a theology that integrated both spiritual and material dimensions. This synthesis often led to an overemphasis on the material aspects of eschatological hope, such as the expectation of a renewed physical world, rather than the more mystical and spiritual realities emphasized in the New Testament.

THE CHALLENGE OF SPIRITUAL REALITIES

In 2 Cor 4:18, Paul exhorts believers to "fix our eyes not on what is seen, but on what is unseen, since what is seen is temporary, but what is unseen is eternal." This verse encapsulates the original Christian focus on spiritual realities that transcend the material world. Yet, as Christianity adapted to a hellenized context, this emphasis on the unseen and eternal was increasingly overshadowed by a more concrete and material eschatology. The challenge for contemporary readers and theologians is to disentangle these historical developments and recover the spiritual depth and relational dynamism that characterized early Christian thought (Van Kooten et al. 2015, 252).

The integration of Hellenistic ideas, while it allowed Christianity to thrive and expand in the gentile world, also shaped its doctrines in ways that sometimes obscured the original intent of its founders. Understanding this complex history is crucial for appreciating both the strengths and limitations of early Christian theology as it navigated the cultural sea of the Hellenistic world.

2

The Early Church Fathers
Humanity, Nuance, and Eschatological Expectations

For what else is Plato than Moses speaking Attic Greek?
—EUSEBIUS, HISTORIAN AND EARLY CHURCH FATHER

STALACTITES AND STALAGMITES: LAYERS OBSCURING ESCHATOLOGY

HELLENISM SEEPS DOWN LIKE stalactites, while the early church fathers themselves rise like stalagmites, each adding layers that obscure the eschatological clarity of the Christian message. Navigating these complexities feels like traversing a cave—dark, disorienting, and fraught with uncertainty. Like those who entered the cave of Trophonius in Greek mythology, emerging pale and shaken yet enlightened, readers may find this chapter unsettling, but it will ultimately lead them to a clearer vision of the truth.

The eschatological landscape of early Christianity was far from unified. While figures like Justin Martyr (ca. AD 100–165) and Irenaeus of Lyons (ca. AD 130–202) embraced premillennialism, anticipating a literal thousand-year reign of Christ after his return, others, like Origen of Alexandria (ca. AD 185–253) and Eusebius of Caesarea (ca. AD 260–340), leaned toward a more spiritualized interpretation of the kingdom of God. This diversity not only complicates the narrative of early Christian eschatology but also challenges modern assumptions about the clarity and uniformity of early beliefs regarding the end-time.

THE FATHERS AND THEIR FRACTURED ESCHATOLOGY

The early church fathers shaped Christian theology in ways both profound and perplexing. These figures navigated doctrinal disputes, philosophical challenges, and a rapidly changing world, leaving behind a legacy that is as varied as it is influential. Their eschatological views—their beliefs about the end-time—are no exception. From the earliest apostolic fathers to the later intellectual giants, what emerges is not a coherent narrative but rather a tapestry of conflicting expectations, personal fervor, and sometimes downright obsessive tendencies.

PREMILLENNIALISM AND LITERAL EXPECTATION

Among the early church fathers, figures like Polycarp (ca. AD 69–155), Ignatius of Antioch (ca. AD 35–110), Clement of Rome (ca. AD 35–99), Justin Martyr, Irenaeus of Lyons, and Tertullian (ca. AD 155–240), grappled with the implications of Christ's return. For some, like Justin Martyr and Irenaeus, eschatology was a matter of premillennialism, a literal thousand-year reign of Christ on earth following his second coming. They envisioned the end-time as a future, tangible reality, often laid out with a clarity and conviction that can come only from a deep belief in prophecy's literal fulfillment. For others, like Polycarp and Clement of Rome, the details of Christ's return were far less concrete. Their eschatological views are often more ambiguous, reflecting a hopeful expectation without the specific timelines or apocalyptic fervor seen in later thinkers.

POLYCARP: A MORAL EXHORTATION OVER URGENCY

A closer look at Polycarp reveals more complexities. Tradition often holds that Polycarp was a direct disciple of the apostle John, yet this claim has been questioned by some scholars. While Irenaeus provides the testimony that links Polycarp to John, the historical evidence is thin and primarily reliant on later sources. As Bart Ehrman points out, such associations were often constructed to lend authority to theological traditions rather than being based on verifiable personal connections (Ehrman 2005, 129). This casts doubt on the claim, suggesting that the relationship may have been more symbolic than actual. Polycarp's eschatological outlook is defined more by moral exhortation than by specific prophetic claims. His writings reflect an expectation of Christ's return, but without the urgency or elaborate details seen in others like Justin Martyr (Wilken 2003, 57).

THE OBSESSION OF IGNATIUS AND THE FANATICISM OF TERTULLIAN

Perhaps no figure exemplifies the human frailty and obsession that sometimes crept into early Christian eschatology more than Ignatius of Antioch. Ignatius was consumed by the idea of martyrdom. In his letters, written on his journey to be executed in Rome, Ignatius practically begs to die, viewing his impending martyrdom not just as a witness to Christ but as his personal entry into the kingdom of God. His letters suggest a realized eschatology, where death and suffering are the primary means of uniting with Christ. In modern terms, one might even call it an obsession, a near-pathological desire to achieve salvation through martyrdom. It's hard not to see the human hunger for significance in his willingness to embrace suffering, especially when other options were available. Tertullian, too, was no stranger to intensity. His defense of premillennialism had a moral urgency that bordered on the fanatical, as though every moment ticked toward an impending divine reckoning (Rankin 1995, 112).

CLEMENT OF ROME: AMBIGUOUS ESCHATOLOGY

However, not all early figures embraced a literal interpretation of eschatology. Clement of Rome, by contrast, focused on unity within the Christian community and moral behavior in light of Christ's return, but his eschatological views were vague at best. He spoke of the resurrection and judgment but didn't offer detailed timelines or delve into specific prophecies. His eschatology, much like Polycarp's, reflects a hopeful yet somewhat undefined expectation. There's a sense that both Clement and Polycarp were more concerned with the ethical implications of faith rather than parsing out when or how the end-time would unfold (Lampe 2003, 269).

SYSTEMATIC FUTURISM: JUSTIN MARTYR AND IRENAEUS

Justin Martyr, by contrast, had no qualms about laying out a future premillennialist eschatology. He envisioned a literal thousand-year reign of Christ on earth following his second coming, drawing heavily on the book of Revelation. Justin's eschatology is systematic and unapologetically futurist. For Justin, the kingdom of God was not yet fully realized but would come in the future, marked by Christ's physical return, the resurrection, and a final judgment (Barnard 1967, 81). His futurist views align with those of Irenaeus of Lyons, who elaborated on the same eschatological themes, offering an even more detailed narrative of the events leading to Christ's return. Irenaeus, in his work *Against Heresies*, lays out a firm premillennialist belief, envisioning a future earthly kingdom where Christ would reign for a thousand years before the final judgment (Steenberg 2008, 149).

SPIRITUALIZATION OF THE KINGDOM: ORIGEN, EUSEBIUS, AND AUGUSTINE

However, as Christian thought developed, particularly in the later church fathers, we see a more intellectualized and, in some ways, spiritualized approach to eschatology. Origen of Alexandria, writing in the third century, famously rejected the literalist interpretations of figures like Justin and Irenaeus, opting instead for a spiritual allegory. For Origen, the kingdom of God wasn't a future physical reality but rather a present, mystical one—a reign of Christ already in the hearts of believers. He transformed what had once been a clear-cut future event into a more esoteric, philosophical concept (Barnard 1967, 84). Eusebius of Caesarea, the fourth-century historian and theologian, straddled the line between realized eschatology and futurism. Some scholars argue that Eusebius saw the establishment of the Christian Empire under Constantine as the fulfillment of Christ's kingdom on earth, effectively merging historical reality with theological expectation (Drake 2002, 435). Yet, even his views are debated, and there remains an uncertainty in categorizing him as a strictly realized or futurist thinker.

Saint Augustine of Hippo (ca. AD 354–430) would ultimately bring about a decisive shift. Writing in the fourth and fifth centuries, Augustine firmly rejected premillennialism and developed a more nuanced, amillennial eschatology. For Augustine, the thousand-year reign of Christ was symbolic, representing the age of the church rather than a literal future kingdom. His intellectual approach marked a significant departure from the fiery expectations of earlier fathers like Justin Martyr and Irenaeus, whose apocalyptic visions often read like countdowns to a cosmic event (Augustine 2003).

What becomes clear is that these figures, both early and later, were not detached theologians simply pondering abstract doctrine. They were human, grappling with their faith, their world, and their fears. Ignatius's obsession with martyrdom, Tertullian's fierce urgency, and Augustine's intellectual rigor all reflect the very human need to make sense of the world, particularly in light of a God who promised to return. Their views often seem contradictory, as if they were staring at the same horizon but seeing entirely different landscapes. Some looked for Christ's imminent reign on earth, while others sought his presence in the spiritual here and now.

This diversity reveals not only the complexity of early Christian eschatology but also the humanity of the men behind these ideas. They were driven not just by theological purity but by personal passions, historical circumstances, and the constant tension between what they hoped for and what they believed they had already received.

PROTO-PRETERISM

The roots of preterism can be traced among those who embraced spiritualized eschatological interpretations. Figures such as Eusebius of Caesarea, Origen of Alexandria, and St. Augustine of Hippo represented a movement toward a natural, organic unfolding of eschatology, drawing inspiration from the tradition of Christ, who often spoke in allegory, spirit, and truth. In contrast, many of the earlier church fathers shaped eschatology like a bonsai tree, using Greek philosophical frameworks and reactionary critique to mold it into something more controlled, restrained, and distant from the authentic spiritual vision found in Christ's teachings.

EUSEBIUS OF CAESAREA: THE FULFILLMENT IN HISTORY

Among those church fathers whose eschatological views laid the groundwork for proto-preterism, Eusebius of Caesarea stands as a significant figure. In his historical works, particularly his *Ecclesiastical History*, Eusebius presents the rise of Constantine and the Christian Roman Empire as a divinely ordained fulfillment of biblical prophecies. He viewed Constantine as more than a ruler; he was an instrument through which God's kingdom was authentically realized on earth. In his panegyric to Constantine, Eusebius ties Constantine's reign directly to the establishment of God's kingdom, seeing historical events as a natural outgrowth of divine will (Drake 2002, 429).

This perspective contrasts with earlier fathers who attempted to shape prophecy into strict frameworks. For Eusebius, prophecy and fulfillment are naturally woven into the fabric of history, not restricted by the rigid boundaries of Greek thought or systematic theology. Rather than forcing eschatology into a predetermined shape, Eusebius allowed it to grow organically, interpreting the rise of Christianity in the Roman Empire as the kingdom of God taking root in the world. This natural growth is closer to Christ's own teachings, which often employed parables and spiritual truths to reveal deeper realities.

Eusebius provides a compelling interpretation of the "last days," a term that appears frequently in prophetic literature. He understood this phrase, which the Septuagint translates as "the end of the days," to signify the end of the Jewish nation and its political structure. He explained that these last days referred not to the end of the world but to the cessation of the Jewish state's national existence, including the fall of the ruling order of Judah and the subsequent establishment of Christ's rule over all nations (Eusebius 1920, 91). The transition from the dominance of Judah to the universal kingship of Christ fulfilled the "expectation of the nations," a hope rooted in the ancient prophecies concerning the Messiah.

ORIGEN OF ALEXANDRIA: ALLEGORY AND SPIRITUAL REALIZATION

Origen of Alexandria also embraced a more authentic and free-form approach to eschatology. For Origen, the kingdom of God was a present spiritual reality, not merely a future physical event. While earlier thinkers like Justin Martyr and Irenaeus attempted to shape Christian eschatology into the rigid structures of premillennialism, Origen rejected such literalist readings, favoring an allegorical interpretation. His eschatology, like a tree growing naturally in the wild, was not bound by the constraints of Greek philosophical thought, but instead allowed to follow the contours of Christ's own spiritualized teachings (Barnard 1967, 106).

Section 1: Historical and Theological Foundations

Origen's writings offer insights into the preterist understanding of prophetic language, particularly regarding "the coming of the Lord" and the use of fire (Origen 1885b 4.6). He argued that references to God "coming down" or the Lord arriving "with fire" were to be understood figuratively rather than literally. He explained that divine fire was a metaphor for the judgment and purification of wickedness, symbolized by "wood, hay, and stubble" being consumed. According to Origen, the purificatory fire accompanied the destruction of Jerusalem, a judgment upon the wicked generation that had rejected Christ. This figurative interpretation aligns with the preterist view that the apocalyptic language used in Scripture was fulfilled in the first century, culminating in the judgment on Jerusalem and the inauguration of a new-covenant era.

Origen also commented on the renewal of all things, as described in Rev 21:5, noting that the destruction of the old Jerusalem was followed by the establishment of the new heavens and new earth. He recognized that the fulfillment of the eschatological promises was tied to the transformation initiated after the events of AD 70, wherein the Jewish nation's judgment marked a shift into a new age.

The "abomination of desolation" mentioned by Jesus as a sign to flee Jerusalem is explained by Origen as a reference to the Roman armies surrounding the city during the war that began under Nero (ca. AD 37–68) and concluded with the destruction of Jerusalem under Vespasian and Titus (Origen 1885a 2.8). Origen notes that Jesus had predicted these events while Jerusalem was still intact, with no immediate sign of destruction. The eventual siege and devastation of the city thus served as the fulfillment of Christ's warnings about the impending judgment. This perspective affirms the preterist view that the prophecies concerning the "abomination of desolation" were realized in the first-century context.

In Origen's view, prophecy found its fulfillment in the inner transformation of believers and the spiritual reign of Christ in their hearts. This approach stands in stark contrast to the systematic eschatology of earlier fathers, which often felt more like a bonsai tree—carefully pruned and shaped by external forces. Origen's allegorical method allowed Christian eschatology to breathe, drawing its shape from spiritual truths rather than external systems. In this way, Origen's vision was closer to the authenticity of Christ's teachings, which used allegory and metaphor to unveil the kingdom of God.

ST. AUGUSTINE OF HIPPO: THE KINGDOM AS THE CHURCH

By the time of St. Augustine, Christian eschatology had begun to take its most natural form. In his famous work *The City of God*, Augustine decisively moved away from the earlier premillennialist interpretations that had dominated early Christian thought, shaping eschatology in line with Christ's own spiritual vision. Augustine's amillennialism represented the culmination of an organically grown theological approach—one that rejected the artificial boundaries of Greek thought and instead embraced the kingdom of God as a present reality through the church.

In Augustine's view, the thousand-year reign of Christ was symbolic, representing the present age of the church rather than a future, literal kingdom. His theological method flowed naturally from Christ's teachings about the kingdom of God being within and among believers. Where earlier thinkers might have taken up the pruning shears, Augustine's eschatology allowed the tree of Christian thought to grow and bear fruit in the life of the church. The final judgment and resurrection remained future events, but Augustine's approach freed eschatology from the rigid and often mechanical frameworks that earlier thinkers had imposed. This shift marks a key moment in the development of proto-preterism, where many biblical prophecies were seen as already fulfilled in a spiritual or historical sense.

THE BONSAI AND THE FREE-GROWING TREE

In comparing these figures, we see two distinct approaches to eschatology. On one hand, there were those early fathers who, influenced by Greek philosophical frameworks, treated eschatology like a bonsai tree—carefully pruning and shaping prophecy into rigid systems. Justin Martyr and Irenaeus, for example, viewed the millennium as a literal future event and confined Christian eschatology within the boundaries of premillennialism. Their eschatology often felt constrained, limited by the need to fit prophecy into predetermined structures, much like a bonsai tree is wired and bent into an artificially created shape.

On the other hand, figures like Origen, Eusebius, and Augustine allowed eschatology to grow naturally, reflecting the organic teachings of Christ. Their interpretations, whether through allegory or historical realization, were not shaped by external constraints but allowed to grow freely from within the spiritual truths of the gospel. Origen's allegories, Eusebius's historical fulfillment, and Augustine's symbolic millennium reflect a more authentic development of Christian eschatology, unbound by the artificial limits of earlier frameworks. Like trees growing in the wild, their theology was shaped by natural forces, not by the careful hands of gardeners seeking to force it into something it was never intended to be.

The roots of proto-preterism are found in the writings of Eusebius, Origen, and Augustine, whose spiritualized and realized eschatology allowed Christian thought to grow freely, unrestrained by external systems. These thinkers, drawing on the spiritual truths of Christ's teachings, moved eschatology away from the artificial frameworks of Greek philosophy and toward a more natural, present-oriented understanding of prophecy. Their vision of the kingdom of God as something already realized—whether through the church, the inner life of believers, or historical events—represents a turning point in Christian eschatology, marking the emergence of proto-preterism. With this examination it becomes apparent that the eschatology of post–AD 70 Christianity was not an unadulterated tradition allowed to grow freely but something closer to a bonsai—a carefully controlled and manipulated theology, shaped by the hands of the church fathers using the tools of Greek philosophical frameworks and a reactionary critique to steer its growth away from the broader, natural course it might have otherwise taken. In contrast to those who sought to shape eschatology into strict, predefined systems, Eusebius, Origen, and Augustine allowed theology to grow in its natural, spiritual form, true to the teachings of Christ.

The writings of the church fathers reveal a tension between preterist elements and the expectation of future events. While none of the fathers fully embraced a preterist framework, their interpretations often reflected the belief that significant aspects of prophecy had already been fulfilled. This dual expectation led to attempts to synthesize preterist and futurist views, resulting in some imaginative ideas, such as the expectation of Nero's return or a second Elijah (Commodianus 1885, 211).

Despite these inconsistencies, the persistence of preterist strains suggests that the original teachings of Christ and the apostles, which emphasized the fulfillment of prophecy in the first century, were never entirely lost. This legacy was preserved through a diligent study of Scripture and the transmission of tradition, even if it was sometimes overshadowed by later doctrinal developments. The early Christian struggle to reconcile these conflicting eschatologies highlights the enduring influence of full preterism as an undercurrent in church history.

The patristic writers, though not explicitly preterists, left behind a legacy rich in preterist thought. Their acknowledgment of the fulfillment of many prophecies within the first century, including the destruction of Jerusalem, the identity of the antichrist, and the implications of the "last days," supports the full preterist position. While later generations increasingly leaned toward futurist expectations, the early testimonies reveal that the preterist understanding of prophetic fulfillment remained a significant, if sometimes obscured, aspect of early Christian eschatology.

3

The Errors and Evils of the Church
A Lukewarm Legacy

I know thy works, that thou art neither cold nor hot: I would thou wert cold or hot. So then because thou art lukewarm, and neither cold nor hot, I will spue thee out of my mouth.

—Jesus, Rev 3:15–16

"HERETICAL, EVIL, AND UNBIBLICAL"

THESE WERE THE WORDS hurled like rocks of condemnation on a Christian apologetics podcast to describe full preterism and its adherents.[1] Words like "heretical," "evil," and "unbiblical" hold profound significance in theological discourse. Yet in certain contexts, these terms are weaponized as rhetorical totems, wielded not to illuminate truth but to shut down inquiry and intimidate those who dare to explore alternative perspectives. Within the debate over full preterism, such accusations often function as hollow signals of condemnation, discouraging believers from asking questions or pursuing deeper understanding.

This misuse of powerful terms distorts their purpose. To study eschatology with an open mind and to consider full preterism as a possible

---

1. Willy, "Heretical, Evil, and Unbiblical."

explanation is neither a moral failing nor a spiritual danger. To claim otherwise is to misrepresent the very heart of biblical inquiry, which calls believers to test all things and hold fast to what is good (1 Thess 5:21).

These accusations, rather than protecting the faith, serve to obscure it. They create barriers where dialogue should thrive, fostering fear instead of understanding. True study requires the courage to engage deeply with Scripture, free from the shadow of labels that are too often used to silence rather than enlighten. This kind of rhetoric comes from a mindset that feeds off in-group bias, where the out group is villainized to solidify the group's sense of superiority (Brewer 1999). Rather than reflecting a secure, inward faith, this approach projects their own internal angst outward, trading depth for tribalism.

Yes, full preterism might be dismissed as heresy by the mainstream, hellenized, Enlightenment-formed churches of today, but evil and unbiblical? These are bold claims that don't stand up to scrutiny. In theology and philosophy, evil is typically understood as anything causing harm, suffering, or moral wrongdoing—whether from moral evil (caused by human actions) or natural evil (natural events). To lump full preterism into the same category as moral atrocities? You'd need to tee up a tricky swing to land that one. And then there's the charge of being unbiblical. Full preterism is nothing if not biblical. It's so rooted in Scripture that even the sharpest scholars and most gifted linguists acknowledge its merit.

N. T. Wright argues that numerous New Testament prophecies, particularly those about the "end-time," likely refer to the fall of Jerusalem in AD 70, emphasizing their historical context rather than a future apocalypse (Wright 1996, 345). R. C. Sproul similarly notes that preterism offers a compelling framework for understanding the timing of prophetic fulfillment, highlighting the importance of New Testament time statements like "this generation shall not pass away" (Sproul 1998, 37). Preterist scholars like Kenneth Gentry argue that full preterism's focus on imminent prophecy aligns with the historical context of the New Testament (Gentry 2010), while Gary DeMar emphasizes that preterism provides the clearest interpretation of biblical time statements regarding Christ's return (DeMar 1999).

Even C. S. Lewis—no theological lightweight—acknowledged the awkwardness of Jesus's supposed "failed" first-century predictions, realizing something didn't add up in the futurist framework (Lewis 1952, 97). So, while it's fair to say someone might not be convinced by full preterism, to call it unbiblical? That's not critique; that's a smear campaign. In appendix A there are 101 of the most glaring statements of imminency. If anyone still accuses full preterists of cherry-picking, they might have to admit the entire New Testament is a cherry orchard.

Many of full preterism's critics enjoy standing on the sturdy ground of mainstream church tradition. They point to the long, storied history of the institutional church as if longevity is proof of correctness. "How could something so ancient be so wrong?" Well, as history teaches us—quite easily.

We've already peeled back the layers of this thinking. The church was never a monolith, never a unified voice. It's a human bureaucracy, and like any bureaucracy, it is prone to failure. Trusting too deeply in this institution can make an idol of it. Let's not forget, God isn't commending any of us for acing a theology exam. It's the quality of our faith and its expression that reflect our relationship with God. Futurist eschatology—this waiting for Jesus to physically return to earth—is as valuable as the empty chant of "Lord, Lord" (Matt 7:21-23). We're not a faith of incantations and intellectual posturing. It's not that mantras or theological sharpness lack value, but when they become rigid dogma, they rob us of humility.

This dogmatic rigidity is the natural fruit of physicalism—the reduction of spiritual realities to the material. And it leads to what we might call a sort of theological narcissism—where faith is less about seeking God and more about glorifying our own theological correctness. It's not just egocentrism but a pathological need to be right in the divine realm, an intellectual idolatry of our beliefs dressed up as spirituality.

That's not to say being discerning or even skeptical isn't productive—it is, when applied with fairness and balance. But if we want to be truly discerning, let's direct that scrutiny towards the very thing that many of these critics elevate: the institutional church. What happens when we shine the same critical light on the church's legacy of heresy, evil, and the unbiblical?

HERESY: DEVIATIONS FROM CHRIST'S TEACHINGS

Christianity under Constantine—a man who had killed his wife and son—ushered in an age of enforced Christianization. His policies crushed dissent from non-Christians and fellow Christians alike. And yet, Eusebius would call this the "kingdom of God on earth" (Eusebius 1920, 117). This paved the way for the Theodosian persecutions, which forcefully purged pagans and non-Christians, murdering their priests and worshippers. The Council of Nicaea didn't resolve this—it formalized it, setting the stage for disinformation trials and public humiliation campaigns, a precursor to the long nightmare of Christendom's violence.

From there, the carnage only intensified. Fast forward to the Massacre of Béziers, where Abbot Arnaud Amalric famously declared, "Kill them all; God will know his own." The Inquisitions unleashed centuries of oppression, murder, and torture in the name of doctrinal purity, and the Thirty Years' War left millions dead over Protestant and Catholic disputes. Then there's the murder of William Tyndale, condemned for translating the Bible into English so that ordinary people could read it. Colonial conquests brought forced conversions, and the list of atrocities goes on: indulgence controversies and a systematic child molestation crisis, with over ten thousand documented US victims between 1950 and 2002, and global estimates exceeding one hundred thousand (John Jay College of Criminal Justice 2004).

Now, how does all of this square with Matt 5, where Jesus equates anger with murder and commands us to love our enemies? What would Jesus call heresy?

EVIL: HARM AND SUFFERING IN THE CHURCH'S LEGACY

These so-called heresies of the church are just the tip of the iceberg. We're talking ten to twenty million dead, countless victims of torture, and over one hundred thousand children abused in just a fifty-year span (1950–2002). Now, think about Rev 3:15–16, where Jesus threatens to spit out the lukewarm church—a church that's just mildly corrupt. Imagine his reaction to this blood-soaked history of atrocities that certain futurists claim authority from.

How would Jesus speak about a legacy steeped in murder, oppression, and abuse? The futurist, standing on the authority of the mainstream church, basks in the cold waters of this dead tradition, chilled by the weight of fear and self-censorship. This chilling effect, where fear deters the spirit of love and truth, is the true inheritance of a church that silences, punishes, and oppresses rather than embodies Christ's message. Jesus didn't cherry-pick good from the Laodicean church; he threatened to spit it out for being lukewarm. And yet, the futurist clings to the legitimacy of this rapacious tradition, claiming power not from God but from a church that would rather crush its enemies than love them. If we are to speak of evil, which legacy truly deserves that title? See appendix B for a little more insight into evil called good throughout the centuries.

UNBIBLICAL: HOW FUTURISM UNDERMINES CLEAR TEACHINGS OF THE BIBLE

In Luke 21:8, Jesus warns, "Take heed that ye be not deceived: for many shall come in my name, saying, I am Christ; and the time draweth near: go ye not therefore after them." Jesus is clear—don't follow those who falsely claim the time is near. Yet, Paul, Peter, John, and others repeatedly said just that: "But the end of all things is at hand" (1 Pet 4:7); "And that, knowing the time, that now is our salvation nearer than when we believed" (Rom 13:11); "The night is far spent, the day is at hand" (Rom 13:12); and "Little children, it is the last time" (1 John 2:18).

Now, according to futurist theology, these apostles were wrong. If the end was *not* near, as futurism claims, then by Jesus's own words, we should not follow them, because they would have been the very ones misleading people. But that's the absurdity of it. Futurism essentially makes liars out of the apostles and, by extension, questions the integrity of Scripture itself. How can one hold that these men were inspired by the Holy Spirit and yet got this wrong? If they said the time was near and it wasn't, then Jesus's warning condemns them—but if they were right, as full preterism holds, then futurism has grossly misinterpreted the timing of prophecy.

ACKNOWLEDGING THE CHURCH'S CONTRIBUTIONS AND CONFRONTING ITS FLAWS

While much of church history reveals darkness, the church also contributed positively, establishing universities, building hospitals, and advocating for abolition. These are no small contributions—they represent genuine expressions of faith lived out in service to others. My aim here is not to chastise every person or every action connected to the institutional church, but to confront the uncomfortable truth that these profound failures are not just fleeting anomalies or historical quirks.

These flaws evidence something deeply embedded in the human psyche—the tendency for bureaucracies, even religious ones, to slip into retrograde motions, driven by pettiness, vicious power struggles, and the pursuit of control. These motives are antithetical to the Spirit of Christ. For those who claim the church's authority as their heritage, it's vital to reckon with how that influence was often secured—by force, fear, and even manipulation. The failures of the past aren't some strange, sci-fi anomaly; they are the predictable results of human nature and power structures, which have consistently warped and degraded the very essence of Christ's teachings.

So, while we honor the church's contributions, let's also recognize that its errors remind us how fragile human institutions are—ever vulnerable to the darker impulses of control, coercion, and corruption that Christ himself condemned.

4

Rationalism and the Decline of the Mystical

Cogito, ergo sum.
—René Descartes

With these famous words, René Descartes laid the foundation for Enlightenment thought, signaling the beginning of a new era in which thinking, rather than feeling or divine inspiration, became the measure of human existence. This phrase birthed a kind of *scientism*—a belief that human integrity relied on rational thought, sidelining the relational and mystical elements that once grounded spiritual life. The Enlightenment acted like a craftsman pouring cement over the roots of the bonsai tree that the early church fathers had already pruned and confined. While the church fathers meticulously shaped eschatology using Greek frameworks, restricting its natural growth, the Enlightenment solidified the materialist view, further confining eschatological thought to the rational, physical world. Just as the kingdom of God is not meant to "come with observation" (Luke 17:20–21), the Enlightenment reinforced a worldview in which only the observable and material had value, choking off the mystical elements that once gave the free tree of faith its potential to flourish naturally.

Rationalism and the Decline of the Mystical

DESCARTES: THE BIRTH OF RATIONALISM

René Descartes (1596–1650), a French philosopher, contributed significantly to the development of *rationalism*—the belief that reason and deduction are the primary sources of knowledge. In his *Meditations on First Philosophy* (1641), Descartes introduced Cartesian dualism, a separation of mind and body, which would become foundational to Enlightenment thinking. Descartes posited that humans, through the act of thinking, could understand the world and their own existence without recourse to the divine or the mystical. This shift toward reason displaced spiritual intuition, leading to what later thinkers would describe as the disenchantment of the world.

SPINOZA: RATIONALIZING THE DIVINE

While Descartes set the groundwork for rationalism, Baruch Spinoza (1632–77) pushed it even further, particularly in his understanding of God. Spinoza's pantheistic view in *Ethics* (1677) rejected the notion of a personal God who intervened in the world. Instead, Spinoza identified God with nature, operating through rational laws rather than mystical or supernatural events. This view, deeply rational and devoid of the personal, mystical experiences that had once been central to Christianity, contributed to a more mechanical understanding of the divine.

LOCKE AND HUME: THE RISE OF EMPIRICISM AND MATERIALISM

John Locke (1632–1704) built on these ideas by advancing empiricism, the notion that knowledge comes exclusively through sensory experience. In *An Essay Concerning Human Understanding* (1689), Locke argued that the mind is a tabula rasa—a blank slate at birth, shaped entirely by experience. Locke's empiricism would lay the groundwork for a materialist worldview, one that valued what could be observed and tested over what was felt or believed through faith.

David Hume (1711–76) carried this empiricist philosophy to its logical extreme. In *An Enquiry Concerning Human Understanding* (1748), Hume expressed skepticism about miracles, arguing that they could not be trusted because they violated the laws of nature that were observable through reason and experience. Hume's outright rejection of the supernatural and his insistence on the primacy of material experience marked a significant turn toward a fully disenchanted worldview.

VOLTAIRE: CRITIQUE AND DISENCHANTMENT

In the same period, Voltaire (1694–1778), one of the most famous figures of the Enlightenment, applied rationalism and empirical criticism to religious institutions. While not outright atheist, Voltaire's work, especially in *Candide* (1759), was a sharp critique of the church's grip on society. He saw superstition and faith in the mystical as barriers to human progress. While Voltaire's critique focused largely on the institutional church, it also reflected a broader disenchantment with the unseen and supernatural aspects of life that had been central to earlier Christian thought.

ADAM SMITH: THE INVISIBLE HAND AND MATERIALISM

The shift from spiritual to material interpretations reached new heights in the work of Adam Smith (1723–90). While primarily known for his economic theories, Smith's *The Wealth of Nations* (1776) advanced a deeply materialist understanding of human interactions. Smith's concept of the *invisible hand*—the idea that individuals pursuing their own self-interest unintentionally contribute to the common good—mirrors the Enlightenment's broader move away from mystical forces toward unseen material mechanisms.

The invisible hand metaphorically represents the Enlightenment's larger shift: trust in unseen material forces like market dynamics over unseen spiritual forces like the kingdom of God.

THE DOMINANCE OF RATIONALISM AND THE DECLINE OF THE SPIRITUAL

In *The Master and His Emissary* (2009), Iain McGilchrist explores how the left hemisphere of the brain has come to dominate Western thought, especially since the Enlightenment. The left hemisphere is concerned with rationality, categorization, and materialism—attributes that align perfectly with the empirical focus of Enlightenment philosophy. Meanwhile, the

Rationalism and the Decline of the Mystical

right hemisphere, which is responsible for intuition, spiritual understanding, and the ability to make poetic connections, has been increasingly constrained in modern culture.

This dynamic is symbolized by the ancient Greek gods Apollo and Dionysus. Apollo represents order, reason, and the observable, while Dionysus stands for chaos, intuition, and the unseen mysteries of life. The Enlightenment leaned heavily toward the Apollonian side, fostering a worldview dominated by the left hemisphere's materialistic and rational outlook. As a result, the Dionysian impulse—the capacity to grasp spiritual truths, perceive interconnectedness, and engage with the poetic and mystical aspects of existence—has withered.

McGilchrist's argument helps explain why contemporary society struggles to comprehend the deeper spiritual insights of faith, such as the truth of full preterism. Full preterism, with its emphasis on spiritual fulfillment and the unseen kingdom of God, requires the kind of right-hemisphere thinking that understands mystery, metaphor, and spiritual realities that transcend the material. However, in a culture dominated by the left hemisphere's focus on reason and empirical evidence, people are conditioned to seek material, future-oriented interpretations of prophecy. This rationalist mindset blinds them to the spiritual nature of Christ's fulfilled kingdom.

The right hemisphere is the domain where we comprehend the mystical and make poetic connections—where spiritual truths are understood not through logic but through a deeper, relational understanding of the world. In our overly rational and empirical context, this side of the brain is constrained, leading people to miss the true nature of eschatology as a realized and spiritual fulfillment. As Jesus said, "The Kingdom of God does not come with observation" (Luke 17:20–21), yet the Enlightenment's emphasis on the observable world forces us to look for material signs where only spiritual truths can be found.

THE DECLINE OF MYSTICISM AND SPIRITUAL ESCHATOLOGY

The Enlightenment marked a turning point in the history of Christian thought, gradually shifting focus away from the mystical and spiritual toward a more material and observable interpretation of theological concepts. Central to this shift was the demand for rationalism and empirical evidence, which undermined the early Christian emphasis on worshipping in spirit and truth.

In John 4:24, Jesus emphasizes, "God is Spirit, and his worshipers must worship in spirit and in truth." Early Christians understood this as a call to look beyond the physical and observable world, embracing a faith grounded in spiritual realities. However, as Enlightenment thinking took root, the mystical aspects of Christianity—such as the resurrection and the kingdom of God—were increasingly interpreted through a materialist lens. The spiritual dimension, once central to eschatology, was eclipsed by a growing emphasis on the physical and observable.

THE "IRON MESSIAH": MATERIALISM'S IMPACT ON CHRISTIAN ESCHATOLOGY

This transformation is powerfully captured in Vladimir Kirillov's poem "The Iron Messiah," originally written in 1918 (Yarmolinsky 1929, 216). The poem vividly portrays a world that has traded its expectation of a divine, mystical messiah for an industrial, materialist savior:

> *There he is the savior, the lord of the earth,*
> *The master of titanic forces—*
> *In the roar of countless steel machines,*
> *In the radiance of electric suns.*
>
> *We thought he would appear in a sunlight stole,*
> *With a nimbus of divine mystery,*
> *But he came to us clad in gray smoke*
> *From the suburbs, foundries, factories.*
>
> *We thought he would appear in glory and glitter,*
> *Meek, blessedly gentle,*
> *But he, like the molten lava,*
> *Came—multiface and turbulent.*
>
> *There he walks o'er the abyss of seas,*
> *All of steel, unyielding and impetuous;*
> *He scatters sparks of rebellious thought,*
> *And the purging flames are pouring forth.*
>
> *Wherever his masterful call is heard,*
> *The world's bosom is bared,*

Rationalism and the Decline of the Mystical

The mountains give way before him,
The earth's poles together are brought.

Wherever he walks, he leaves a trail
Of ringing iron rail;
He brings joy and light to us,
A desert he strews with blossoms.

To the world he brings a new sun,
He destroys the thrones and prisons,
He calls the peoples to eternal fraternity,
And wipes out the boundaries between them.

His crimson banner is the symbol of struggle;
For the oppressed it is the guiding beacon;
With it we shall crush the yoke of fate,
We shall conquer the enchanting world.

In Kirillov's vision, the anticipated spiritual messiah, symbolizing peace and divine mystery, is replaced by an industrial figure—a master of "titanic forces" and "steel machines." The Iron Messiah embodies the materialist power of modernity, clothed not in light and divine mystery but in "gray smoke" from factories and foundries. This messianic figure is not meek or gentle but multifaceted, turbulent, and impetuous, wielding control over the earth's resources and reshaping the physical world with technological prowess.

This transformation mirrors the Enlightenment's impact on Christian eschatology. Early Christians viewed the kingdom of God as a spiritual reality—something that does not come with observation (Luke 17:20–21)—but the Enlightenment shifted the focus to the observable and material. In this new worldview, salvation was not a mystical, spiritual fulfillment but a mechanized, material force, reshaping the world through progress and industrial power.

Kirillov's poem acts as a powerful metaphor for the decline of mystical eschatology in the face of rationalism and materialism. The spiritual kingdom, once imagined as something mysterious and beyond the grasp of human logic, was replaced by a concrete, industrial savior—an embodiment of the world's shift away from the unseen toward the observable. As the Iron Messiah scatters "sparks of rebellious thought" and "crushes the yoke of fate," he heralds a new era in which the mystical has been replaced by the rational and material.

This shift, epitomized by the rise of Enlightenment thought, has profound implications for the understanding of eschatology. The mystical aspects of faith—those that cannot be seen or measured—have been relegated to the margins, while materialist interpretations of concepts like the resurrection and the kingdom of God have come to dominate Christian thought.

Many modern Christian apologetics, rather than appealing to spiritual or mystical insight, rely heavily on logical philosophy and natural science to defend the faith. This approach reflects the deep influence of Enlightenment rationalism on contemporary theology, where arguments are often constructed around evidence, reason, and material explanations. While this may bolster the faith's intellectual credibility in a rationalist society, it further distances Christianity from its original emphasis on spirit and truth (John 4:24), suppressing the mystical and relational aspects that were once central to Christian belief.

ROMANTICISM AS A COUNTERFORCE: REDISCOVERING THE INTUITIVE AND RELATIONAL

The Enlightenment's emphasis on reason and empirical evidence created a vacuum for those yearning for a deeper connection with the intuitive and mystical aspects of human experience. Romanticism emerged as a reaction against this cold rationalism, seeking to reintroduce emotion, intuition, and the relational elements of life that Enlightenment thinkers often dismissed as irrational or secondary to material reality (Berlin 1999, 26–27). In Christian theology, this Romantic counterforce represented a return to the personal and mystical dimensions of faith—those that could not be easily quantified or explained through reason alone.

A key figure representing this Romantic turn in Christian thought is Søren Kierkegaard. Kierkegaard's writings, particularly in *Works of Love* (1995), emphasize the importance of subjective experience in faith. For Kierkegaard, the relationship between the individual and God transcends doctrinal systems and rational explanations, requiring an emotional and relational commitment that resonates with the Romantic ideal. In contrast to the Enlightenment's focus on external laws and institutions, Kierkegaard's vision of faith rebalanced the scales by focusing on the inner life, where spiritual truths are felt rather than logically deduced (Taylor 1989, 17).

Rationalism and the Decline of the Mystical

This Romantic approach to faith also found expression in the mystical connection to nature, which had been a central element of religious experience long before the Enlightenment. Many great religious figures sought their most profound revelations in nature: Moses on Mount Sinai, Elijah on Mount Horeb, Jesus in the mountains and waters. These encounters emphasize the sacredness of nature as a source of divine inspiration and mystical insight—a sharp contrast to the mechanical, industrial world celebrated in Vladimir Kirillov's Iron Messiah. Where Moses, Jesus, and Elijah found connection with the divine through the natural world, Kirillov's messianic figure is "clad in gray smoke" and surrounded by "countless steel machines." This industrial savior, emblematic of modernity's materialist worldview, stands in stark opposition to the Romantic vision of nature as a place of spiritual renewal.

The Romantics viewed nature not merely as a collection of resources to be harnessed but as a manifestation of the divine. In this sense, nature was a living text, capable of revealing truths that were beyond the reach of rational discourse (Ferber 2010, 57). The Romantic critique of the Enlightenment highlights that not all truths can be observed or measured—some need to be intuited and felt. For Christianity, this means reengaging with a relational faith, one that prioritizes the personal connection between the believer and God over abstract, logical proofs of God's existence.

While the Enlightenment sought to distance theology from the mystical and emotional, Romanticism argues that emotion and intuition are crucial components of spiritual life. Kierkegaard's emphasis on the leap of faith exemplifies this Romantic vision, where faith becomes an act of trusting in the unknowable and embracing the mystery of the divine, rather than reducing God to a rational formula.

In contrast to the Iron Messiah of Kirillov's industrial future, the Romantics call for a return to nature and intuition as essential avenues to spiritual understanding. For them, the soul's connection to the divine cannot be reduced to rational calculation or industrial might. The mountains, wildernesses, and waters where Moses, Elijah, and Jesus encountered the divine symbolized a deeper reality that the Romantics seek to reclaim—a reality where faith is lived and experienced through relationship and spiritual connection, not just reasoned from principles or proofs (Berlin 1999, 26–27).

In rebalancing the focus of Christian theology, Romanticism urges a rediscovery of the mystical, highlighting the need for relational, intuitive faith that can challenge the overreliance on reason and the neglect of the inner, mystical world that characterized the Enlightenment. As such, Romanticism doesn't merely reject rationalism but complements it, insisting that a full understanding of faith must incorporate both the heart and the mind.

MEME THEORY: CULTURAL INHERITANCE AND ESCHATOLOGICAL SHIFTS

In his groundbreaking work *The Selfish Gene* (1976), Richard Dawkins introduced the concept of memes as units of cultural inheritance, analogous to genes in biological reproduction. Just as genes propagate traits through generations via natural selection, memes are cultural ideas or behaviors that spread through societies by replication. According to Dawkins, memes include beliefs, rituals, and social practices that dominate culture by replicating effectively.

In Scottish culture, the celebration of Hogmanay—the Scottish New Year—serves as a perfect example. Customs like "first-footing," where the first person to enter a friend's home after midnight is considered to bring good luck, and the singing of "Auld Lang Syne" as the clock strikes twelve, are cultural memes that help preserve and transmit Scottish identity over time. These traditions encapsulate the values of community, continuity, and good fortune, binding each generation to the ones before. Similarly, in American culture, the meme of the American dream plays an integral role in shaping national values. This belief—that anyone can achieve success through hard work and determination—has been passed down through generations as a powerful cultural ideal. It encapsulates the ethos of individualism, ambition, and the pursuit of personal prosperity, not only driving personal motivation but also shaping collective national identity. The American dream meme reflects a cultural narrative that is continuously replicated and adapted in stories, politics, and education, reinforcing its presence in American life.

In the context of Christian theology, the Enlightenment fostered the growth of certain theological memes, particularly those surrounding the material interpretation of key eschatological events like the second coming of Christ and the physical resurrection. These interpretations—rooted in a materialist worldview—became self-replicating memes, entrenched through repeated theological reinforcement. As Dawkins argues, memes that resonate with existing cultural frameworks are more likely to spread, and in the Enlightenment period, the emphasis on empirical evidence and observable reality created fertile ground for materialist interpretations of Christian prophecy.

Memes, like biological genes, do not require truth to propagate; they need only to be effective in spreading. In this way, the futurist expectation of Christ's return—a tangible, physical event to occur at some point in the future—became a meme that ignored earlier mystical and realized eschatological perspectives. These realized perspectives, which saw Christ's kingdom as already spiritually fulfilled, were gradually overshadowed by the materialist expectation of a visible return, which aligned better with the Enlightenment's rationalist framework.

EGOCENTRISM AND THE PERSONAL FABLE

Developmental psychology offers a lens through which we can understand why certain eschatological memes, such as the futurist expectations, gained dominance. One concept that applies here is *egocentrism*, the tendency to view oneself as central to events. The *personal fable*, a term introduced by David Elkind in the context of adolescent psychology, refers to the belief that one's experiences are unique and of central importance (Elkind 1967). This psychological tendency can explain why individuals often interpreted eschatological prophecies as being directly relevant to their own time, seeing themselves as the pivotal generation within the divine timeline.

This egocentric bias helps perpetuate the futurist expectation meme. Believers, viewing themselves as the main characters in the eschatological narrative, were more likely to embrace interpretations that positioned their generation as witnessing Christ's physical return. This sense of personal significance kept the futurist narrative alive and continuously passed down through cultural inheritance.

CONFIRMATION BIAS AND MEMETIC REINFORCEMENT

Another key psychological theory relevant to the perpetuation of futurist eschatology is confirmation bias. This refers to the tendency of individuals to seek out information that confirms their preexisting beliefs, while ignoring evidence that contradicts them (Nickerson 1998). When Christians with futurist expectations read Scripture, they may have selectively interpreted passages to support their belief that Christ's return was imminent.

Over time, this confirmation bias helped reinforce the meme of a future physical return, making it a dominant narrative within Christian theology.

As Dawkins describes in his theory, memes that fit with established cultural norms—like the Enlightenment's preference for materialism—are more likely to replicate successfully (Dawkins 1976, 192). The futurist expectation meme, continually confirmed by selective readings of Scripture, became self-reinforcing, locking many Christians into a materialist interpretation of prophecy.

NARRATIVE PSYCHOLOGY: THE APPEAL OF A CENTRAL ROLE

Narrative psychology examines how people construct stories to make sense of their lives and the world around them. Humans naturally place themselves at the center of these narratives, especially in stories about ultimate meaning, like eschatology. By seeing themselves as central figures in Christ's return narrative, believers could make sense of their place in history. This desire to be part of a cosmic climax provided an additional psychological mechanism for the perpetuation of futurist eschatology (Bruner 1990. 56–57).

The meme of Christ's physical return thus became embedded not just as a theological concept but as a personal story for believers. By imagining themselves in the pinnacle of the eschatological timeline, Christians made the future-oriented, materialist interpretation of prophecy more attractive and memorable, ensuring its survival and dominance within Christian thought.

IN-GROUP FAVORITISM AND COALITION BUILDING

Psychological research provides further insights into why these ideas spread. In-group favoritism, the preference for members of one's own group, is a deeply ingrained psychological tendency (Brewer 1999). In the context of futurist eschatology, this bias reinforced the idea that *we*—the current generation—are the chosen ones to witness the second coming of Christ. By framing eschatology as relevant to the present generation, futurist interpretations not only satisfied personal and psychological needs but also strengthened group identity, as believers united around the hope of Christ's imminent return.

This coalition-building behavior, where individuals rally around shared beliefs that strengthen group cohesion, further entrenched the meme of a physical return. The cultural transmission of these ideas was not just intellectual but also social, as believers reinforced each other's expectations through community structures and shared narratives.

THE NEED FOR A RETURN TO SPIRIT AND TRUTH

The Enlightenment significantly reshaped Christian theology, cementing a worldview dominated by rationalism and materialism. In the process, it distanced Christianity from its mystical roots and suppressed the spiritual, relational, and intuitive aspects of faith that had once defined early Christian worship. By elevating reason and empirical observation, Enlightenment thinkers reduced key theological concepts—such as the resurrection and the kingdom of God—to materialist interpretations, perpetuated through cultural memes that ignored deeper, spiritual meanings.

In the wake of this transformation, Romanticism emerged as a counterforce, advocating for the intuitive, mystical, and relational aspects of human experience that had been neglected. As we have seen, thinkers like Søren Kierkegaard called for a rebalancing of faith, where subjective experience and personal connection with the divine take precedence over cold, rational systems. Kierkegaard's vision resonates with the original Christian call to worship in spirit and truth, as expressed in John 4:24. Such a faith embraces the mystical, the unseen, and the relational, in contrast to the rigid materialism that has long dominated theological discourse.

The Enlightenment's influence on Christian thought is like cement poured over a bonsai tree. Just as the church fathers meticulously pruned eschatology using Greek frameworks, Enlightenment rationalism further constrained Christian theology, stifling its natural spiritual growth. The cement of Enlightenment rationalism hardened around the tree, freezing it into a fixed, materialist form that stifled the living, dynamic nature of true spirituality. If Christian theology is to flourish once again, it must break free from the rigid confines imposed by rationalist and materialist thinking.

A return to spirit and truth—a return to the mystical and relational understanding of faith—holds the key to recovering the richness of Christian spirituality. By rediscovering the intuitive and personal dimensions of faith, as advocated by Romanticism, we can remove the cement and allow Christian theology to grow naturally and spiritually once again, just as the

SECTION 1: HISTORICAL AND THEOLOGICAL FOUNDATIONS

early church envisioned. Only then can the kingdom of God be fully understood in its spiritual fulfillment, unshackled from the materialist expectations that have long dominated the narrative.

5

Addressing the Critique of Over-Spiritualizing

We are far too easily pleased. Our desires are not too strong, but too weak. We are half-hearted creatures, fooling about with drink and sex and ambition when infinite joy is offered us.

—C. S. LEWIS, *WEIGHT OF GLORY*

A COMMON CRITIQUE OF full preterism is that it "over-spiritualizes" Scripture, focusing too much on spiritual realities and neglecting the anticipated physical return of Christ. Critics argue that our eschatological perspective neglects the physical and tangible expectations of a future return of Christ, focusing too heavily on spiritual realities. However, this criticism ignores a significant thread running throughout Scripture, where spiritual truths are often emphasized over physical realities. The Bible continuously invites us to see beyond the material, encouraging a deeper spiritual understanding.

Section 1: Historical and Theological Foundations

BIBLICAL EMPHASIS ON SPIRITUAL LIFE AND DEATH

The biblical narrative consistently elevates spiritual interpretations over physical events. Consider Adam's death in Genesis—while he lived physically after his disobedience, he experienced a spiritual death as he was separated from God (Witała 2021, 33). Paul's ministry of reconciliation (2 Cor 5:18–19) emphasizes restoring this spiritual connection, focusing on a life in harmony with God's spirit rather than on physical states of existence (R. Hays 1996, 22). Similarly, Paul speaks to the church in Ephesus of being "dead in sins" (Eph 2:1), highlighting spiritual death as a more critical issue than physical mortality.

Furthermore, the concept of being "born again" (John 3:3–6) stresses spiritual renewal as essential to eternal life. Jesus frequently downplays physical death in favor of spiritual realities, as seen in statements like "let the dead bury their dead" (Luke 9:60), implying that those who are spiritually dead have no hope, regardless of their physical condition. This recurring theme in the New Testament sets the stage for understanding the true heart of biblical eschatology: it is not the physical realm but the spiritual that holds ultimate significance.

THE USE OF ALLEGORY IN CHRISTIAN TRADITION

Allegory is a long-standing tradition in Scripture and Christian thought. Jesus himself employed parables—spiritual stories with hidden meanings—to convey profound truths. The mustard seed (Matt 13:31–32), the prodigal son (Luke 15:11–32), and many other parables reveal the depth of Jesus's use of allegory to communicate the nature of the kingdom of God.

The early church fathers, such as Origen and Augustine, also relied on allegorical interpretation to understand the deeper meanings of Scripture. Origen believed that Scripture operated on multiple levels—literal, moral, and spiritual (Balthasar 2001, 26–28). Augustine, in *The City of God*, similarly understood many prophecies as pointing not to physical fulfillments but to spiritual realities (Brown 2000, 388–89). Allegory became a tool to unlock the mysteries of God's plan, highlighting the spiritual dimensions beneath the surface of the text.

The charge of over-spiritualizing is not new; it is rooted in a long and rich tradition of interpreting Scripture in ways that look beyond the physical to the heart of God's message.

Addressing the Critique of Over-Spiritualizing

SPIRITUALIZING FOOD: SUPREMACY OF SPIRIT OVER MATERIALISM

The relationship between food and religion or spiritual practice is ancient and intrinsic. For millennia, humanity has associated food with both catastrophic downfalls, as in Gen 2:17, and divine elevation, such as the immortality conferred by ambrosia in Greek mythology. Across ancient cultures, food and fasting held spiritual significance, showing discipline and symbolizing sustenance and the quickening presence of the divine.

In dharmic traditions, such as Hinduism, Buddhism, and Jainism, the relationship between food and spirituality is explicit. Hinduism divides food into categories like *sattvic* (pure, nourishing foods), *rajasic* (stimulating foods), and *tamasic* (sedative, dulling foods) (Jacobs 2018). For example, Jainism goes so far as to reject root vegetables like onions and potatoes because pulling them from the ground harms countless microorganisms. This aligns with their principle of ahimsa, or nonviolence, which informs their strict vegetarianism. It's not just what you eat, but how and why you eat that matters.

In contrast, Jewish kosher laws, derived from halakah (Jewish law), emphasize obedience to divine command rather than health or well-being. Animals must have cloven hooves and chew cud (pigs are forbidden because they do not chew cud), and many sea creatures, like monkfish and shellfish, are prohibited. Even kelp and seaweed pose challenges for keeping kosher due to the risk of contamination from microscopic nonkosher crustaceans (Klein 1989, 363). Kosher meat must be prepared by a shochet (a kosher butcher), and the process must follow strict guidelines to minimize the animal's suffering.

While some argue that kosher laws were designed to prevent unsanitary practices, especially in times before refrigeration, their purpose goes far deeper. Kosher laws were about sanctification, not necessarily health. Leviticus 20:7 underscores this: "Sanctify yourselves therefore, and be ye holy: for I am the Lord your God." Each kosher meal is an opportunity to rededicate oneself to living in covenant with God, reinforcing a sense of being set apart. The kashrut ensures Jewish continuity, much like how cultural memes replicate and shape behavior (Dawkins 1976).

Section 1: Historical and Theological Foundations

FROM FOOD LAWS TO ESCHATOLOGY: TRADITION AS A CULTURAL MEME

Kosher laws once represented being set apart, yet in the *Olam haBa* (world to come), they no longer apply as they once did. Nevertheless, they remain a strong cultural symbol, much like the persistent futurist expectations that continue to shape Christian belief despite scriptural evidence for an imminent first-century fulfillment (Matt 16:28; Rev 1:1–3). The continued observance of these traditions, whether dietary or eschatological, serves as a powerful meme, passed down through generations, shaping community identity.

FOOD AS A SHADOW OF SPIRITUAL REALITIES

The biblical discussion around food laws offers profound insights into the larger theological question of physical versus spiritual significance. As Paul argues in Rom 14:17, "The kingdom of God is not eating and drinking, but righteousness and peace and joy in the Holy Spirit." The kashrut served as a shadow of deeper spiritual realities. Just as circumcision was a physical sign of a deeper spiritual truth, the food laws pointed to a spiritual purity, not merely a dietary one (Dunn 1998, 706).

Christ's teachings further emphasize this, as seen when he says, "Do not labor for food which perishes, but for the food which endures to everlasting life" (John 6:27). The kashrut was a shadow of the true sustenance that comes from Christ, "the bread of life" (John 6:35).

THE SPIRITUAL HEART OF SCRIPTURE

Paul's declaration that "there is nothing unclean of itself" signals a radical shift in understanding (Rom 14:14). What matters is not what we eat but the righteousness, peace, and joy that come from serving Christ. Food, while a part of religious practice, does not commend us to God. Rather, it is the content of our hearts and our love for others that define our spiritual standing. The kashrut laws served as a shadow pointing toward something greater, but now, through Christ, we live in the fullness of spiritual truth. In this way, full preterists' focus on spiritual realities over physical expectations is not an "over-spiritualization" but rather a return to the true heart of biblical theology. The physical is temporary, but the spiritual is eternal.

SECTION 2

Key Full Preterist Interpretations of Prophecies

This section reveals the timing and nature of the resurrection, the second coming of Christ, and the myriad other eschatological elements central to preterist thought, illuminating how each found its realization within the first century. Drawing upon a wealth of academic sources and scholarly insights, these perspectives are informed by rigorous analysis of historical, theological, and cultural contexts. As we tour these passages, we see the grand mosaic of history resolving, as if prophecies once shrouded in mystery are now laid bare in their historical context. The result is a panorama of fulfilled promises, where cryptic symbols take on shape and meaning, leaving no trace of enigma—only revelation.

6

Mystery Babylon Was Old-Covenant Israel

> How is the faithful city become an harlot! It was full of judgment; righteousness lodged in it; but now murderers.
>
> —Isa 1:21

Nowhere is the brilliance of full preterism more blindingly evident than in the revelation that mystery Babylon is none other than Jerusalem in old-covenant Israel. This isn't some veiled riddle left for future world empires to crack—Revelation lays it bare, a damning portrait of a city turned harlot. The city where the Lord was slain (Rev 11:8) could be only Jerusalem, making Babylon's veil thinner than ever. What we're seeing is an indictment not just against a city but a nation, guilty of spiritual adultery. Like an unfaithful bride, Jerusalem wore the face of piety but harbored within the spirit of rebellion, fornication, and betrayal. Babylon is the poetic mask, Israel the adulterous heart beneath. Revelation 14:8 brands her as a fornicator, echoing the accusations of Hos 1:2, where God calls out Israel's faithlessness. Here lies the key: only Israel, in covenant with God, could commit such divine infidelity, abandoning the bridegroom in a ruinous affair with the idols of the world. Jerusalem, once chosen, now forsaken—her lovers are many but her loyalty none.

THE SYMBOLISM OF BABYLON

The use of Babylon as a symbol offers significant insight into Jerusalem's spiritual status in Revelation. Revelation 17:5–6 states:

> And upon her forehead was a name written, MYSTERY, BABYLON THE GREAT, THE MOTHER OF HARLOTS AND ABOMINATIONS OF THE EARTH. And I saw the woman drunken with the blood of the saints, and with the blood of the martyrs of Jesus: and when I saw her, I wondered with great admiration.

The harlot imagery and the association with fornication point directly to the adulterous relationship between old-covenant Israel and God. Throughout the Old Testament, Israel is described as a harlot when it turns away from God to worship idols and align itself with other nations (Hos 1:2). The use of Babylon as a symbol is deeply significant. Babylon is a historic enemy of God's people, and by aligning Israel with Babylon in Revelation, the text reveals Israel's spiritual downfall (Wright 2011, 161). Babylon is presented as a fornicator (Rev 14:8), a description that aligns with old-covenant Israel's spiritual unfaithfulness (Gentry 1998, 215–16; Preston 2006, 55–56).

THE CITY WHERE THE LORD WAS SLAIN

The explicit reference to the "great city" where the Lord was crucified in Rev 11:8 provides a direct link to Jerusalem, identifying it as the spiritual Babylon that betrayed its covenant: "And their dead bodies shall lie in the street of the great city, which spiritually is called Sodom and Egypt, where also our Lord was crucified."

This passage explicitly identifies the "great city" where the Lord was slain, which, without question, is Jerusalem. This provides strong evidence that the symbolic Babylon is, in fact, Jerusalem (Preston 2006, 48). The references to Sodom and Egypt underscore this symbolism. Israel had already been likened to Sodom for its moral depravity (Isa 1:10; Ezek 16:44–48) and to Egypt for its role in oppressing God's people.

Additionally, Deut 32:32 describes Israel: "Their vine is of the vine of Sodom, and of the fields of Gomorrah: their grapes are grapes of gall, their clusters are bitter."

This prophetic language ties Israel's spiritual corruption to that of Sodom, reinforcing the identification of Israel as Babylon in Revelation.

THE AVENGING OF THE SAINTS' BLOOD

The avenging of righteous blood in Rev 19:1–2 resonates with Jesus's words in Matt 23, where he condemns Jerusalem for shedding the blood of God's prophets, further identifying Israel as the prophetic Babylon:

> And after these things I heard a great voice of much people in heaven, saying, Alleluia; Salvation, and glory, and honour, and power, unto the Lord our God: For true and righteous are his judgments: for he hath judged the great whore, which did corrupt the earth with her fornication, and hath avenged the blood of his servants at her hand.

The avenging of the blood of the saints is a significant element of Revelation's narrative, and Jesus himself references this concept in Matt 23:35–36:

> That upon you may come all the righteous blood shed upon the earth, from the blood of righteous Abel unto the blood of Zacharias son of Barachias, whom ye slew between the temple and the altar. Verily I say unto you, All these things shall come upon this generation.

Here, Jesus speaks directly to the religious leaders of Jerusalem, condemning them for shedding the blood of the prophets and righteous men. This further strengthens the identification of Jerusalem as the Babylon of Revelation, guilty of martyring God's servants (Preston 2006, 70).

OLD TESTAMENT PRECEDENTS

In addition to Isaiah and Ezekiel, Jer 39 and 52 provide valuable context. These passages describe the literal destruction of Jerusalem at the hands of Babylon, a historical event that provides the background for the symbolic use of Babylon in Revelation. Similarly, Isa 13:17–22 speaks of the fall of Babylon, which in preterist interpretation foreshadows the destruction of Jerusalem in AD 70 (Gentry 1998, 212; Wilson 2005, 177).

Section 2: Key Full Preterist Interpretations of Prophecies

BABYLON OR ROME? SCHOLARLY DEBATE

In scholarly discourse surrounding Revelation, the question of whether Babylon refers to Rome or Jerusalem has remained a focal point of debate. Giancarlo Biguzzi argues that Babylon is best understood as a symbol of Rome, but this view faces significant challenges, especially when considering the broader scriptural context (2006). As Russell aptly notes, Rome was never betrothed to God (1983, 483), while Ford emphasizes that the image of the harlot is more appropriately applied to Jerusalem or Israel, invoking the rich imagery of covenantal unfaithfulness found throughout prophetic literature (1975, 285).

A compelling parallel exists between the harlot of Ezek 16 and the harlot of Rev 17–18. Both passages describe the adornments, influence, behavior, and ultimate destruction of a city depicted as a harlot. Ezekiel's description of Jerusalem adorned in gold and fine garments mirrors the description of Babylon in Revelation, with its lavish presentation and subsequent punishment. Yet, as we extend this analysis, it is important to note that Tyre and Nineveh are also called harlots in Scripture, which complicates the claim that this designation could apply only to nations in covenant with Israel.

However, this does not undermine the spiritual significance of the harlot imagery, as the case of Cyrus the Great demonstrates. Cyrus, despite being a foreign king, was called the Messiah (מָשִׁיחַ, māšîa⌧ [Isa 45:1]), suggesting that such titles are spiritual designations, not confined to legal frameworks. Chilton argues that both Tyre and Nineveh had been converted to the worship of the true God (1987, 87–88), but critics contend that this was merely contact and not covenant, falling short of the relationship depicted in Ezekiel's Jerusalem or Revelation's Babylon.

Furthermore, Thomas raises an important linguistic point: the term for adultery, μοιχεία (*moicheia*), is not used in Rev 17–18, where πόρνη (*pornē*, harlot) is applied (1995, 286). This broader term, πόρνη, could encompass all forms of false religion and unfaithfulness, allowing the imagery to extend beyond Israel alone, encompassing all forms of spiritual corruption. This linguistic choice reinforces the view that Babylon is not strictly Rome but represents a broader spiritual reality.

Futurist interpretations often focus on Ezek 16 and the restoration of Jerusalem in a terrestrial sense. However, this view, rooted in Enlightenment rationality, can obscure the more intuitive spiritual sense of Revelation, which suggests a fulfilled vision rather than a future material restoration. The temple imagery in Revelation is particularly instructive here. While Ezekiel envisions a new temple at the heart of a restored Jerusalem, Revelation downplays the significance of the temple altogether, stating, "I saw no temple in the city, for its temple is the Lord God the Almighty and the Lamb" (Rev 21:22). This spiritual reinterpretation of the temple is far more powerful if we consider Revelation to have been written before the destruction of the Second Temple in AD 70, rather than after, as Aune suggests (1998, lvii).

Indeed, the timing of Revelation's composition plays a significant role in this debate. While Aune connects Babylon to Rome based on the parallels between Babylon's conquest of Jerusalem in 587 BC and Rome's conquest in AD 70 (1998, 946), this view assumes that Revelation was written post–AD 70. Yet, a minority of scholars argue that the book was written before this event, making the prophetic imagery of the temple's destruction far more poignant and immediate.

Collins adds another layer by suggesting that Rome arrived too late to be considered the mother of harlots (2016, 251). While Rome certainly persecuted the martyrs of Jesus, it did not spill "the blood of the prophets" or of "all who were slain upon the earth" (Ogden 2006, 289, 290)—a crime more fitting for Jerusalem, which had long been accused of such actions. Similarly, Walvoord contends that Babylon in Revelation is depicted in two dimensions: in Rev 17 as an ecclesiastical or spiritual entity, and in Rev 18 as a political one (1997). Critics may argue that these two descriptions clash—how can a spiritual city in one chapter be a physical one in the next? But this could simply be Revelation articulating the spiritual reality manifesting physically, emphasizing that Babylon represents more than a mere location; it signifies a corrupt system of power.

Some scholars point to the seven mountains in Rev 17:9 as a reference to Rome, but these mountains are also described as seven heads (Rev 17:7) belonging to the beast (Rev 13:1; 17:3, 7), not the harlot Babylon. It is Babylon who sits on both the hills and the beast (Rev 17:3), and also "on many waters" (Rev 17:1), representing control over "peoples, and multitudes, and nations, and tongue" (Rev 17:15). Therefore, as Carrington notes, Babylon is less about a fixed geographical location and more about a power that spans multiple nations and peoples (2008, 228). With the sea beast generally understood to represent Rome in mainstream scholarship, identifying Babylon as Rome as well becomes unnecessary and redundant.

Section 2: Key Full Preterist Interpretations of Prophecies

Thus, while Biguzzi and others attempt to identify Babylon with Rome, the weight of evidence—both scriptural and theological—points instead to old-covenant Israel/Jerusalem as the true identity of Babylon. As Gregg suggests, Revelation reflects a deeper spiritual reality, one where the old-covenant city—now corrupted—must fall to make way for the new Jerusalem (1997, 492). Babylon is not merely a location; it is the embodiment of a system in rebellion against God, and old-covenant Israel, having played the harlot, stands at the heart of this mystery.

JERUSALEM AS BABYLON, THE FULFILLED PROPHECY

The evidence is overwhelming: Babylon in Revelation is not a symbol for Rome or any future world power, but for old-covenant Israel, specifically Jerusalem. The consistent biblical theme of spiritual adultery, the specific identification of the city being where the Lord was crucified, and the Old Testament's prophetic language all point to this conclusion. Just as Israel was likened to Sodom and Egypt for its spiritual unfaithfulness, so too is it identified as Babylon in Revelation, a city marked for destruction as judgment for its rejection of Christ and the prophets.

This understanding of Revelation within a full preterist framework brings clarity to the symbolic language of prophecy, showing how the events of AD 70 fulfill God's final judgment on Israel. Rather than looking for future fulfillments, this interpretation brings the focus back to the spiritual truths revealed in Scripture, where the old covenant passes away and the new covenant in Christ is fully realized.

7

The End of the Age
(*Olam haZeh*)

In my end is my beginning.
—T. S. Eliot, *Four Quartets*

This chapter provides an in-depth exploration of the biblical "end of the age" narrative, focusing on how the "last days" were not a distant, future event but an imminent reality in the first century. Scripture demonstrates that the events described as the "end of the age" correspond to the closing of the old covenant and the emergence of the new covenant in the kingdom of God. This shift was not a literal, cataclysmic end to the universe but a profound spiritual transformation that redefined the relationship between God and his people (Russell 1983, 104–5). It was a move from a system bound to physical laws, sacrifices, and holy places, to one that is spiritual, unconfined, and eternal.

THE LAST DAYS REALIZED IN THE FIRST CENTURY

The Bible is unequivocal in identifying the first century as the time of the last days. At Pentecost, Peter declares the fulfillment of Joel's prophecy before the gathered crowd: "And it shall come to pass in the last days, saith God, I will pour out of my Spirit upon all flesh" (Acts 2:17).

Peter's proclamation leaves no doubt that the "last days" were already present in their time, not a far-off era. This is further reinforced by Joel's prophecy in Joel 2:28–31, where he describes apocalyptic signs such as the sun being darkened and the moon turning to blood (Marshall 1978, 65). Jesus echoes this same imagery in Matt 24:29: "Immediately after the tribulation of those days shall the sun be darkened, and the moon shall not give her light, and the stars shall fall from heaven" (France 2007, 937).

These descriptions do not signify the literal end of the physical universe but the end of the old-covenant system. Jesus's concluding statement in Matt 24:34 confirms this: "This generation shall not pass, till all these things be fulfilled."

OLD TESTAMENT PROPHETS AND THE TIMING OF FULFILLMENT

The Old Testament prophets frequently spoke of events that were far off. Numbers 24:17 states, "I shall see him, but not now: I shall behold him, but not nigh." Daniel 10:1 similarly notes that the appointed time for his vision was "long" (Goldingay 1989, 271).

Daniel's prophecy spans four kingdoms, beginning with the Babylonian empire of Nebuchadnezzar and culminating in the Roman Empire (Dan 2:36–45). This prophecy clearly points to the first century as the time when the heavenly kingdom would be established, as confirmed in Dan 7:23–27 (Collins 1993, 308–9).

While the Old Testament prophets described far-off events, the New Testament writers emphasized that their time marked the fulfillment of these prophecies. Hebrews 10:37 asserts, "For yet a little while, and he that shall come will come, and will not tarry" (Bruce 1990, 259). This is a stark contrast from the distant expectations of the Old Testament, marking a decisive shift in prophetic fulfillment. The events long anticipated were now coming to fruition within the lifetime of those who heard Jesus's words (Beale 1999, 135–37).

THE FULFILLMENT OF DANIEL'S PROPHECY: NO GAP, NO DELAY

Daniel's prophecy of the seventy weeks (Dan 9) serves as a foundational element in eschatological understanding, particularly in how we interpret the closing of the old-covenant age. In full preterist interpretation, this prophecy is seen as a continuous timeline that does not contain the speculative gap inserted by futurist views, which often suggest an unexplained break between the sixty-ninth and seventieth weeks. The futurist theory proposes a distant, yet-to-be-fulfilled conclusion that complicates the prophecy with unnecessary postponement, clouding what is otherwise a seamless chronological revelation (Ladd 1974, 139–40). Daniel's seventy weeks flow continuously, culminating in the first century with the destruction of the temple in AD 70. This view is supported by the historical events surrounding the Roman siege of Jerusalem, aligning the prophetic timeline with first-century events (Josephus 1981).

Daniel's seventy-weeks prophecy is comprised of seven weeks, sixty-two weeks, and a final week (all adding to make a seventy-week period). Each day in the seventy weeks represents a year, so it spans 490 years, culminating in the first century but with a significant event in the middle of the last prophetic week (the last seven-year period)—the "cutting off" of Messiah (Dan 9:26). The three periods coincide with particular prophetic eras. First, forty-nine years (the prophetic seven weeks) are given to rebuild the temple.

Then, there is 434 years (the prophetic sixty-two weeks) of perseverance under Persian, Greek, and Roman occupation. In Gen 15:13–16, God told Abraham that the Canaanites (referred to specifically as Amorites) would be given 400 years before judgment because their "iniquity was not yet full." Similarly, in Dan 9:24–27, Israel was given 434 years of preparation before the final week, culminating in the coming of the Messiah and the judgment on Jerusalem in AD 70. Both periods reflect God's mercy and patience, allowing time for repentance, but in both cases, judgment came when the measure of guilt was "filled up" (Matt 23:32; Rev 6:9–11).

The final seven years (the prophetic final week) is the climactic period of Messiah's ministry and the judgment on Israel. We know Jesus was crucified 3.5 years into his ministry (ca. AD 33). This would be the first half of the final seven-year period. Here, he "causes sacrifice and offering to cease" (Dan 9:27), effectively nullifying the old covenant's system through his sacrificial death.

Section 2: Key Full Preterist Interpretations of Prophecies

This "halving" of the week appears in Dan 12:7 and is echoed in Rev 12:14, where 3.5 years or "a time, times, and half a time" symbolizes periods of intense trial, covenantal transition, and judgment. The imagery of a divided week not only reflects the separation between Jesus's ministry and the coming judgment but aligns with apocalyptic language where the "3.5 years" or "1,260 days" represent periods of transformative trial within a larger fulfillment.

The judgment of Israel in the Roman-Jewish war began in AD 66 and lasted 3.5 years culminating in the AD 70 destruction of the temple. The siege and destruction of Jerusalem in AD 70 bring the prophecy to its full completion, with the temple permanently dismantled and the sacrificial system irreparably disrupted, in accordance with Josephus's historical accounts (1981). This would be the second half of the final seven-year period.

This leaves us with a period of around thirty-three years (ca. AD 33–66) that appear unaccounted for. In strict chronology, the second period of 3.5 years would follow the first, bringing us to AD 37. Is there an unexplained gap after all?

The "cutting off" and intentional segmenting of the final seven-year period into two periods of 3.5 years is not without theological significance. This would grant a period of grace equal to the mortal lifespan of Jesus. It is also interesting to note how close the mortal lifespan of Jesus (est. 33.5 years) is to the difference between the Canaanites' 400-year period of grace and Israel's 434 years (the prophetic sixty-two weeks) of grace. More to the point, the proposition of an unaccounted delay is anticipated and strongly repudiated by Jesus, Peter, and Paul (Matt 24:48; Luke 12:45; 2 Pet 3:4; Heb 10:36–37).

Indeed, this period is accounted for:

> He spake also this parable; A certain man had a fig tree planted in his vineyard; and he came and sought fruit thereon, and found none. Then said he unto the dresser of his vineyard, Behold, these three years I come seeking fruit on this fig tree, and find none: cut it down; why cumbereth it the ground? And he answering said unto him, Lord, let it alone this year also, till I shall dig about it, and dung it: And if it bear fruit, well: and if not, then after that thou shalt cut it down. (Luke 13:6–9)

> Or despisest thou the riches of his goodness and forbearance and long-suffering; not knowing that the goodness of God leadeth thee to repentance? (Rom 2:4)

> The Lord is not slack concerning his promise, as some men count slackness; but is long-suffering to us-ward, not willing that any should perish, but that all should come to repentance. (2 Pet 3:9)

God's gracious patience, as further reflected in Matt 23:37–39; 24:14; Luke 21:24; Rom 11:25–26; and Rev 2:21, effectively underscores this point. God extends mercy and patience, echoing Messiah's earthly ministry, before the final judgment on Jerusalem in AD 70.

THE ROLE OF ELIJAH IN FIRST-CENTURY FULFILLMENT

A key aspect of prophetic fulfillment is the role of Elijah. Many futurists expect Elijah to return in a future event, but Jesus clarifies that this prophecy was fulfilled in John the Baptist. Jesus clearly identifies John the Baptist as the prophesied Elijah in Matt 11:13–14, stating, "For all the prophets and the law prophesied until John. And if ye will receive it, this is Elias, which was for to come." Again, in Matt 17:10–13, Jesus clarifies this connection by answering the disciples' question directly: "But I say unto you, That Elias is come already, and they knew him not," confirming that John the Baptist fulfilled Elijah's role. This ties directly to Mal 4:5, where Elijah's return is prophesied to occur before the "great and dreadful day of the LORD" (J. Hays 2016, 450–52). This recognition definitively closes out any future expectation of Elijah's return, reinforcing the full preterist understanding that these prophecies were completed in the first century with the coming of John.

Futurists require another coming of Elijah; however, this is outside the scope of biblical prophecy. John the Baptist came to prepare the way for Christ, fulfilling the role of Elijah before the time of judgment (Keener 1999, 342–43). This completion removes any need for future fulfillment. Jesus's identification of John as Elijah signifies the imminent destruction of Jerusalem in AD 70, marking the end of the old covenant and the beginning of the new (Wright 1996, 345–47).

FIRE AS COVENANT END, NOT COSMIC DESTRUCTION

Futurists frequently misinterpret Peter's language in 2 Pet 3:10–12, which describes the heavens passing away and the elements melting with fervent heat. This passage is often taken as a literal prediction of the end of the physical universe. However, it's crucial to recognize the Hebraic hyperbole and Greek Stoic influence at play.

In Jewish literature, apocalyptic language like this was used to describe major covenantal transitions rather than literal cosmic destruction (Beale 1999, 100–102). The phrase "heavens and earth" refers to the old-covenant system, not the physical cosmos (Russell 1878, 65–67). In 2 Peter, "the elements" (Greek: *stoicheia*) can be understood as the fundamental principles or ordinances of the Mosaic law (Davies 2004, 112–14).

The fire Peter describes, then, represents the purging judgment that came upon Jerusalem in AD 70, symbolizing the end of the old covenant rather than a physical apocalypse. Peter's vivid, fiery imagery parallels the Stoic concept of *ekpyrosis*—the cyclical destruction and renewal of the cosmos by fire—though in a Jewish context, this fire symbolizes covenantal refinement rather than cosmic annihilation (Osborne 2002, 619).

Paul also confirms this understanding in 1 Cor 10:11: "Now all these things happened unto them for examples: and they are written for our admonition, upon whom the ends of the world [ages] are come." Paul's use of "the ends of the world" should be rendered as "ages," referring to the end of the old-covenant age, not the physical universe. The destruction of Jerusalem, the heart of the old-covenant system, is the event that marked the final dissolution of the old covenant (Wright 1996, 345).

Peter's warning in 2 Pet 3:3–4 against scoffers questioning the coming of the Lord also reveals the immediacy of these events. These scoffers, who mocked the idea of Jesus's return in judgment, were addressed to Peter's contemporaries in the first century (Davies 2004, 118). This wasn't a message for future generations but a direct warning to the early Christian community, reinforcing the fact that they were living in the "last days" of the old covenant (France 2007, 920).

FROM TEMPLE WORSHIP TO WORSHIP IN SPIRIT

With the old covenant's end, Jesus redefined worship and the kingdom of God, shifting the focus from physical locations to a spiritual reality. This is most clearly seen in Jesus's conversation with the Samaritan woman at the well in John 4:21–24, where Jesus tells her that the time has come when worship will no longer be tied to mountains or temples but will be done "in spirit and in truth" (Wright 2004, 38).

This marks a pivotal shift from the physical worship system of the old covenant to the spiritual worship in the kingdom of God. Isaiah 2:2 also prophesied this change: "And it shall come to pass in the last days, that the mountain of the Lord's house shall be established in the top of the mountains." This metaphor refers to the spiritual kingdom being elevated above all earthly systems, not a literal mountain, signaling the supremacy of God's new spiritual order (Motyer 1993, 356–58).

The destruction of the temple in AD 70 was the definitive sign that the old-covenant system had come to an end. With the temple gone, worship could no longer be confined to a physical place (Evans 2001, 210–12). The kingdom of God, as Jesus had foretold, was not of this world (John 18:36) but was fully realized in the hearts of believers through the Holy Spirit (Carson 1991, 589). This shift to a spiritual kingdom is essential to the full preterist understanding of prophecy, as it highlights the fulfillment of God's promises in the first century without requiring a future physical kingdom (Beale 1999, 110). In the *Olam haBa*, worship would prioritize the inward reality over ritual or place as well as authenticity, and faithfulness to God over mere external performance.

THE JUDGMENT ON "THIS GENERATION"

The Olivet Discourse in Matt 24; Mark 13; and Luke 21 is one of the most critical sections of the New Testament concerning the end of the age. In this discourse, Jesus speaks directly to his disciples about the coming judgment on Jerusalem and the end of the old covenant. He refers to this time as the "days of vengeance," when all that had been written in the Old Testament would be fulfilled (Luke 21:22): "For these be the days of vengeance, that all things which are written may be fulfilled."

In Matt 24:34, Jesus makes a clear statement about the timing of these events: "Verily I say unto you, This generation shall not pass, till all these things be fulfilled." Speaking directly to his disciples, Jesus is addressing a first-century audience and specifying that they themselves would witness these events. The phrase "this generation" firmly places the prophecy within the lifespan of those who heard it, pointing unmistakably to the historical events surrounding Jerusalem's destruction in AD 70 (France 2007, 935).

Jesus directly connects the events of Matt 24 to Daniel's prophecy, warning that they would occur within the generation of his audience (Wright 1996, 361). In Matt 24:36, Jesus acknowledges that no one knows the exact day or hour, "But of that day and hour knoweth no man." Many interpret this as suggesting an indefinite postponement, but in Rev 1:1–3, the Father confirms that the time for these events is near (Beale 1999, 181).

Revelation clarifies that these events "must shortly come to pass" because "the time is near" (1:1–3). The continuity of Daniel's prophecy and the clear timeline provided by Jesus leave no room for a future delay, aligning the events with the first century (France 2007, 934).

The fulfillment of this prophecy came with the Roman siege of Jerusalem in AD 70, when the city was destroyed, the temple burned, and the old-covenant system was completely shattered (Josephus 1981). Daniel 12:7 also speaks of this moment, saying, "When the power of the holy people has been completely shattered, all these things shall be finished." This event marked the final eschatological domino in the end-times narrative, with the destruction of the temple serving as the ultimate sign that the age of the old covenant had come to an end (Collins 1993, 400).

Even early church fathers like John Chrysostom acknowledged the fulfillment of these prophecies in their generation. Chrysostom wrote that the desolation and vengeance foretold by Jesus had already occurred, aligning with the preterist view that these events were realized in the first century, not postponed for a distant future (Osborne 2002, 456).

THE RECONCILED QUICK AND DEAD

The concept of judgment is central to the end of the age, and both Jesus and his apostles framed their ministry as taking place in the "last days." Paul writes in 2 Tim 4:1 that Christ would judge "the quick and the dead at his appearing and his kingdom." The significance of this verse cannot be understated as it informs us that the judgment happens at the time of his appearing and his kingdom. This means the second coming and the judgment are contemporaneous events. This judgment was not something far off but was imminent (J. Hays 2016).

In Matt 16:27–28, Jesus says, "For the Son of man shall come in the glory of his Father with his angels; and then he shall reward every man according to his works. Verily I say unto you, There be some standing here, which shall not taste of death, till they see the Son of man coming in his kingdom." These verses are pivotal in understanding the preterist perspective, as Jesus directly states that some of those present would witness his coming in judgment within their lifetimes (Carson 1991, 89). By asserting that some standing before him would witness his coming, Jesus dispels the notion of an indefinitely postponed fulfillment and firmly places his return within the scope of his disciples' lives.

The language here leaves little room for a futuristic interpretation. Jesus directly affirms that his coming in judgment would occur within a short time frame. This declaration echoes the kingdom-focused urgency found throughout the gospels, where the nearness of the kingdom and the impending judgment are emphasized repeatedly. As such, these verses underscore that the coming of the kingdom, with all its associated events, was intended as a completed reality within the first century.

The destruction of Jerusalem in AD 70 was the fulfillment of this promise. The "quick and the dead" were judged as Christ brought an end to the old-covenant system, vindicating his followers and punishing those who rejected him. This judgment marked the full establishment of Christ's kingdom, not in a physical sense but as a spiritual reality where believers are reconciled to God (Beale 1999, 85).

JUDGMENT FOR THE BLOOD OF THE RIGHTEOUS

The avenging of the martyrs is a key theme in both the Old and New Testaments. In Deut 32:43, God promises to avenge the blood of his servants: "Rejoice, O ye nations, with his people: for he will avenge the blood of his servants, and will render vengeance to his adversaries." This theme is carried forward by Jesus in Matt 23:35–36, where he speaks of the coming judgment upon that generation: "That upon you may come all the righteous blood shed upon the earth. . . . Verily I say unto you, All these things shall come upon this generation."

This prophecy finds its fulfillment in the destruction of Jerusalem in AD 70. The martyrs' blood was avenged as God's judgment fell upon those who had rejected and killed his prophets and apostles (Wright 1996, 587; Keener 1999, 552). The destruction of Jerusalem served as the ultimate expression of divine judgment against the old-covenant system and those responsible for the persecution of God's people (Josephus 1981, 580–84).

This event is further confirmed by Rev 6:9–10, where the souls of the martyrs cry out for vengeance: "How long, O Lord, holy and true, dost thou not judge and avenge our blood on them that dwell on the earth?" The answer to their plea comes in Rev 6:11, where they are told to rest for a little season until their fellow servants are also killed. This "little season" refers to the short period before the destruction of Jerusalem, when God's judgment would be completed. The avenging of the martyrs was not delayed for some

Section 2: Key Full Preterist Interpretations of Prophecies

distant future but was realized in the judgment that fell upon Jerusalem in the first century (Beale 1999, 98).

THE LITTLE SEASON AND THE GREAT TRIBULATION

A crucial feature of Revelation's structure is the appearance of what it calls a "little season" (Rev 20:3), a brief but explosive period following the symbolic 1000-year reign. This "little season" is not some distant apocalyptic storm on the horizon. Rather, from a full preterist lens, it aligns precisely with the years AD 66 to 70—the final Jewish-Roman conflict that culminated in the destruction of Jerusalem and the temple.

What many miss is that this "little season" is the very same event Jesus described as the Great Tribulation in Matthew 24:21. Revelation 6:9–11 also references this moment with identical language. The martyrs under the altar are told to "rest yet for a little season" until the number of their brethren should be fulfilled—clear persecution language. This anticipates the chaos to be unleashed when Satan is loosed "for a little season" (Rev 20:3), deceiving nations and provoking final confrontation. The convergence of these texts suggests that the "great tribulation" and the "little season" are not distinct epochs, but one and the same.

This understanding is strengthened by historical and scriptural convergence. In Rev 6, the martyrs are not simply waiting—they are told that their blood will be avenged when the full measure is complete (cf. Matt 23:35–36: "Fill up then the measure of your fathers"). This time of vengeance and reckoning finds its outworking in the war and siege of Jerusalem. Josephus described the city as if "possessed by demons," and the infighting among zealots, false messiahs, and factions echoes the spiritual chaos of Satan being loosed for one final assault.

Thus, the little season represents a final window of covenantal judgment—a period where restraint is removed (2 Thess 2:6–8), persecution intensifies, deception spreads, and the old age gasps its last breath. This "short time" (Rev 12:12) is not a worldwide tribulation, but a terminal moment for the Old Covenant order. What Revelation dramatizes symbolically, history confirms prophetically: Satan's brief release did not mean he triumphed, but that the full measure of judgment was poured out and the age of the Spirit could come in fullness.

DANIEL'S RESURRECTION PROPHECY IN LIGHT OF FULFILLMENT

One of the most important prophecies in understanding the end of the age is found in Dan 12:2, which describes the resurrection: "And many of them that sleep in the dust of the earth shall awake, some to everlasting life, and some to shame and everlasting contempt." This passage has often been interpreted as predicting a future, physical resurrection at the end of time. However, Jesus redefines the timeline of this resurrection in the Gospel of John (Carson 1991, 284–85).

In John 5:25, Jesus says, "Verily, verily, I say unto you, The hour is coming, and now is, when the dead shall hear the voice of the Son of God: and they that hear shall live." This verse ties directly into Daniel's prophecy, with Jesus asserting that the resurrection is not a far-off event but something already underway in his time. The "hour" was not some distant moment in the future but had already arrived with Christ's ministry, and those who "heard" his voice would be spiritually resurrected (Wright 1996, 209).

This aligns with the full preterist interpretation, where the resurrection is understood as a spiritual event, not a literal, physical rising of bodies from graves. The context of John 5:25 suggests that Jesus was speaking of the spiritual resurrection of believers who would be made alive in Christ, paralleling the spiritual rebirth he spoke of in John 3:3–7 with Nicodemus. This resurrection was the fulfillment of Daniel's prophecy, realized through the end of the old covenant and the establishment of the new covenant in AD 70 (Beale 1999, 1158).

SEALED AND UNSEALED: DANIEL AND JOHN'S PROPHETIC TIMELINES

The distinction between Daniel's sealed prophecy and John's open scroll in Revelation further clarifies the timing of these events. In Dan 12:9, Daniel is told to seal up the words of the prophecy because the time of its fulfillment is "far off." However, in Rev 22:10, John is instructed, "Do not seal up the words of the prophecy of this scroll, because the time is near."

This shift in timing is significant. Daniel's prophecy was sealed because it concerned events that would take place hundreds of years after his time, culminating in the first century (Goldingay 1989, 321). In contrast, John is told that the fulfillment is near because it is about to occur in his

Section 2: Key Full Preterist Interpretations of Prophecies

lifetime. The destruction of Jerusalem in AD 70 marked the end of the old covenant and fulfilled the prophecies that Daniel had been told to seal up. The stark difference in language—Daniel's "far off" versus John's "near"—demonstrates that we are not waiting for these events to happen; they have already been fulfilled (Beale 1999, 1158).

This also raises a critical point about the logic of futurism. If the 560 years between Daniel's time and John's were considered "far off," then the 2,000 years that have passed since John's vision cannot reasonably be called "near" (Wright 1996, 331). The full preterist view resolves this inconsistency by asserting that the time of fulfillment was indeed near for John, as it took place in the first century, just as Jesus and the apostles had predicted (France 2007, 940).

8

The Mark of the Beast and 666

Man sees the deed, but God knows the intention.
—Thomas à Kempis, Christian writer and author of *The Imitation of Christ*

Few symbols in biblical prophecy are as arresting as the number 666 and the mark of the beast in Rev 13:16–18. These images have stirred apprehension and debate for centuries, representing human frailty, rebellion against divine authority, and submission to worldly power. The influence of this prophecy has left an indelible influence on the collective consciousness of humanity. For instance, when Ronald Reagan and his wife Nancy moved to 666 St. Cloud Road in Bel-Air, Los Angeles, they had the address changed to 668 to avoid the number's ominous associations (Watt 1989, 370).

This chapter explores the significance of the mark and the number 666 in its original first-century context, contrasting early Christian interpretations with modern theories about technology, such as RFID chips and digital commerce. From the Roman Empire to Nero Caesar and beyond, the symbolic meaning of this number has shaped understandings of power, control, and spiritual allegiance.

SECTION 2: KEY FULL PRETERIST INTERPRETATIONS OF PROPHECIES

> And he causeth all, both small and great, rich and poor, free and bond, to receive a mark in their right hand, or in their foreheads: and that no man might buy or sell, save he that had the mark, or the name of the beast, or the number of his name. Here is wisdom. Let him that hath understanding count the number of the beast: for it is the number of a man; and his number is Six hundred threescore and six. (Rev 13:16–18)

THE HISTORICAL CONTEXT OF 666

The number 666 has long been interpreted through gematria, a system where letters correspond to numerical values. This practice was common in ancient cultures, and many scholars agree that 666 is likely a cryptic reference to Nero Caesar, a Roman emperor notorious for his persecution of Christians. When the Hebrew spelling of Nero's name is used, the numerical values add up to 666. This is supported by ancient manuscripts that also reference 616, an alternate spelling of Nero's name. The reign of Nero, infamous for its extreme brutality towards Christians, became symbolic of ultimate defiance against God—a direct affront that rendered him the embodiment of the "beast" itself. Christians saw in Nero's actions not just personal cruelty but a calculated attempt to extinguish the budding Christian faith, making him a natural symbol of apocalyptic opposition. He is said to have used Christians as human torches to light his gardens, crucified them, and had them fed to wild animals in the Colosseum. The use of gematria allowed early Christians to reference him covertly, avoiding direct accusations that could lead to further persecution.

Moreover, as David Chilton notes in *The Days of Vengeance*, the number 666 symbolically represents human imperfection and rebellion against God. In contrast to 777, a divine number symbolizing completeness, 666 is man's attempt to usurp divine authority, but ultimately failing to reach God's perfection (Chilton 1987, 451).

THE MARK OF THE BEAST

The mark of the beast is another element that has sparked widespread debate. Revelation 13:16 states that "the beast . . . forced all people, great and small, rich and poor, free and slave, to receive a mark on their right hands or on their foreheads." This mark is often interpreted as a symbol of loyalty to the Roman Empire, with early Christians refusing to participate in imperial worship, and thus risking economic exclusion and persecution.

In ancient Rome, the emperor's image appeared on coins, and certificates of sacrifice to the emperor were required for participation in trade. While the mark was depicted as a physical identifier, its deeper significance lies in what it represented: an allegiance to earthly powers and values in contrast to the kingdom of God. John's readers would have understood that their ultimate loyalty was to Christ, a commitment that would often mean exclusion from Roman economic and social life.

ELIJAH, NERO, AND THE BEAST: A MISUNDERSTOOD ESCHATOLOGICAL FRAMEWORK

Early Christians associated the figures mentioned in prophetic writings—such as Elijah, the "beast" or "little horn" in Daniel, and the antichrist—with eschatological fulfillment in the first century. Jesus identified John the Baptist as the prophesied "Elijah" who was to come (Matt 11:7–15), leaving Nero as the likely candidate for the beast of Revelation. Several church fathers, such as Commodianus and Sulpicius Severus, identified Nero with the beast and the "man of sin," interpreting his actions as embodying the mystery of lawlessness (Sulpicius Severus 1894 2.28–29). Although some erroneously expected a future return of Nero, this demonstrates a recognition that the events surrounding the Roman emperor were significant eschatological markers (Chrysostom 1889).

The early identification of Nero as the "man of sin" and "beast" was further reinforced by the writings of Victorinus and others, who noted that the "restraint" described in 2 Thess 2 referred to the Roman Empire and that the man of lawlessness was linked to the Roman Caesars. Augustine confirmed that this restraining power was associated with the stability of the Roman Empire and that its dissolution would give rise to the antichrist spirit, explicitly shining the spotlight on Nero (Augustine 2003, 877).

THE MAN OF SIN AND THE RESTRAINER

Second Thessalonians 2 describes a "man of sin" whom the Lord would destroy at his coming, and the text indicates that a restraining power was preventing his full manifestation. Several early writers, including Tertullian and Victorinus, interpreted this restrainer as the Roman Empire itself. The "mystery of lawlessness" was seen as already at work, with Nero's actions serving as the precursor to the final unveiling of lawlessness (Tertullian 1869a, 3:563). This association with the Roman state and Nero supports a preterist reading of the "man of sin," suggesting that these events were not awaiting a future end but were unfolding within the first-century context.

MODERN MISCONCEPTIONS: RFID CHIPS AND TECHNOLOGY

In modern times, various interpretations of the mark of the beast have arisen, including the belief that it might refer to RFID (radio-frequency identification) chips or other forms of technology. For instance, Ken Peters, in his revelation on the *Prophecy Club*, shared that the mark of the beast could be some kind of RFID chip implanted in the hand between the thumb and index finger. He likened this technology to the prophetic mark described in Revelation, as it allows individuals to engage in commerce digitally.[1]

Others have pointed to the Google Chrome logo or mobile phones as possible manifestations of the mark of the beast, emphasizing the control that such technologies exert over modern life. However, these interpretations often overlook the symbolic nature of Revelation's imagery. As Wright (2011) and other scholars argue, the text is deeply rooted in first-century concerns, especially regarding loyalty to Christ over Rome. To suggest that John envisioned a literal microchip is to engage in eisegesis, reading modern issues into the text rather than interpreting it in its historical context.

THE BEASTS OF REVELATION: ROMAN EMPIRE AND ISRAEL

The two beasts in Rev 13—the beast from the sea and the beast from the earth—are often interpreted as symbols of the Roman Empire and apostate Israel, respectively. The beast from the sea (Rev 13:1) represents the oppressive power of the Roman Empire, while the beast from the earth (Rev 13:11) represents Israel's corrupt religious leadership, who collaborated with Rome in persecuting early Christians.

By placing 666 in the context of these beasts, Revelation highlights the struggle between God's kingdom and the imperial powers that demand

---

1. Peters, "I Saw the Tribulation," 1.21.33.

allegiance. Those who receive the mark of the beast align themselves with these corrupt systems, rejecting Christ's lordship.

SPIRITUAL SIGNIFICANCE OF THE MARK

The mark of the beast is not necessarily a physical mark, such as an RFID chip, but rather a spiritual allegiance. Receiving the mark symbolizes accepting the ungodly ways of the world and rejecting Jesus as Lord. The forehead and hand, representing belief and action, are symbolic of this alignment. In contrast, the 144,000 sealed in Rev 7 represent those who are baptized into Christ, standing in direct opposition to those who receive the mark of the beast.

LITERARY DEVICES IN REVELATION

Revelation's apocalyptic style is rich with literary devices. The number 666 serves as an allusion to other symbolic uses of numbers in the Bible, particularly in contrast to the number 7, which signifies divine completeness. Furthermore, John contrasts the 144,000 sealed with those who bear the mark of the beast, highlighting the stark division between loyalty to Christ and allegiance to worldly powers.

DIAL 666 FOR DEBATE: A HITCHCOCKIAN CRITIQUE

In discussing the mark of the beast and the number 666, various interpretations have been put forward over the centuries. One particularly detailed analysis is provided by Hitchcock, who critiques the preterist view that Nero Caesar is the beast of Rev 13 (2007). According to Hitchcock, the identification of Nero with 666 is problematic for several reasons. He points out that the calculation requires the use of Hebrew gematria, whereas John's audience was primarily Greek speaking. Hitchcock questions why John would choose to render the name in Hebrew instead of using a more straightforward Greek calculation. Additionally, Hitchcock emphasizes that when Nero's name is calculated in Greek, the value is 1005, not 666. This discrepancy, he argues, undermines the preterist claim that the beast refers to Nero.

SECTION 2: KEY FULL PRETERIST INTERPRETATIONS OF PROPHECIES

However, while Hitchcock presents a thorough critique, his analysis is not without its own limitations. He seems to underplay key historical evidence, such as the use of gematria in early Christian communities to refer to Nero in cryptic terms. As noted by Gumerlock, there is evidence from a fifth-century biblical genealogy that some in the early church were already associating Nero's name with 666 (Gumerlock 2006). This challenges Hitchcock's assertion that the Nero connection was a more recent scholarly development. The association of Nero with the number 666 served as both a protective cipher, allowing early Christians to identify their persecutor symbolically without overtly challenging Roman authority. This approach, rooted in both religious conviction and survival strategy, underscores how the early church operated within a world hostile to their faith.

Moreover, Hitchcock's futurist leanings sometimes color his conclusions. His reliance on a future, global fulfillment of the beast's worship ignores the first-century historical context in which the early Christians lived under the oppressive rule of Rome and, in particular, Nero. While Hitchcock raises valid points about inconsistencies in the preterist position, it is worth noting that his own interpretations are shaped by the expectation of future events that may bias his readings of the text.

Nonetheless, Hitchcock's depth of analysis and attention to detail, especially in linguistic matters such as the use of gematria, should be commended. His work forces us to wrestle with the complexities of Rev 13 and challenges preterists to account for some of the textual difficulties in applying 666 to Nero Caesar. Yet, when considering Hitchcock's objections, it remains clear that early Christian writers did use symbolic language and cryptographic techniques to convey hidden meanings, which were often rooted in their immediate historical context.

A LASTING ALLEGIANCE: BEYOND THE MARK AND INTO REVELATION'S MESSAGE

In conclusion, while modern interpretations of the mark of the beast often gravitate towards technological concerns—such as RFID chips, microchips, or the influence of digital commerce—the original context of Revelation offers a far more profound and spiritually symbolic message. For early Christians living under the Roman Empire, the mark of the beast represented a forced submission to the imperial system, which demanded allegiance not only to the emperor but to a way of life that conflicted with the teachings of Christ.

Through this lens, Revelation's imagery of the beast and its mark can be understood as a symbolic depiction of the spiritual allegiance required by the empire. The act of receiving the mark, whether on the hand or forehead, symbolizes one's thoughts and actions being aligned with the world's values, rather than with the kingdom of God. As such, the mark of the beast signifies a profound rejection of Christ's lordship and a submission to the corrupted, earthly powers represented by Rome and the forces allied with it.

The debate surrounding the number 666 also invites a broader consideration of gematria and the symbolic use of numbers in Jewish and Christian apocalyptic literature. While scholars like Hitchcock offer compelling critiques of the preterist identification of Nero Caesar as the beast, these critiques often overlook or dismiss the deep historical context in which these cryptic numbers would have been understood by early Christians. The use of 666 to represent Nero in Hebrew and the alternative reading of 616 suggest that early believers found ways to cryptically express their opposition to the Roman state without drawing unnecessary attention. As Gumerlock's research has shown, the association between Nero and 666 was already present in the early church, further complicating attempts to dismiss this connection as a modern invention.

At the heart of this debate is the recognition that Revelation speaks through symbols, allegories, and apocalyptic imagery meant to convey spiritual truths to a persecuted and suffering people. In this context, the mark of the beast is less about a literal future technology or mark and more about loyalty—whether to the kingdom of God or to the kingdom of man. Early Christians faced existential pressure to conform to the Roman imperial system, and receiving the mark of the beast was a potent way to describe this submission to Rome's authority and values.

Finally, while Hitchcock's detailed critique of the preterist position provides valuable insights and forces a closer examination of the text, his futurist bias at times limits the scope of his analysis. He dismisses the historical relevance of Nero's reign and the immediate context of first-century persecution. Yet, his attention to the numerological significance of 666 and his exploration of gematria deepen our understanding of the complexities of Revelation and how apocalyptic literature uses symbols and numbers to convey layers of meaning.

Section 2: Key Full Preterist Interpretations of Prophecies

In the end, Revelation invites us to move beyond literalistic interpretations and instead embrace its symbolic richness. The text challenges us to think deeply about spiritual allegiance, loyalty, and the ever-present tension between the kingdoms of this world and the kingdom of God. Understanding the mark of the beast requires more than decoding a number—it requires discerning the spiritual battle that has always confronted humanity, not only in the first century but in every age. In every age, Revelation calls readers to discern where their true allegiance lies: not merely in visible marks or modern technologies but in the alignment of their thoughts, actions, and devotion. As Christians resisted the pull of Rome, today's believers are called to confront their own cultural idols, recognizing that true allegiance to Christ is a matter of spiritual conviction, not material conformity.

9

The Sun, Moon, and Stars

When I consider thy heavens, the work of thy fingers, the moon and the stars, which thou hast ordained; What is man, that thou art mindful of him?

—Ps 8:3–4

IN APOCALYPTIC LITERATURE, ESPECIALLY in Revelation, the falling of the sun, moon, and stars is not a literal description of astronomical events but a symbolic representation of spiritual and political upheaval. The Old Testament prophetic tradition frequently used cosmic signs to signify the downfall of nations and power structures. This chapter will explore how these celestial symbols represent the end of the old covenant and the fall of Jerusalem in AD 70, drawing on both Jewish and Greco-Roman influences.

SYMBOLISM IN THE SUN, MOON, AND STARS

The use of sun, moon, and stars as symbols for earthly powers is well established in biblical prophecy. A prime example of this can be found in Gen 37:9–11, in which Joseph dreams of the sun, moon, and eleven stars bowing down to him. His father Jacob (Israel) interprets these symbols as representing himself (the sun), Joseph's mother (the moon), and Joseph's brothers (the stars). This symbolic interpretation of celestial bodies representing people, familial leadership, and authority within the nation of Israel sets a precedent for understanding similar imagery throughout prophetic texts: "Behold, the sun and the moon and the eleven stars made obeisance to me" (Gen 37:9).

The sun, moon, and stars are again used to represent Israel and her leadership in Rev 12:1: "And there appeared a great wonder in heaven; a woman clothed with the sun, and the moon under her feet, and upon her head a crown of twelve stars."

Here, the woman represents Israel, and the twelve stars represent the twelve tribes of Israel, further reinforcing the idea that celestial symbols are used to depict nations and rulers. David Chilton notes that this type of imagery points to the covenantal structure of Israel, with its tribal leadership depicted as the stars in the heavens (Chilton 1987, 85–86).

This same symbolic use is evident in Isa 13:10, which describes the fall of Babylon: "For the stars of heaven and the constellations thereof shall not give their light: the sun shall be darkened in his going forth, and the moon shall not cause her light to shine."

Similarly, Ezek 32:7-8 foretells the destruction of Egypt: "And when I shall put thee out, I will cover the heaven, and make the stars thereof dark; I will cover the sun with a cloud, and the moon shall not give her light."

In both cases, the darkening of the sun, moon, and stars symbolizes the collapse of nations and their leadership, a theme that is carried into Revelation.

As we trace these celestial symbols from the Old Testament into the New, a pattern emerges, reflecting the progression of Israel's history and its covenantal journey. These prophetic symbols don't merely denote celestial bodies but mark key shifts in authority, governance, and covenantal standing. In the New Testament, these symbols reappear, indicating spiritual transformation and the culmination of Israel's narrative with the transition to a new covenant. The recurring use of the sun, moon, and stars to signify ruling powers underscores the metaphorical language of cosmic change as covenantal transition—a key to understanding the apocalyptic language that follows.

The Sun, Moon, and Stars

THE ABSURDITY OF LITERAL INTERPRETATION

Apocalyptic literature thrives on symbolic, often hyperbolic, imagery to express spiritual and societal upheaval rather than physical destruction. In the context of prophecy, symbols like falling stars or darkened suns communicate the collapse of systems of power and authority rather than literal, observable events in the cosmos. This symbolic approach reflects the intended message of Revelation: that monumental change often comes in spiritual or institutional forms, reshaping society in ways more profound than physical ruin.

If we were to take these cosmic signs literally, the consequences would be astronomically absurd. Stars, which are millions of times larger than the earth, would obliterate the planet if even one were to "fall." The idea of literal stars falling to Earth, a relatively modest planet in the cosmos, would result in total destruction long before any further prophecy could be fulfilled. This absurdity further underscores the symbolic nature of these signs, which represent the political upheaval and spiritual judgment associated with the fall of Jerusalem in AD 70.

THE GRECO-ROMAN INFLUENCE IN LUKE'S ACCOUNT

While Mark and Matthew follow the Jewish apocalyptic tradition, Luke's Gospel (21:25–26) appears to adopt a Greco-Roman orientation. As Van Iersel suggests, Luke may have shifted the meaning from the dysfunction of the luminaries as Jewish symbols to more general signs in the heavens, possibly alluding to the Greco-Roman deities Helios and Selene, who governed the sun and moon (1996). This interpretation reflects the influence of Greco-Roman astrology, where celestial phenomena were viewed as omens for significant earthly events. This reorientation highlights how different gospel writers interpreted the apocalyptic language of the sun, moon, and stars based on their intended audiences.

Luke's audience, potentially including many from Greco-Roman backgrounds, would understand celestial events as signs of divine activity affecting human affairs, aligning with how Roman and Greek societies viewed omens. Unlike Mark and Matthew, who emphasize Jewish eschatological motifs, Luke's language frames these cosmic signs in a way that non-Jewish audiences could interpret as signaling dramatic shifts ordained by higher powers.

Section 2: Key Full Preterist Interpretations of Prophecies

This gives us a deeper understanding of how the cosmic imagery in the New Testament can be interpreted through different cultural lenses. Where Mark saw the fall of Jerusalem, Luke might have been appealing to a broader Greco-Roman audience, reinterpreting the sun, moon, and stars in ways they could understand as divine portents rather than covenantal judgments.

Luke's approach not only bridges Jewish and Greco-Roman perspectives but also frames these cosmic symbols as culturally resonant indicators of upheaval. By weaving together these traditions, Luke broadens the prophetic vision, portraying apocalyptic signs in ways that resonate with a diverse audience. This blending of Jewish and Greco-Roman elements sets the stage for Revelation's intensified use of cosmic imagery, where symbolic judgments on the old order signal the dawn of a transformative covenant.

COSMIC METAPHORS OF JUDGMENT AND RENEWAL

The falling of the sun, moon, and stars in Revelation reflects the Old Testament tradition of using cosmic imagery to symbolize the collapse of political powers and religious structures. As seen in Gen 37:9–11 and Rev 12:1, these celestial bodies symbolize Israel, its leadership, and authority. While literal interpretations of stars falling to earth would result in absurdity and destruction, the symbolic meaning aligns with the spiritual and political judgments associated with the fall of Jerusalem.

As Yarbro Collins highlights, this language evokes catastrophe on a cosmic scale but in symbolic terms, referring to the end of the old covenant and the transition into a new era (1984, 56–58). Meanwhile, Van Iersel's exploration of Luke's Greco-Roman influences adds depth to our understanding of how different cultures interpreted these cosmic symbols.

The cosmic imagery throughout Revelation not only symbolizes the political and spiritual upheaval surrounding Jerusalem's fall but also embodies the sweeping covenantal transformation that Christ's coming brought. The sun, moon, and stars illustrate a profound shift from the old order, represented by Israel's leadership and sacrificial system, to a new era of spiritual worship in the kingdom of God. These apocalyptic symbols do not signal the end of the physical universe but rather announce a new reality where worship transcends earthly structures. Thus, the cosmic language in Revelation challenges readers to move beyond literal interpretations and embrace the deeper, spiritual fulfillment that Christ's kingdom represents—a covenant bound not by geography or temple but by faith.

10

The Identity of Beasts
Sea, Scarlet, and Land

By their fruits ye shall know them.
—MATT 7:20

IN REVELATION'S SYMBOLIC TAPESTRY, the sea, scarlet, and land beasts emerge not merely as antagonists but as personifications of the systems that sought to undermine the early Christian community. These apocalyptic figures are critical to understanding the spiritual, political, and religious forces at work in the first-century world of early Christianity. The sea beast, closely aligned with the scarlet beast, represents the Roman Empire in its vast political and military power. This beast's authority and reach, given by the dragon (Satan), brought persecution upon the early church, marking the empire's role as a central oppressor in the narrative of Revelation. The scarlet beast, which is ridden by Babylon, a symbol of false religion and moral corruption, emphasizes the spiritual and economic corruption that Rome propagated throughout its empire. Together, these two beasts exemplify the oppressive regime that early Christians faced, combining imperial might with religious apostasy.

On the other hand, the land beast, while still working in tandem with the sea beast, has a more nuanced role as a religious enforcer. It acts as a

Section 2: Key Full Preterist Interpretations of Prophecies

counterfeit religious power, misleading people into worshiping the sea beast and perpetuating false doctrines. With horns like a lamb but the voice of a dragon, the land beast embodies spiritual deception, symbolizing either the Jewish authorities who aligned with Rome or false religious systems that mimicked the true faith but ultimately sought to undermine it.

This chapter examines the identity and significance of these beasts within the full preterist framework, which sees the prophetic visions of Revelation as largely fulfilled in the first century. By exploring the roles of the sea beast, scarlet beast, and land beast, we aim to reveal how these symbols illustrate the broader spiritual, political, and religious conflicts that defined early Christian persecution, particularly the events surrounding the destruction of Jerusalem in AD 70.

THE BEAST OF THE SEA

The sea beast introduced in Rev 13 has been a subject of significant scholarly debate. The historical-critical perspective widely agrees that the beast from the sea in Rev 13:1 symbolizes the Roman Empire. Pierre Prigent supports this view, noting that the identification of the beast with Rome is held by the "very great majority of commentators" (1981, 313). The Roman Empire, with its dominance, was a persecutor of Christians, which aligns with the beast's role as a blasphemous, oppressive force.

As early as the reign of Augustus, emperors were declared divine, establishing a pervasive imperial cult that required subjects to offer sacrifices or worship the emperor as a god. Refusal to participate in this cult, a defining aspect of Christian resistance, underscored the depth of the conflict between the empire's demands and the early church's allegiance to Christ.

However, from a full preterist perspective, this symbol is not just a generic empire but a specific representation of Nero Caesar's reign, which marked the height of Rome's persecution against Christians leading up to the destruction of Jerusalem in AD 70. The sea is often associated with chaos and foreign nations in biblical imagery (Ps 74:13), and in Dan 7, the four beasts rising from the sea represent successive world empires (vv. 3–7). The fourth beast, corresponding to Rome, serves as a backdrop for John's vision of the sea beast in Revelation.

THE BEAST'S BLASPHEMY AND PARODY OF CHRIST

The beast in Rev 13:3 suffers a "fatal wound" yet miraculously recovers, a parody of Christ's death and resurrection, as Schejbal notes. The Greek phrase ὡς ἐσφαγμένην used here parallels the description of the Lamb (Jesus) in Rev 5:6, further emphasizing that the beast is attempting to imitate Christ's resurrection to deceive the world (Schejbal 2018, 45–50).

This fake resurrection is followed by the world marveling and worshipping the beast. This reflects the Roman imperial cult, where emperors like Nero were venerated as gods (John 19:12–15). The blasphemous names on the beast's heads likely represent the divine titles claimed by Roman emperors (Rev 13:1–4), a theme commonly linked with Nero in preterist thought.

Furthermore, Rev 13:8 extends this narrative by noting that those who worship the beast are not innocent but complicit in the persecution of Christians, echoing Rev 6:10, where the martyrs call for justice (Schejbal 2018, 45–50). This complicity with the beast highlights the pervasive influence of Rome's persecution.

THE "WAS, IS NOT, AND IS TO COME" BEAST

In Rev 17, the beast is described as one that "was, is not, and is to come" (v. 8), a direct parody of God's eternal nature. Schejbal emphasizes that this is a mocking echo of the way God and Christ are referred to earlier in Revelation (Rev 1:4, 8; 4:8), signifying that the beast desires to be like God (2018, 45–50). Rome's relentless persecution of Christians, including a brief cessation of widespread oppression after Nero's death, cemented its influence as a seemingly immortal empire, resonating with the phrase "was, is not, and is to come." This perception of Roman endurance symbolized the empire's longevity and its enduring threat, despite changes in leadership, which early Christians recognized as a cyclical oppression. After Nero's death, Rome's persecution of Christians continued under future emperors, particularly Vespasian and Titus, fulfilling the "is to come" aspect of the beast. Vespasian's reign marks the resurrection of Rome's oppressive power, especially through the destruction of Jerusalem in AD 70.

Section 2: Key Full Preterist Interpretations of Prophecies

SEA AND SCARLET

The sea beast and the scarlet beast in the book of Revelation are closely related in their shared symbolism of opposition to God, but they represent different aspects of that opposition. Both beasts share the imagery of seven heads and ten horns, symbolizing Rome's political structure and power dynamics, particularly as described in Rev 13 and Rev 17. However, their distinctions lie in the nature of the opposition they symbolize.

The sea beast in Rev 13 represents Rome's political and military might, which directly persecuted the early Christian church. It rises out of the sea, traditionally a symbol of chaos and the gentile nations, showing how Rome's imperial power emanated from the chaotic and diverse territories it ruled. This beast is empowered by the dragon (Satan), emphasizing the role of political oppression in Satan's plan to defeat God's people.

On the other hand, the scarlet beast in Rev 17 is portrayed as being ridden by the woman Babylon, a symbol of spiritual corruption and false religion. The scarlet beast represents the same empire but focuses on the spiritual and moral degradation of Rome as it aligns with false religious systems and economic decadence, symbolized by the harlot. While the sea beast wields direct political and military power, the scarlet beast portrays Rome's spiritual corruption and cultural influence, which seduced nations and peoples into worshipping the empire and abandoning God.

This connection to Babylon amplifies the image of Rome as an epicenter of both spiritual and societal debauchery. Babylon, historically known for its grandeur and apostasy, serves as the prototype of a power that subjugates both spiritually and economically, portraying Rome as a parallel to the ancient city's sins. Rome's reach encompassed vast territories, drawing nations into its orbit and promoting idolatrous practices that permeated cultural and religious life across the empire (Chilton 1987, 389–90).

Thus, the two beasts are part of the same system of Rome's imperial power, but they highlight different facets of Rome's oppression—one political and the other spiritual. Their interrelatedness emphasizes Rome's comprehensive opposition to God, where both political force and spiritual deception are tools used to lead people away from the truth.

SEVEN HEADS AND TEN HORNS

The seven heads of the sea beast, described as representing both seven hills and seven kings (Rev 17:9–13), are an unmistakable reference to Rome, historically known as the city of seven hills. The five fallen kings could correspond to the Roman emperors Julius Caesar, Augustus, Tiberius, Caligula, and Claudius, while Nero would be the sixth, the one reigning during the writing of Revelation.

Regarding the ten horns, preterists often identify these as the leaders of Rome's ten provinces (Muller 2007, 160–62). Egypt, Syria, Gaul, Spain, Italy, and Britain were among Rome's crucial territories. These provincial leaders allied themselves with Rome's persecution of Christians (Rev 13:12–14), but they were ultimately defeated by the Lamb (Rev 17:14).

SYMBOLISM OF THE BEAST'S RESURRECTION

In terms of the fatal wound suffered by the beast, several interpretations exist, including Cestius Gallus's defeat at the hands of the Jews, though preterists find a more fitting explanation in the rapid spread of Christianity throughout the empire, even within the imperial household (Rom 1:8, Phil 4:22). Christianity's rise could be seen as a mortal blow to Rome's authority, yet the recovery of the beast represents Rome's continued persecution, under Vespasian, which intensified after Nero's reign (Prigent 1981, 248–50).

Finally, Rev 13:14 tells us that the beast was wounded by a sword, which could symbolize the word of God (Eph 6:17), emphasizing that the ultimate defeat of the beast lies in the spiritual realm rather than merely the political.

SUMMARY OF SEA BEAST

The sea beast of Rev 13 represents the Roman Empire, with particular focus on Nero Caesar as a personification of Rome's oppressive, blasphemous power. From a full preterist perspective, this beast signifies Rome's persecution of Christians leading up to the destruction of Jerusalem in AD 70, and the beast's recovery is tied to Rome's resurgence under Vespasian. The symbolism in Revelation, including the beast's blasphemy, wound, and worship, portrays Rome as a counterfeit divine power that sought to challenge the true authority of Christ, but which ultimately falls in the face of the Lamb's victory.

Section 2: Key Full Preterist Interpretations of Prophecies

LAND BEAST

In Rev 13:11, the land beast is introduced as a figure who exercises authority on behalf of the sea beast. This second beast has two horns like a lamb, but speaks like a dragon. This description symbolizes deception—appearing harmless and even Christlike, but speaking and acting with the authority of Satan. The land beast represents an earthly power aligned with the sea beast but with a distinct role in spiritual deception and false prophecy.

SYMBOLISM AND SPIRITUAL CONFLICT

De Waal suggests that the land beast symbolizes a counterfeit of the Holy Spirit, working to deceive the world into worshiping the sea beast (Rome) and its blasphemous claims (2015, 20–22). This idea is rooted in the way the land beast performs miraculous signs, including calling down fire from heaven (Rev 13:13), mimicking the acts of the true prophets of God, such as Elijah. According to De Waal, this conflict is deeply spiritual, not merely political, and will not always be evident to the senses. The land beast serves as a religious enforcer of Rome's political power, deceiving people into worshipping the empire and abandoning Christ.

This spiritual deception becomes clear when examining how the land beast sets up the image of the beast and demands worship of it, mirroring the Roman imperial cult, where citizens were required to declare Caesar as Lord (John 19:12–15). The mark of the beast represents a spiritual allegiance, contrasting those who bear the mark with the 144,000 who are sealed by God (Rev 7:4; 14:1). In a preterist interpretation, this is a direct challenge to the faith of early Christians, who were persecuted for refusing to participate in emperor worship.

INTERPRETATIONS OF THE LAND BEAST

Historically, scholars like Irenaeus have identified the land beast as an individual false prophet. Koester notes that Irenaeus, working within a literary framework of early Christian writings, viewed the land beast as the false prophet, juxtaposed with Christ (2017, 333–34). Since Christ was an individual, Irenaeus assumed that both the sea and land beasts would also be individuals. This led him to interpret the land beast as antichrist, aligning it with the man of lawlessness in 2 Thess 2:1–12 and the antichrist from the Johannine Epistles.

However, Koester questions this individualistic reading, noting that the beast from the land in Rev 13 functions more as a corporate entity, representing false religious systems or those complicit in political power. He notes that while Irenaeus made sense of early Christian writings, John's vision presents a broader symbolic struggle rather than a single opponent. The land beast is a false prophet not limited to one individual but representing the system of false religion that promotes emperor worship and secular power.

THE ROLE OF THE LAND BEAST IN REVELATION'S PROPHETIC FULFILLMENT

From a full preterist perspective, the land beast represents Jewish leaders and local authorities who aligned themselves with Rome to maintain their power. This interpretation is strengthened by the land beast's connection to the sea beast—both work in tandem to deceive the world, particularly in enforcing the imperial cult. The two horns like a lamb but speaking like a dragon could symbolize the religious authorities in Jerusalem, who outwardly professed faith but ultimately rejected Christ and collaborated with the Roman Empire.

Historically, Jewish authorities cooperated with Roman power, especially in opposition to early Christians, in a significant and unique alignment. This connection is embodied in the land beast's complicit role, as it acts to enforce the imperial cult's demands while appearing religious. This dual role captures the alliance between Roman authority and local religious leadership, which upheld Roman authority and worked to suppress Christian influence (France 2007, 253–54). Therefore, the land beast is seen as representing the corrupt Jewish leaders who partnered with Rome to suppress Christianity. This interpretation aligns with the historical role that Jewish leaders played in the persecution of early Christians (Acts 17:5–7). While the sea beast represents Rome's political power, the land beast represents the religious forces that aided the empire's agenda.

Section 2: Key Full Preterist Interpretations of Prophecies

WIDER IMPLICATIONS AND SPIRITUAL DECEPTION

The land beast also performs miraculous signs, which reflect the spiritual deception inherent in false religions that mimic the power of the Holy Spirit. According to De Waal, these signs are part of the spiritual warfare that defines the end-times conflict (2015, 14). The beast's power to call down fire from heaven echoes the true prophets of Israel but is ultimately a counterfeit designed to lead people away from God. This deception is so deep that it even seems to challenge the church's prophetic witness (Rev 11).

The land beast, as a counterfeit of the Holy Spirit, aims to undermine the church's witness, mimicking the miracles of Christ to lead people into false worship. This spiritual conflict is not easily discernible to the physical senses, as De Waal suggests, and it calls for spiritual discernment to recognize the false religious systems at work.

SUMMARY OF LAND BEAST

The land beast in Rev 13 is not simply a political figure but a religious entity that works in collaboration with the sea beast (Rome) to deceive people into worshiping secular power. Through the imperial cult and false religious systems, the land beast promotes allegiance to Rome and opposition to Christ. Scholars like Irenaeus saw this beast as an individual false prophet, while modern interpretations, including Koester and De Waal, emphasize the systemic nature of the spiritual deception. This preterist interpretation highlights how Jewish religious leaders and local authorities allied with Rome to suppress Christianity, portraying the land beast as an enforcer of spiritual apostasy in the first century.

THE TRIUMPH OVER EMPIRE AND APOSTASY

In Revelation, the sea beast, scarlet beast, and land beast reflect layers of opposition to God's kingdom. The sea beast symbolizes Rome's political and military dominance, while the scarlet beast underscores its spiritual and moral corruption. The land beast, more subtly but no less powerfully, represents the anti-Christian religious authorities who aligned with imperial Rome, creating a counterfeit authority to mislead the people and oppose the early church.

The Identity of Beasts

Viewed through full preterism, these beasts' roles find their culmination not in a distant future but in the first-century upheavals that reshaped faith and history. The Lamb's victory over these beasts is a profound affirmation: even the strongest empires and most deceptive authorities are temporary, destined to fall before the eternal kingdom. Revelation assures its readers that, while oppressive forces may rise, their power is fleeting compared to the enduring triumph of Christ's reign. The Lamb's victory, timeless and unyielding, promises that all forces opposing God's kingdom, no matter their strength or longevity, are but fleeting in the scope of eternity.

11

The Two Witnesses of Revelation 11

> The lips of truth shall be established for ever: but a lying tongue is but for a moment.
>
> —Prov 12:19

THE TWO WITNESSES IN Rev 11 stand as central figures in the apocalyptic vision, bearing testimony against a world in rebellion against God. These figures, often seen through a symbolic lens, have sparked much debate regarding their identity and role within the larger eschatological framework. While some see them as literal individuals, others argue they are representative of larger entities, such as the church or Holy Scripture. Regardless of interpretation, the two witnesses serve as prophetic voices that invoke the legacy of Old Testament figures such as Moses and Elijah, while also pointing to the broader mission of God's people and the unfolding of divine judgment.

THE SYMBOLISM OF MOSES AND ELIJAH

In Rev 11, the two witnesses are imbued with the miraculous powers of Elijah and Moses. Elijah's ability to shut the heavens, preventing rain for three and a half years (1 Kgs 17:1) and Moses's power to turn water into blood (Exod 7:14–21) during the plagues of Egypt both reflect the authority of these Old Testament figures. As Eric Fugett points out, the pairing of Moses and Elijah is significant not only for their miraculous deeds but for their roles as bearers of divine law and prophecy (2003, 45). Moses represents the law, having delivered the commandments to the Israelites, while Elijah embodies the prophetic tradition, calling Israel back to God through acts of judgment.

The two witnesses in Revelation mirror these roles by exercising divine authority throughout their 1,260-day mission. The reference to 1,260 days—a period equivalent to three and a half years—recalls the drought in Elijah's time (Luke 4:25; Jas 5:17), highlighting the importance of the number three and a half within the biblical context. This time period, often associated with tribulation and prophetic witness, is essential to understanding the witnesses' role in the eschatological timeline.

THE LEGAL AND PROPHETIC FUNCTION OF TWO WITNESSES

The number two in the depiction of the witnesses has deep significance in both Old and New Testament traditions. According to Deut 19:15, two or more witnesses were required to establish a valid testimony in court. This legal principle is echoed throughout the Bible, where two witnesses are often needed to confirm truth or establish guilt. In fact, this motif appears in pivotal moments of judgment, such as in Gen 19, where two angels visit Sodom before its destruction. Their arrival is not simply a visit but a symbolic act that precedes divine judgment on the city's unrighteousness. The presence of these two figures underscores the severity and inevitability of the judgment to come, just as the two witnesses in Revelation foreshadow the impending consequences for those who persist in opposition to God's will.

Throughout Scripture, pairs are established to underscore the certainty of a testimony: two angels announced the resurrection of Jesus (Luke 24:4), two spies were sent by Joshua into Jericho (Josh 2:1), and two witnesses are depicted here to fulfill both the legal and spiritual dimensions of truth. Notably, the two witnesses in Revelation echo the prophetic tandem of Moses and Aaron, who confronted Pharaoh, and of Joshua and Zerubbabel, the two "olive trees" described in Zech 4, who were empowered to restore Israel. This pattern of dual testimony underscores the power and authority of a message when confirmed by two, aligning with the theme in Revelation that God's judgment is indisputable and divinely sanctioned.

In Revelation, the two witnesses serve not only as prophets but also as legal testifiers, bearing witness against the world's rebellion. This courtroom imagery reinforces the notion that their testimony is vital to the unfolding judgment described in the book of Revelation.

As Muller explains, their "standing before the Lord of the earth" signifies their proximity to God and their divine commission (2002, 6). Their role is not merely to proclaim repentance but also to act as legal witnesses in the divine courtroom, where their testimony is used to build the case against those who oppose God. This legal motif runs throughout Revelation, with the witnesses serving as crucial figures in this cosmic drama. The witnesses' dual role invokes the requirement for truth and purity in testimony, intensifying their duty as divine agents within God's judicial proceedings against unfaithful Israel.

MARTYRDOM AND RESURRECTION: THE THREE AND A HALF DAYS

One of the most significant elements of the two witnesses' narrative is their death and subsequent resurrection. After prophesying for 1,260 days, the witnesses are killed by "the beast from the abyss," a figure often associated with Satan or the political powers through which he operates (Rev 11:7). Their bodies lie in the street of the great city, spiritually called "Sodom and Egypt," where their Lord was crucified. This city, clearly identified as Jerusalem, represents a place of both spiritual corruption and judgment.

The witnesses lie dead for three and a half days, mirroring the three-and-a-half-year period of their prophecy. This number, as Fugett points out, appears repeatedly in biblical texts, symbolizing a temporary period of trial or suffering before a divine resolution (2003, 58). The three and a half days also echo Jesus's time in the grave before his resurrection, further linking the witnesses' fate to Christ's own passion and victory over death. This connection aligns their fate with a pattern of spiritual endurance symbolized throughout Scripture, where three and a half frequently marks the culmination of a divine test (Dan 12:7; Rev 12:6).

Their resurrection after three and a half days is a powerful symbol of God's ultimate authority over life and death. The world, which rejoices at the death of the witnesses, is struck with fear as they are raised and ascend to heaven in the sight of their enemies. This act not only demonstrates God's power but also serves as a final warning to those who continue in rebellion.

THE SACKCLOTH AND THE CALL TO REPENTANCE

The attire of the two witnesses is also laden with symbolic meaning. Throughout the Bible, sackcloth is associated with mourning, repentance, and prophetic proclamation. Prophets such as Jeremiah and Jonah wore sackcloth as they called the people to repentance, urging them to turn back to God before it was too late. The witnesses' wearing of sackcloth (Rev 11:3) underscores the recurring invitation throughout Revelation for humanity to repent before the impending divine judgment, underscoring the mercy woven even into these calls of wrath.

Sackcloth also symbolizes the suffering that accompanies their mission. The prophetic ministry is not without hardship, and the witnesses face hostility from those who dwell on the earth. The "inhabitants of the earth," a phrase consistently used negatively in Revelation, represent those who are opposed to God and his people. The witnesses' message torments the consciences of these individuals, causing psychological and spiritual anguish. Yet, despite this, they refuse to repent, rejoicing instead at the death of the witnesses (Rev 11:10).

FIRE FROM THE MOUTHS: DIVINE JUDGMENT

One of the most striking images associated with the two witnesses is the fire that proceeds from their mouths, consuming their enemies (Rev 11:5). While fire is often associated with Elijah, who called down fire from heaven to destroy the messengers of King Ahaziah (2 Kgs 1:10–17), the idea of fire emanating directly from the mouths of the witnesses suggests something more. As Muller notes, this imagery is closely tied to the word of God, which is described as a fire in the mouth of the prophet Jeremiah: "I am making my words in your mouth a fire, and this people the wood it consumes" (Jer 5:14) (2002, 11).

The fire from the witnesses' mouths represents the power of their prophetic word, which brings judgment upon the unrepentant. This theme of judgment runs throughout the narrative of the two witnesses, who are empowered to strike the earth with plagues, stop the rain, and turn water into blood. Their actions echo the plagues of Egypt and the judgments that

SECTION 2: KEY FULL PRETERIST INTERPRETATIONS OF PROPHECIES

befell those who refused to heed God's word in the Old Testament. This symbolism is enriched by understanding that the Old and New Testaments together present a cohesive witness to God's ultimate authority, his expectations, and his promises fulfilled through Christ.

THE WITNESSES AS SYMBOLS OF SCRIPTURE

While some interpret the two witnesses as representing the church, there is also a strong argument to be made for understanding them as symbols of the Old and New Testaments. Ekkehardt Muller (2002) and Kenneth Strand (1981) argue that the two witnesses may represent the word of God and the testimony of Jesus, reflecting the unity of the Old and New Testaments. This interpretation emphasizes the witnesses' role in proclaiming God's truth and judgment throughout history, culminating in the events of Revelation.

The use of singular nouns such as "body" and "mouth" in connection with the witnesses further supports this idea, as it highlights their unity in bearing divine testimony. Despite being two figures, they act as one entity, delivering one message and sharing one fate. This unity in duality mirrors the way Scripture operates as a cohesive testimony to God's plan of salvation, encompassing both the old and new covenants.

THE WITNESSES' MISSION AND THE ESCHATOLOGICAL FULFILLMENT

The mission of the two witnesses, like that of Moses and Elijah, is one of preparing the people for judgment. Their testimony, empowered by the Spirit, is both a call to repentance and a warning of impending doom. As Muller observes, their proximity to the Lord of the earth reflects their divine inspiration and commission (2002, 9). Though their message is rejected by many, their resurrection and ascension serve as a final vindication of their mission and the truth of their testimony.

From a full preterist perspective, the story of the two witnesses aligns with the events leading up to the destruction of Jerusalem in AD 70. The witnesses' death and resurrection symbolize the triumph of the early church over the forces of opposition, while their ascension prefigures the ultimate victory of Christ's kingdom. The period of 1,260 days corresponds to the

Roman-Jewish War, further linking the narrative to the historical events of the first century.

THE ENDURING LEGACY OF THE TWO WITNESSES

The two witnesses of Rev 11 stand as powerful symbols of prophetic testimony, divine judgment, and the ultimate victory of God over evil. Whether interpreted as individual figures, representatives of the church, or symbols of Scripture, their role in the eschatological drama is undeniable. Their mission of proclaiming truth in the face of opposition, their death and resurrection, and their ascension into heaven all point to the larger theme of God's sovereignty and the certainty of his plan.

In the end, the witnesses embody the call to repentance that runs throughout the Bible, urging humanity to turn back to God before the final judgment. Their narrative serves as both a warning and a promise—a reminder that though the world may rejoice at their temporary defeat, God's truth will ultimately prevail and his witnesses will stand victorious. In them, the church finds an enduring model of unwavering faith, a reminder that each believer bears the responsibility of truth even when facing opposition, embodying the witnesses' spirit in every generation.

12

Every Eye Will See Him

The real voyage of discovery consists not in seeking new landscapes, but in having new eyes.

—Marcel Proust

I once was lost, but now am found; was blind, but now I see.

—John Newton

The prophecy in Rev 1:7—"Behold, he cometh with clouds; and every eye shall see him, and they also which pierced him: and all kindreds of the earth shall wail because of him. Even so, Amen"—is often viewed through a futurist lens, with many imagining a physical return of Christ. However, when examined through the lens of full preterism, this prophecy points to the judgment of covenant Israel in AD 70, when the Roman siege of Jerusalem served as a visible manifestation of Christ's authority.

This chapter explores how spiritual sight and covenantal judgment form the basis for understanding this prophecy. Rather than a distant physical event, this "coming" is best understood as divine judgment witnessed by those who rejected Christ, particularly those responsible for his crucifixion.

THE NATURE OF SPIRITUAL SIGHT: SEEING THE UNSEEN

In John 9:39–41, Jesus declares: "For judgment I am come into this world, that they which see not might see; and that they which see might be made blind."

This emphasizes his mission to grant spiritual sight to the humble while rendering blind those who, in their pride, claim to see clearly. This echoes the whitewashed tombs imagery from Matt 23:27, where those who appear outwardly righteous are inwardly corrupt.

Paul captures this theme in 2 Cor 4:18: "While we look not at the things which are seen, but at the things which are not seen: for the things which are seen are temporal; but the things which are not seen are eternal."

Spiritual vision is key to perceiving Christ's reign and judgment, as those with true sight can discern the significance of the destruction of Jerusalem in AD 70. Beale asserts that Revelation's symbolic language, including the "clouds" metaphor, reflects divine authority rather than literal events (1999, 284). The destruction of the old-covenant system required spiritual discernment to see Christ's authority in action.

Spiritual sight unveils truths that are often invisible to the physical eye, illuminating the deeper, covenantal messages behind historical events. Just as physical sight perceives the external, spiritual sight discerns the divine hand at work in moments of judgment.

ACTS 1:11 AND REVELATION 1:7: A MISUNDERSTOOD DISCREPANCY

Critics of the preterist interpretation often point to Acts 1:11, where the angel tells the disciples, "This same Jesus, which is taken up from you into heaven, shall so come in like manner as ye have seen him go into heaven" (Acts 1:11). At first glance, this seems to suggest a future physical return, matching the way Jesus ascended. However, a deeper reading reveals that the "like manner" of his return refers to authority and power rather than the specific physical details of the ascension, aligning with ancient Jewish thought that emphasized continuity of function rather than identical physical replication (Wright 1996, 635).

The ascension in Acts was witnessed by a small group of disciples, and Jesus's return in AD 70 was similarly witnessed—by covenant Israel—but not in a literal or physical sense. The Rev 1:7 passage—"every eye shall see him, and they also which pierced him"—ties directly to those who rejected and crucified Christ, many of whom were alive to witness Jerusalem's destruction. James McGrath argues that this passage speaks of a judgment event rather than a physical return, consistent with apocalyptic language (2012).

To interpret "those who pierced him" as literally resurrected spectators watching a five-foot-five-inch Jewish man descend on a cumulus cloud renders the text almost absurd, missing the profound spiritual depth intended. Preston critiques this view with a touch of humor, suggesting that such a literal approach reduces the majestic return of Christ to a surreal physical spectacle, rather than the transformative, spiritual revelation it was meant to convey (2008, 102).

"COMING ON THE CLOUDS": JUDGMENT IMAGERY IN SCRIPTURE

The phrase "coming with the clouds" in Rev 1:7 draws on rich Old Testament imagery. In Isa 19:1, "the LORD rideth upon a swift cloud, and shall come into Egypt: and the idols of Egypt shall be moved at his presence." Similarly, Ps 104:3 describes God as one "who maketh the clouds his chariot." These and other passages, such as Nah 1:3 and Joel 2:1–2, employ cloud imagery to symbolize divine judgment, not a literal event. This language is echoed in Matt 24:30, where Jesus, speaking of the coming destruction of Jerusalem, uses clouds to signify his coming in judgment.

Throughout the Old Testament, clouds symbolized both divine judgment and protective presence. When God appeared to lead Israel through the wilderness, he was "in the cloud," guiding and safeguarding his people (Exod 13:21). In apocalyptic texts, however, clouds typically represent judgment upon rebellious nations, as in Nahum and Isaiah, transforming a sign of guidance into a foreshadowing of retribution for covenant unfaithfulness.

In the preterist view, the "clouds" represent God's authoritative judgment rather than a future physical descent. Corbett argues that cloud imagery reflects God's presence in judgment, particularly in cases where covenant nations, such as Israel, are judged (n.d., s.v. "Secondly").

THE INTERACTION WITH THE HIGH PRIEST: A COVENANT JUDGMENT

In Mark 14:61–62, Jesus tells the high priest: "I am: and ye shall see the Son of man sitting on the right hand of power, and coming in the clouds of heaven." Jesus's statement to the high priest was not merely a foretelling of judgment but a legal proclamation of accountability. As a covenantal representative of Israel, the high priest symbolically bore witness to Israel's rejection of their promised Messiah. The phrase "coming in the clouds" would resonate with the Jewish authorities as a familiar signal of divine reckoning, reflecting a fate tied to their covenant responsibilities.

This prophecy directly addresses the Jewish leadership and was fulfilled in the destruction of Jerusalem, when the old-covenant system was judged. The high priest and other leaders who rejected Christ would witness this judgment firsthand.

This passage ties directly to Luke 17:20–21, where Jesus says: "The kingdom of God cometh not with observation: Neither shall they say, Lo here! or, lo there! for, behold, the kingdom of God is within you."

This kingdom is not visible in a literal sense but is a spiritual reality. The high priest's "seeing" of Christ "coming on the clouds" was not about physical sight but recognizing the divine judgment that came upon Israel.

THE INVISIBILITY OF GOD AND THE SPIRITUAL KINGDOM

Scripture consistently emphasizes the invisibility of God and the spiritual nature of his kingdom. First Timothy 1:17 refers to the "King eternal, immortal, invisible, the only wise God," pointing to the nonphysical nature of divine rule.

Similarly, Heb 12:28 speaks of an "unshakable kingdom": "Wherefore we receiving a kingdom which cannot be moved, let us have grace, whereby we may serve God acceptably with reverence and godly fear." This kingdom, established through Christ, is not one bound by physical realities but exists in the hearts of believers. Beale emphasizes that the spiritual nature of Christ's reign is key to understanding Revelation, where physical and spiritual realities are conveyed through symbolic language (1999, 19–20).

Section 2: Key Full Preterist Interpretations of Prophecies

EVERY EYE SHALL SEE HIM—THROUGH JUDGMENT

The prophecy of Rev 1:7—that "every eye shall see him"—finds its fulfillment in the covenantal judgment upon Israel in AD 70. The destruction of Jerusalem, witnessed by the generation that rejected Christ, was a manifestation of his divine authority. The cloud imagery, the interaction with the high priest, and the emphasis on spiritual sight all point to a nonphysical, spiritual coming of Christ in judgment.

By employing the symbolic language of clouds and spiritual vision, Scripture reveals that "every eye shall see him" is not to be understood literally but as a profound spiritual realization. Those with spiritual sight witnessed this judgment, while those who were blind to Christ's authority remained in darkness.

In the context of covenant judgment, "seeing" denotes a recognition that transcends physical vision—it is an acknowledgment of divine justice. Just as the plagues of Egypt revealed God's power to both Israel and Pharaoh, the fall of Jerusalem in AD 70 served as an undeniable testament of Christ's authority to all of Israel, even those who were spiritually blind.

13

Wipe Away Every Tear

Tears are words that need to be written.

—Paulo Coelho

In Rev 21:4, the vision of God wiping away tears transcends personal consolation and instead signals the restoration of a covenantal relationship that had been ruptured by sin. Throughout the Old Testament, tears represented the grief of Israel, not just over individual struggles but over their spiritual separation from God. Israel's history of rebellion, exile, and captivity gave birth to tears, and their ultimate restoration in Christ wipes them away forever. This chapter will explore the profound theological implications of these tears, moving from the fall of humanity in Genesis to the eschatological fulfillment seen in Christ's first-century work.

TEARS BORN FROM SIN

The tears of Israel flow from the nation's covenantal failures. They were not simply personal lamentations but a reflection of their spiritual death—a state of alienation from God that began with Adam and Eve in the garden of Eden. From the moment Adam and Eve sinned in the garden of

Eden, death entered the world. However, this death was not simply physical; it was also spiritual, representing separation from God (Wright 2008, 32–33). Genesis 2:17 foretold that Adam and Eve would die on the day they disobeyed, yet their biological lives continued. What transpired was a deeper estrangement from divine life, a separation that Israel continued to experience throughout its history. As Paul explains in Eph 2:1, those who live in sin are "dead in trespasses and sins," echoing Jesus's rebuke, "Let the dead bury their dead" (Luke 9:60), reinforcing the idea that sin is a kind of spiritual death (Aune 1997, 52).

Wright elaborates that covenantal rupture is not merely Israel's personal or national failing but represents a theological journey that transitions from estrangement to redemption through divine restoration (2008, 147–48). This echoes Paul's writings on reconciliation, where Israel's grief reflects a deeper, collective lament of separation and ultimate restoration.

Jeremiah, often called the "weeping prophet," lamented the spiritual and physical exile of Israel, a nation that had forsaken its covenant with God. In Jer 9:1, he cries, "Oh that my head were waters, and mine eyes a fountain of tears!" because of the people's rebellion and the impending Babylonian captivity. Similarly, Lamentations, authored by Jeremiah, captures Israel's collective lamentation: "Streams of tears flow from my eyes because my people are destroyed" (Lam 3:48). These tears, borne from sin and failure, reveal a deeper spiritual death—a state of separation from God that dates back to Gen 3 (Beale 1999, 1045). As Israel's sin led to death, exile, and captivity, their tears reflect the burden of the broken covenant and their spiritual disconnection.

THE BURDEN OF THE LAW AND COVENANT

The old covenant brought both blessings and curses. Israel's inability to keep the law resulted in the curses being enacted upon them, bringing about their tears. Psalm 119:136 states, "Rivers of waters run down mine eyes, because they keep not thy law." The law was not only the divine standard but also a reminder of Israel's inability to maintain righteousness. Israel's tears are also tied to their experience of exile and captivity, consequences of breaking the covenant. The Babylonian exile epitomized this estrangement. In Ps 137:1, the exiled Israelites lament, "By the rivers of Babylon, there we sat down, yea, we wept, when we remembered Zion." This was a physical exile, but more poignantly, it symbolized the spiritual exile that Israel had brought upon itself by failing to keep God's law (Bauckham 1993, 276).

The valley of dry bones in Ezek 37 illustrates the nation's spiritual death: "Our bones are dried, and our hope is lost: we are cut off for our parts" (v. 11). This vision was not merely about physical death but about spiritual death, a death marked by hopelessness and separation from God. As Beale points out, this dry bone imagery underscores Israel's need for a divine resurrection—one that would come through Christ (1999, 1046). The exile and captivity represent tears that are not easily wiped away, as they reflect the spiritual bankruptcy of a people unable to uphold their covenant (Wright 2019, 212).

THE PROMISE OF RESTORATION AND WIPING AWAY OF TEARS

The prophets consistently spoke of a coming restoration where the tears of exile and death would be wiped away. Ezekiel's vision of dry bones being brought to life (Ezek 37:5) is a powerful image of this promised resurrection. This is not merely physical but spiritual resurrection—Israel being restored to covenantal life through divine intervention. The New Testament makes this explicit in Acts 5:20, where the apostles are instructed to "go, stand and speak in the temple to the people all the words of this life." Through Jesus Christ, the tears caused by Israel's failure to uphold the law are wiped away, as the law is fulfilled in him (Matt 5:17). Beale notes that the prophetic imagery, particularly that of resurrection, operates as a metaphor for the restoration of divine covenant (1999, 1052). Through Jesus, the fulfillment of these covenantal promises signifies the end of Israel's tears and alienation, symbolically transitioning them into the new-covenantal life.

The New Testament reveals that the wiping away of Israel's tears was realized in Christ's first-century fulfillment of the covenant promises. Jesus declared, "Ye shall weep and lament, but the world shall rejoice: and ye shall be sorrowful, but your sorrow shall be turned into joy" (John 16:20). This promise was fulfilled when the old covenant, symbolized by the destruction of the temple in AD 70, gave way to the new covenant—a reality in which spiritual death was conquered. As Paul proclaims in 1 Cor 15:54, "Death is swallowed up in victory." This was not a promise for some far-off future but for that generation, who would live to witness the culmination of Christ's kingdom.

SECTION 2: KEY FULL PRETERIST INTERPRETATIONS OF PROPHECIES

As we look to Rev 21:4, the imagery of God wiping away every tear finds its eschatological culmination. The "former things"—death, sorrow, and pain—are no more, for the new Jerusalem represents the fulfillment of the covenant. This is not just a future event, but something realized in Christ's first-century kingdom work. Paul echoes this theme in Rom 8:2, "For the law of the Spirit of life in Christ Jesus hath made me free from the law of sin and death." The tears of Israel, born from sin, are wiped away as they are liberated from the bondage of the law and brought into the freedom of God's children.

BIRTH PANGS AND THE JOY OF NEW LIFE

The birth pangs motif in Scripture further enriches this discussion. Just as the world groaned under the weight of sin, so did Israel anticipate a new birth through Christ. Romans 8:22 captures this well: "For we know that the whole creation groaneth and travaileth in pain together until now." These birth pangs symbolize the transitional suffering that precedes the full manifestation of God's kingdom. Beale further contextualizes the birth pangs in apocalyptic literature as indicative of the end of one covenant era and the beginning of another (1999, 1047). Such imagery signals the impending manifestation of God's kingdom, where the community of faith anticipates the spiritual fulfillment of covenantal promises. This imagery reinforces the idea that the wiping away of tears is not just a future hope but a present reality in the life of the church, as it experiences the full restoration of God's promises (Beale 1999, 1050). The New Testament church experienced this labor, witnessing the destruction of Jerusalem and the birth of the new covenant (Matt 24:7–8). This is why Peter can write to the believers, encouraging them to endure, for their trials will give way to inexpressible joy (1 Pet 1:6–9).

Jesus Himself likened this process to the labor of a woman in John 16:20–22, saying, "Ye shall be sorrowful, but your sorrow shall be turned into joy." This speaks directly to the new Jerusalem, where the tears of the old covenant's pain and judgment are replaced by the joy of eternal life. The culmination of this new birth is not only the wiping away of tears but the defeat of death itself. As Paul declares in 1 Cor 15:54, "Death is swallowed up in victory."

The birth pangs of this new era, described in Matt 24:7–8; Rom 8:22; and Rev 12, symbolize the transitional suffering of the first-century church.

These birth pangs indicated the dawning of a new creation—the new Jerusalem—where the tears of persecution, exile, and separation would be wiped away forever (Aune 1997).

FIRST-CENTURY FULFILLMENT: THE END OF TEARS

The idea that the tears of Rev 21:4 were wiped away in the first century is supported by the repeated emphasis on imminency throughout the New Testament. Jesus assured his disciples that this generation would not pass until all things were fulfilled (Matt 24:34). Revelation 1:3 and 22:6 emphasize that the time is near for these events, pointing to their fulfillment in the lives of the first-century believers (Bauckham 1993, 276).

The apostles, who lived through the destruction of Jerusalem and the establishment of the new covenant, were witnesses to the wiping away of tears as the old-covenant order passed away. Wright emphasizes that the New Testament's language of imminency aligns with the apostles' anticipation of seeing the old covenant's final dissolution within their generation (2013, 1267). Their witness to these events marked a definitive end to covenantal exile and inaugurated the new Jerusalem as a spiritual, realized kingdom. Christ's resurrection and the destruction of the temple represented the fulfillment of the prophecies of Isaiah, Ezekiel, and Daniel, all of which pointed to the restoration of God's people. The new Jerusalem described in Revelation is not a distant physical city but a present spiritual reality in the church, where death, sorrow, and pain are no more.

Thus, the wiping away of tears in Rev 21:4 is not a promise for a far-off future but the fulfillment of God's plan for Israel and the world, realized in the first century. The tears of death, exile, and captivity have been wiped away through the victory of Christ. The new Jerusalem is here, and the kingdom has come in its fullness.

FIRST-CENTURY FULFILLMENT AND THE END OF TEARS

The promise of wiping away tears in Rev 21:4 is not simply an abstract hope for a distant future. It is grounded in the first-century fulfillment of God's promises to his covenant people. The overwhelming weight of biblical prophecy, particularly in the New Testament, emphasizes that the time for the restoration of Israel and the end of spiritual death came in the

Section 2: Key Full Preterist Interpretations of Prophecies

generation that witnessed the culmination of Christ's ministry, his resurrection, and the destruction of Jerusalem.

Jesus consistently foretold that the kingdom of God was at hand. In Matt 24:34, he declared, "This generation shall not pass, till all these things be fulfilled." The destruction of the temple, the sign of the end of the old-covenant order, occurred within that generation. This corresponds to the birth pangs spoken of in Matt 24:7–8 and Rom 8:22, where the world, groaning under the weight of sin, was about to give birth to the new creation. This theme is emphasized by Paul, who speaks of the imminent fulfillment of the promises: "The night is far spent, the day is at hand" (Rom 13:12).

When Christ proclaimed, "Ye shall be sorrowful, but your sorrow shall be turned into joy" (John 16:20), he was not speaking of a distant hope but of a reality that would be realized in the lifetime of his apostles. The tears shed over the destruction of Jerusalem and the persecution of the early church would be wiped away as the new covenant was fully established in Christ's reign. Peter's assurance that the faithful would receive the salvation of their souls (1 Pet 1:9) is not some far-off reward but a fulfillment for those living in that time, as they endured the "birth pangs" of a new age.

The tears of Israel, born out of the captivity and spiritual exile they faced for centuries, were wiped away as the first-century church witnessed the final vindication of God's people. The valley of dry bones in Ezekiel's vision (Ezek 37:11) came to life as the spiritual resurrection promised through Christ was fulfilled. This wasn't simply a metaphor for distant eschatological hope but an immediate, tangible reality for those believers who saw the old-covenant order pass away and the new covenant firmly established (Acts 5:20).

Thus, the fulfillment of Rev 21:4—the wiping away of tears, the end of death, and the defeat of sorrow—was realized in the first century. The new Jerusalem is not a future city but a present reality in the church, where the old order of sin and separation has passed away. As the prophets, apostles, and Jesus himself foretold, the tears of Israel were wiped away when the kingdom of God was fully inaugurated through Christ's victory over death, not just for a future generation but for the believers who lived to see the destruction of the old-covenant world and the dawn of the new.

The New Testament repeatedly emphasizes the nearness of these events: "The time is at hand" (Rev 1:3); "These things must shortly come to pass" (Rev 22:6). These were not abstract statements but concrete promises to the first-century church, which saw the fulfillment of all that had been prophesied. Jesus's words to his disciples—"Blessed are the eyes which see the things that ye see" (Luke 10:23)—stand as a testament that the era of tears has ended, the covenant has been restored, and the kingdom has come in its fullness.

14

No More Sea, New Heaven and New Earth

The Kingdom of God, in its fullest sense, is a realm where justice and peace are eternally established, and the old order has completely passed away.

—WILLIAM BARCLAY, *REVELATION OF JOHN*

THE VISION OF A new heaven and new earth in the book of Revelation pulses with the energy of a new dawn—the dissolution of the old and the birth of the new. As John peers into the future, the sweeping symbolism speaks not just of cosmic change but of covenantal renewal, a shift in the very fabric of spiritual reality. It is the end of the old covenant, the shattering of the former world order, and the establishment of something gloriously different.

THE VISION OF A NEW COVENANT

> And I saw a new heaven and a new earth: for the first heaven and the first earth were passed away; and there was no more sea. (Rev 21:1)

No More Sea, New Heaven and New Earth

This verse, often misunderstood as the obliteration of the material universe, actually heralds the passing of the old order—the end of the Jewish age with its covenantal framework. As Wright suggests, the imagery of the new heaven and new earth is deeply covenantal (2015, 49). It represents a transformation, a renewal of relationship, not a literal end to the physical world but the dawning of a new covenant between God and his people. The universe doesn't burn away; the covenant does. Beale highlights that John's vision of the new heaven and new earth isn't a literal cosmic obliteration but a profound transformation of covenantal reality (1999, 1040–42). The imagery, therefore, represents the passing of the old-covenant order, which defined Israel's relationship with God, and the full establishment of a new covenant through Christ. This symbolic renewal echoes the prophetic vision in Isa 65:17, where a new creation symbolizes restored relationship rather than a remaking of physical substance.

This imagery finds roots not only in the cosmic metaphors of creation but in the unraveling of history itself. Just as God's presence hovered over the chaotic waters in Genesis, bringing order to disorder, so too do the new heaven and new earth represent order restored, with God's covenant now fully established. What was once broken, marred by sin and rebellion, is now made new—a heavenly landscape where justice and peace reign.

THE SEA OF CHAOS AND ROME'S FALL

But John adds an intriguing phrase—there was "no more sea." What does this mean? To the ancient Jewish mind, the sea was the embodiment of chaos, a symbol of unruly, oppressive forces. Throughout the Old Testament, the sea is consistently depicted as a symbol of chaos and opposition to God's order. Psalms describe God's triumph over sea monsters (Ps 74:13–14), and Isa 57:20 speaks of the "wicked like the troubled sea." This imagery establishes the sea as a representation of hostile forces, particularly gentile powers that rose against God's people. Chilton points out that, in Revelation, the sea is the embodiment of the Roman Empire's oppressive rule—Rome rising as the last of the chaotic "beasts" that John foresees being eliminated as God's kingdom establishes true order and peace (1987, 456–57).

Daniel, too, paints this vivid picture of the sea giving rise to wild beasts (Dan 7:2–3), these beasts being empires, kingdoms, oppressive regimes. Rome was one such beast, rising from the chaotic seas of gentile

Section 2: Key Full Preterist Interpretations of Prophecies

nations, swallowing lands and peoples whole. But in John's vision, the sea is gone. Rome's power, the power of chaos, oppression, and tyranny, has been extinguished.

The sea—the embodiment of all that is foreign and opposed to God's rule—is no more. With its removal, there is no longer any room for disorder or rebellion against the true King. As "the kingdoms of this world have become the kingdoms of our Lord, and of His Christ" (Rev 11:15), the sea, representing Rome and gentile nations, fades from view, swallowed by the kingdom of God. Wright explains that Revelation's vision reflects Daniel's prophecy (Dan 2:44) that God's kingdom would arise and ultimately replace all earthly empires (2012, 122–23). This imagery of "no more sea" signals the end of the gentile dominance over Israel, with God's kingdom now taking precedence over every human power. As the kingdoms of the world give way to God's eternal reign, the forces that once fueled division and chaos are now subdued under divine authority.

In this moment, we are witnesses to the final breaths of the old-covenantal world, a world governed by human institutions and empires. The new heaven and new earth are nothing less than the declaration that God reigns—completely, finally, and irrevocably. And just as the kingdoms of this world have fallen, so too has the chaos that sustained them.

A COVENANT FULFILLED

Scholar Rikk Watts explains that the sea in Revelation often represents rebellious nations opposing God (2000). However, in the new heaven and earth, these rebellious forces have been subdued, signifying the complete establishment of God's reign where there is no longer a place for such opposition. This vision of a world without the sea signals the end of oppressive, chaotic forces like Rome, and the full establishment of God's kingdom.

A NEW COVENANT

The new heaven and new earth, therefore, speak of the fulfillment of the promises made to Abraham, to Israel, and to the world. As F. F. Bruce points out, the renewal of heaven and earth is the sign of God's covenantal faithfulness, not to burn the world but to transform it (1985, 105). This is the covenant that Christ's death and resurrection have brought into being,

No More Sea, New Heaven and New Earth

and in this covenant, "old things have passed away; behold, all things are become new" (2 Cor 5:17).

The new heaven and new earth aren't the destruction of creation, but the dawn of something more—a realm where God and his people are finally united in perfect harmony. The kingdom is no longer far off; it is here. The new world is a place where the former things are no longer remembered, where the sea—the old chaos, the empire of Rome—is but a forgotten dream.

John's vision is not just of a new covenant but a cosmic reordering. The heavens and earth, symbolic of the divine and human relationship, are now realigned. The sea, symbolic of division, is removed, and what remains is peace. The kingdoms of this world have indeed become the kingdom of God.

15

The Millennial Reign Explained

Of the increase of his government and peace there shall be no end.
—Isa 9:7

The millennial reign of Christ, often debated and dissected through the centuries, holds a profound place within the eschatological landscape of Revelation. To understand this reign, one must first unlock a critical piece of the prophetic puzzle: the binding of Satan. It is within this binding that the key to deciphering the millennial reign lies.

THE BINDING OF SATAN: UNLOCKING THE PROPHECY

Revelation 20 opens with a vivid image of Satan, the great deceiver, being bound and cast into the abyss: "And I saw an angel come down from heaven, having the key of the bottomless pit and a great chain in his hand. And he laid hold on the dragon, that old serpent, which is the Devil, and Satan, and bound him a thousand years" (Rev 20:1–2).

This "thousand years" is widely contested, with interpretations ranging from literal to symbolic. Augustine argues that this period is symbolic, representing the era of the church's victory over Satan, not a literal

The Millennial Reign Explained

thousand-year period (Augustine 2003, 898–99). Within the full preterist perspective, the millennial reign is a period spanning from Christ's anointing until the first Roman-Jewish war, culminating in the destruction of Jerusalem in AD 70. The binding of Satan, therefore, is not future but past—initiated by Christ's victory over the powers of darkness.

CHRIST'S VICTORY AND SATAN'S BINDING

To understand Satan's binding, we must consider the seismic shift in authority that occurred during Christ's ministry. Throughout the gospels, Jesus spoke of binding the "strong man," Satan himself:

> No man can enter into a strong man's house, and spoil his goods, except he will first bind the strong man; and then he will spoil his house. (Mark 3:27)

> When a strong man armed keepeth his palace, his goods are in peace: But when a stronger than he shall come upon him, and overcome him, he taketh from him all his armour wherein he trusted, and divideth his spoils. (Luke 11:21–22)

In these verses, Jesus reveals that he, as the "stronger man," had come to bind Satan, making way for the plundering of his domain—the liberation of humanity from his oppressive rule (Chilton 1987, 512–13). In the early church, the imagery of binding held profound theological weight. By binding Satan, Christ restricted the adversary's ability to control nations and obstruct the spread of the gospel. Beale notes that in the Jewish apocalyptic tradition, binding a cosmic enemy was a signal of divine sovereignty—Satan's restraints imply the dawn of God's unchallenged rule, enabling the new-covenantal age to flourish (1999, 990–91). The victory over Satan was not a far-off promise but a present reality, demonstrated by Jesus's ministry of casting out demons and breaking the bonds of sin.

This shift in authority is further underscored in John 12:31–32, where Jesus declares, "Now is the judgment of this world: now shall the prince of this world be cast out. And I, if I be lifted up from the earth, will draw all men unto me."

The casting out of Satan here signals a pivotal moment in redemptive history. The power Satan once held over the nations was stripped from him. The cross became the fulcrum upon which the old-world order would turn,

Section 2: Key Full Preterist Interpretations of Prophecies

leading to the fall of Jerusalem and the final establishment of Christ's reign (Wright 2015, 196–97).

INTERPRETING REVELATION AS LAYERED VISIONS

It is important to approach John's visions in Revelation not as a strict chronology of sequential events but as layered perspectives or tapestries, each offering a unique angle on a unified narrative. Rather than a linear, step-by-step timeline, Revelation functions more like a series of tableaux—symbolic scenes stacked and intertwined to deepen our understanding.

Take, for example, Rev 13, where Satan empowers the beast, often identified with Nero Caesar (666) and linked to Rome's persecution of Christians. Then, in Rev 14, we hear of Babylon's fall and the arrival of the harvest—imagery often tied to the end of the age (as echoed in Matt 13:39). Yet in Rev 18, Babylon's fall is described once again, this time in vivid, conclusive detail. If we were to read these chapters in a strict chronological order, we'd be left with multiple "falls" of Babylon and multiple "ends," a sequence that risks confusion. Instead, these chapters seem to show us the same themes or events from different vantage points, layering meaning rather than unfolding a simple timeline.

When we arrive at Rev 20, with its account of the thousand-year reign and Satan's binding and release, a similar question arises: If the harvest is indeed the end of the age, how would it make sense for Satan's binding and release to follow this final harvest? Seen through a linear lens, this would appear out of order. However, if we approach Revelation as a nonlinear vision, this difficulty vanishes. Satan's binding and release may be understood as symbols of the same period of judgment already depicted elsewhere, simply viewed from a fresh angle, rather than a new phase occurring after the age's conclusion.

By interpreting Revelation as a collection of layered visions rather than a sequential timeline, we can see John's experience as a series of snapshots into a complex, multifaceted reality. Each chapter enriches our perspective on a shared period of turmoil, judgment, and redemption. This approach honors the symbolic nature of apocalyptic literature, allowing us to view these visions as simultaneous and cyclical, each reinforcing and expanding upon the others, rather than as a rigid chain of events.

In this way, Revelation is not a progression of events 1, 2, 3, 4, etc., but rather a woven tapestry of interconnected themes. Each vision strengthens and illuminates the others, layering symbolic imagery around the same core truths, inviting us to see beyond a simple linear framework.

THE SHIFT IN AUTHORITY

Before Christ's anointing and his ministry, Satan had significant authority over the kingdoms of the earth. This is evident in Matt 4:8-9, where Satan offers Jesus dominion over the world: "Again, the devil taketh him up into an exceeding high mountain, and sheweth him all the kingdoms of the world, and the glory of them; And saith unto him, All these things will I give thee, if thou wilt fall down and worship me" (Matt 4:8-9).

Yet, after Christ's resurrection, the tables are turned. No longer does Satan have such authority. Jesus now declares in Matt 28:18, "All power is given unto me in heaven and in earth."

The authority that Satan once boasted of had now been stripped from him, for Christ alone holds dominion. This shift in power fulfills the promise of Old Testament prophecy that foretold the Messiah's eventual reign over all nations (Ps 2:8-9). By claiming authority over heaven and earth, Jesus brings to life the prophetic hope that the dominion of oppressive spiritual forces would be displaced by the kingdom of God. Jesus's dominion is illustrated again in Luke 22:31-32, where Satan needs to petition Jesus for permission to sift Simon Peter: "And the Lord said, Simon, Simon, behold, Satan hath desired to have you, that he may sift you as wheat: But I have prayed for thee, that thy faith fail not."

Satan, no longer a kingmaker, must now appeal to Christ, demonstrating the profound shift in authority that has taken place.

THE PROBLEM OF SATAN'S CONTINUED ACTIVITY

Yet, some may object—if Satan is bound, why does he still seem to be active? After all, we see Satan entering into Judas in Luke 22:3-4, hindering Paul's journeys in 1 Thess 2:18, and even blinding the minds of unbelievers in 2 Cor 4:4.

This is where we must wrestle with the metaphor of Satan being "bound." For early Christians, the binding of Satan did not signify an absolute cessation of his actions but represented his restricted capacity to deceive on a global scale. Augustine argued that Satan's binding does not preclude all activity but rather limits his ability to deceive the nations (2003, 861). A chained dragon may still roar, but it cannot roam freely. As Wright notes, Satan's power was curtailed primarily to allow for the spread of the gospel among the nations (2015, 316). This partial restriction means that while he could still act through individuals, his influence on the broader scope of nations had been dramatically limited. Luke 10:18 gives us a glimpse of this cosmic shift when Jesus says: "I beheld Satan as lightning fall from heaven."

This fall from heaven, a status shift, signals Satan's diminished influence in the celestial realm. While he may still cause havoc on earth, his ultimate power has been significantly curtailed.

The parable of the wheat and tares also helps explain this phenomenon. Though the kingdom of heaven has been established, the sons of Satan still remain intermingled with the sons of the kingdom: "The kingdom of heaven is likened unto a man which sowed good seed in his field: But while men slept, his enemy came and sowed tares among the wheat, and went his way" (Matt 13:24–25).

The wheat and tares represent the dual realities of the kingdom's establishment and the lingering presence of evil. This dual existence of righteousness and rebellion reflects an ongoing spiritual warfare—a conflict limited in Satan's scope but persistent within individuals. As Gentry explains, the parable underscores that while Satan's cosmic influence is bound, his deception can still find footholds among those resistant to the gospel (1998, 287).

TIME INDICATORS AND THE FULFILLMENT OF GENESIS 3:15

Time indicators in the New Testament also support the view that Satan's defeat was imminent. John 12:31–32 tells us that the judgment of the world is at hand, and Satan is soon to be cast out. Similarly, Rom 16:20 promises that "the God of peace shall bruise Satan under your feet shortly"—a clear reference to the impending fulfillment of the prophecy in Gen 3:15, where the serpent's head would be crushed.

The binding of Satan, therefore, is not an eschatological event to be fulfilled in the distant future but a present reality, tied to the authority shift that occurred through Christ's life, death, and resurrection. His binding restricts Satan's ability to deceive the nations, setting the stage for the destruction of Jerusalem and the ultimate establishment of Christ's kingdom.

The Millennial Reign Explained

WHY THE 1000 YEARS IS SYMBOLIC

The "1000 years" mentioned in Revelation 20 appears only in that chapter, repeated six times in rapid succession, and nowhere else in Scripture is a literal 1000-year reign taught. In a book teeming with symbolism—the beast, the dragon, the harlot, the lake of fire—this sudden injection of literalism seems unwarranted. Revelation's apocalyptic genre demands a symbolic, covenantal lens rather than a rigid chronological one. The millennium, like the 144,000 (12 x 12 x 1000), is a symbolic construct, rooted in meaning, not mathematics.

The number 1000 has deep symbolic heritage in Scripture. It signifies covenantal fullness, completion, and divine scope, not exact measurement. God owns "the cattle on a thousand hills" (Psalm 50:10), keeps covenant "to a thousand generations" (Deut 7:9), and to Him "a thousand years are as one day" (2 Peter 3:8). These are not meant to be literal counts, but expressions of totality and divine vastness. Just as the New Jerusalem is described as a perfect cube (Rev 21:16)—mirroring the dimensions of the Holy of Holies—the millennium represents a spiritual space of divine reign, not a worldly utopia.

Importantly, the reign of Christ was already active long before Revelation 20. In 1 Corinthians 15:25, Paul writes, "He must reign till he hath put all enemies under his feet." This reign was ongoing in the first century—Christ had already ascended (Acts 2:34–36), been seated at the right hand of God (Eph. 1:20–22), and given "all authority in heaven and on earth" (Matt. 28:18). If we insist that the 1000 years is literal and still future, then Christ has either not begun His reign—or, worse, failed to subdue His enemies within the timeframe. But the testimony of Scripture is clear: He reigns now, and has been reigning since the first century. To suggest the 1000 years is still future either denies His current reign or implies His failure to subdue His enemies within that time—both positions contradict the testimony of Scripture.

Furthermore, this millennium is not described as a utopia. It's not a peaceful golden age. Revelation 20:4–6 speaks of "souls" reigning with Christ—martyrs, not earthly rulers. The scene is deeply spiritual and sacrificial, not political. These are those "beheaded for the witness of Jesus," reigning even as they await final vindication. Their reign coincides with persecution and suffering, not ease. This aligns perfectly with Revelation 6:9–11, where the martyrs cry out for justice and are told to "rest yet for a little season" until the full number of their fellow servants are killed. This echoes Jesus' words in Matthew 23:32: "Fill ye up then the measure of your fathers." It is a climactic generation of guilt, not glory.

The millennium is not a delay in Christ's reign, nor is it a future earthly kingdom. It is the symbolic duration of His triumph through the Church, from His ascension around AD 30 to the covenantal judgment on Jerusalem in AD 70. This is the mediatorial reign of Christ (1 Cor. 15:25), exercised until all enemies were placed beneath His feet. But His kingship does not conclude—it is transfigured, continuing as a peaceable and uncontested reign, no longer mediating between rival covenants, but dwelling fully in His people. The number 1000 is not a calendar span—it is a symbol of the completeness of His redemptive mission. A literal reading creates theological contradictions. A symbolic reading, rooted in the historical-grammatical method and grounded in the context of apocalyptic literature, upholds the richness of the gospel and the already-present Kingdom

The millennial reign, therefore, is not a distant future hope but a realized reality within the first-century church. By witnessing the Roman Empire's persecution and Jerusalem's fall, early Christians perceived the prophecy's fulfillment as unfolding before their eyes. The millennial binding of Satan freed them to spread the gospel across nations, a testament to God's transformative authority within history.

16

The Martyrs in Revelation

The light shines in the darkness, and the darkness has not overcome it.
—John 1:5

IN THE HEART OF Revelation, the martyrs stand as towering figures—souls who bear witness not only to their faith but also to the fulfillment of prophecy. They are not mere casualties of persecution; they are woven into the very fabric of biblical eschatology. Their blood cries out from beneath the altar, echoing the voices of prophets long silenced, but now vindicated. In this chapter, we will explore their identity, their role in the preterist understanding of prophecy, and how they stand as pillars of the ultimate judgment against the old world.

Throughout biblical history, the blood of the righteous stood as a testament against covenant-breaking powers, from Abel to the prophets. The preterist view sees these martyrs as the final witnesses, bridging the old covenant age with the new, where their sacrifice acts as the ultimate indictment against those who rejected the Messiah.

Section 2: Key Full Preterist Interpretations of Prophecies

THE MARTYRS: WITNESSES OF FAITH AND FULFILLMENT

> And when he had opened the fifth seal, I saw under the altar the souls of them that were slain for the word of God, and for the testimony which they held. (Rev 6:9).

Here we see the martyrs—those whose testimony, even unto death, marks them as the witnesses of the true faith. The preterist perspective emphasizes that these are not just any martyrs; they are the first Christians, the ones who stood firm in the face of Rome's oppressive power and Jewish rejection of Christ. Among them, we see Stephen, the first martyr, whose stoning in Acts 7 symbolizes the beginning of this great and terrible testimony of blood.

These early martyrs serve as the "firstfruits" of a greater judgment, embodying the prophetic cry for justice that would be realized in the fall of Jerusalem. In the preterist framework, the blood of Stephen, Peter, James, and Paul echoes through Revelation's visions as the signal of a divine reckoning. As Chilton notes, the martyrs embody the essence of judgment, with their blood marking the fulfillment of Christ's words against the apostate leaders of Israel (1987, 437).

The connection between Stephen and the martyrs of Revelation is a critical one. Stephen, whose face shone like an angel as he was accused, becomes a Christlike figure, echoing Jesus's own forgiveness as he declares, "Lord, lay not this sin to their charge" (Acts 7:60). Yet, in the grand narrative of eschatology, their blood still calls for justice, and justice, in the preterist worldview, is swift.

The martyrs stand in the long line of those whom Jesus condemns in Matt 23. "That upon you may come all the righteous blood shed upon the earth, from the blood of righteous Abel unto the blood of Zacharias" (Matt 23:35). These words are filled with foreboding—a declaration of vengeance for the slain prophets, a judgment that will befall that generation. The martyrs in Revelation are, in this sense, not only the witnesses to Christ but also the inheritors of the prophetic tradition, the final casualties of the old covenant's rebellion against God.

The Martyrs in Revelation

THE PRETERIST UNDERSTANDING OF MARTYRDOM

In the preterist worldview, the significance of the martyrs is deeply tied to the destruction of Jerusalem in AD 70. Their deaths are seen as the culmination of Israel's rejection of its Messiah and the prophets, leading to the ultimate judgment—the fall of the city and the end of the old-covenant age. Gentry points out that the martyrs stand as witnesses against Israel's unfaithfulness, accusing it of persecuting prophets and rejecting Christ (1998, 288). Their sacrifices prompt the divine judgment that ultimately brings about Jerusalem's downfall.

This identification of the martyrs with the early Christian church is crucial. They are the ones who stood against the Roman beast and the corrupt Jewish authorities who opposed the message of the gospel. Their deaths mark the turning point—their blood the seed of the church and the final testament against the fallen city of Jerusalem. Gentry argues that the martyrs in Revelation were the victims of the great persecution under Nero and the Jewish authorities, which culminated in the destruction of Jerusalem and the vindication of the martyrs (1998, 170–71).

This act of vengeance for the martyrs is also connected to Christ's prophetic words in Matt 23. Just as Jesus declared that "all the righteous blood shed upon the earth" would be avenged on that generation, the martyrs' deaths in Revelation cry out for the fulfillment of this promise. The preterist view holds that this vengeance was executed in the destruction of Jerusalem, when the old order collapsed and the blood of the martyrs was avenged (DeMar 1999, 367).

IDENTITY OF THE MARTYRS

Who are these martyrs? While Revelation does not give specific names, the preterist perspective ties them to figures such as Stephen and the early Christian apostles who were slain for their testimony. Stephen's stoning marks the beginning of this long line of witnesses. Peter, Paul, James—all of these figures could be seen among the souls under the altar. Their deaths were not in vain; they were the final witness to the impending judgment that would fall on the old-covenant world.

Stephen's death is especially poignant, as it echoes the rejection of the prophets. Just as Israel had rejected and slain the prophets of old, so too did they reject Stephen and the early Christian martyrs. Chilton suggests that Stephen's martyrdom marked more than a single tragic loss; it signaled the start of Christ's prophecy coming to fruition against Jerusalem, as the shedding of prophets' and apostles' blood filled the cup of divine judgment (1987, 437).

FILLING THE MEASURE OF JUDGMENT

Jesus, speaking to the scribes and Pharisees, declares, "Fill ye up then the measure of your fathers" (Matt 23:32).

> Wherefore, behold, I send unto you prophets, and wise men, and scribes: and some of them ye shall kill and crucify; and some of them shall ye scourge in your synagogues, and persecute them from city to city: That upon you may come all the righteous blood shed upon the earth, from the blood of righteous Abel unto the blood of Zacharias son of Barachias, whom ye slew between the temple and the altar. Verily I say unto you, All these things shall come upon this generation. (Matt 23:34–36)

Here, Jesus is condemning the Jewish leaders for following in the footsteps of their forefathers, who had killed the prophets. He uses the language of "filling up" the measure of their guilt—continuing the pattern of rebellion and murder against God's messengers. He declares that all the righteous blood spilled from Abel to Zechariah will be avenged on that generation.

The theme of "filling the measure" resonates deeply within the Jewish tradition, symbolizing the accumulation of sin to a tipping point that necessitates divine intervention. Historically, this concept recurs throughout prophetic texts, where the collective sins of a nation reach a threshold, prompting God's judgment. Just as in Gen 15:16, where the Amorites' iniquity was "not yet complete," the Jewish leaders' persecution of the prophets and early Christians reaches a climax in this generation, necessitating judgment.

THE CRY FOR JUSTICE: MARTYRS BENEATH THE ALTAR

> How long, O Lord, holy and true, dost thou not judge and avenge our blood on them that dwell on the earth? (Rev 6:10)

The souls of the martyrs, slain for their testimony, cry out for justice:

> And white robes were given unto every one of them; and it was said unto them, that they should rest yet for a little season, until their fellowservants also and their brethren, that should be killed as they were, should be fulfilled. (Rev 6:11)

This passage in Revelation reflects a similar theme: the martyrs under the altar are told to wait for a "little season," until the measure of suffering and death—the full number of martyrs—is complete. Only then will divine vengeance be exacted upon those responsible for their deaths. The phrase "until . . . should be fulfilled" resonates with Jesus's words in Matt 23 about filling the measure of their father's guilt.

This cry for justice, echoing through Rev 6, is central to the narrative's eschatological unfolding. Bauckham explains that Revelation's martyrs personify Israel's prophets whose blood cries out against covenantal injustice (1993, 83). Their cry is the culmination of a prophetic tradition demanding that God's kingdom be vindicated against its oppressors.

THE MATTHEW 23 AND REVELATION 6 CONNECTION

Matthew 23 emphasizes that the current generation is filling up the same measure of guilt that their forefathers began, by persecuting and killing the prophets. Jesus warns that once this measure is full, divine judgment will come upon them.

Revelation 6 mirrors this concept, with the martyrs asking how long until their blood is avenged. They are told to wait "a little while" until the number of those killed for their testimony is complete—the measure of martyrdom must be filled before judgment falls.

Both passages convey the idea that a "measure" of sin or guilt must be filled before God's wrath is poured out. In Matthew, the judgment is upon the Jewish leaders of that generation for rejecting and killing the prophets and Christ's followers. In Revelation, the martyrs are those killed under Roman and Jewish persecution, and their deaths "fill up" the measure that leads to the destruction of Jerusalem (in the preterist view) and the end of the old-covenant order.

Section 2: Key Full Preterist Interpretations of Prophecies

VINDICATION AND COVENANT RENEWAL

The connection to the martyrs in Matt 23 and Revelation emphasizes a prophetic pattern—just as the blood of the prophets was avenged, so too was the blood of the martyrs. The preterist perspective sees this as a fulfillment not only of Christ's warnings but of the entire narrative of biblical prophecy.

The martyrs in Revelation stand as the ultimate witnesses—the final proof of God's righteous judgment. They are tied to the first Christian martyrs, such as Stephen, and their deaths herald the end of the old-covenant age and the vindication of Christ's followers. They are catalysts for the covenant's renewal. Their sacrifice serves to ratify the old covenant's end, making way for the new. As Wright argues, the destruction of Jerusalem, symbolized through the vindication of the martyrs, marks a historical pivot from judgment to restoration, where the new covenant is fully realized and justice is eternally established (2015, 317). As their blood is avenged in the destruction of Jerusalem, the new-covenant age is born. In the preterist view, these martyrs fulfill the prophetic declarations of Jesus in Matt 23, where the blood of the righteous is finally answered.

17

Feast Fulfillment

For everything there is a season, and a time for every matter under heaven.
—Eccl 3:1

JEWISH FEASTS AND THE FULFILLMENT OF COVENANT EXPECTATIONS

THE JEWISH FEASTS MARK profound moments of remembrance and worship in Israel's history, each festival pointing to God's provision, guidance, and the promise of something more to come. For Christians, these feasts take on even deeper meanings, often seen as foreshadowing elements of Christ's life and ministry. In the full preterist perspective, these feasts not only point to Christ's work but also signal the complete realization of the new covenant. By understanding these sacred times, we can see a deliberate timeline that reaches fulfillment in Christ's two notable three-and-a-half-year ministries. His first ministry, beginning when he was around thirty, invited reconciliation and renewal, a time to prepare for God's kingdom (Beale 1999, 1039). The second, from AD 66 to 70, culminated in the destruction of Jerusalem and the temple, ending the era of temple-based worship and judgment upon the old covenant (Wright 2018, 121). Each feast captures aspects of these transformative periods, showcasing a divinely orchestrated plan woven into Israel's calendar—Christ's initial offer of reconciliation and his decisive judgment upon old-covenant Israel, fully realized through Jerusalem's fall.

Passover (Pesach)

The Passover, rooted in Israel's deliverance from Egypt, centers on the sacrifice of a lamb to protect the firstborn, symbolizing liberation through God's provision. In full preterist thought, this feast finds its ultimate fulfillment in Christ as the "Lamb of God," whose crucifixion represents a final, universal Passover. His sacrifice liberates believers not from physical bondage but from the binding power of sin, signifying the new covenant's initiation. Just as Israel was led to freedom, Christ's death frees all who follow him, marking a transition from the old system of sacrifice to the new (Keener 2020, 246).

In this final "Passover," Christ's sacrifice transcends the physical deliverance from Egypt, offering liberation from sin and inaugurating the new covenant. The blood of the Passover lamb, once bound to Israel alone, now covers all who believe, marking a universal covenant and fulfilling the prophetic shadow of God's ultimate deliverance.

Unleavened Bread

The Feast of Unleavened Bread followed Passover, commemorating the removal of leaven (symbolic of sin) from Israel's homes. This act of purification reflected Israel's call to holiness as God's people. Full preterists see Christ's sinless life and his "broken" body in the crucifixion as embodying this feast. As leaven was cast out, so too is sin's power removed, inviting a life of purity and dedication within the new covenant. The early church embodied this purity, free from "the leaven of malice and wickedness" (1 Cor 5:8), reflecting a community transformed by Christ's redemptive work.

Firstfruits

Taking place shortly after Unleavened Bread, Firstfruits was an offering of the season's first harvest, signifying gratitude and the anticipation of a fuller harvest to follow. In this spirit, Paul calls Christ the "firstfruits of those who have fallen asleep" (1 Cor 15:20), suggesting that his resurrection is the beginning of the new-covenant age of resurrection. Full preterists see this as the initial signal of resurrection life, fulfilled and inaugurated through Christ's victory over death.

Christ's resurrection, as the "firstfruits," introduces a new era of spiritual renewal. By defeating death, he inaugurates the age of the Spirit, where life extends beyond physical death, pointing to a future fully realized within the new covenant. This fulfillment anticipates the end of the old-covenant system and the dawn of an eternal relationship with God. His resurrection anticipates the complete redemption realized at the close of the old-covenant age in AD 70.

Pentecost (Shavuot)

Pentecost, celebrated fifty days after Passover, marked the giving of the law and the wheat harvest. In the New Testament, this feast marks the outpouring of the Holy Spirit, signaling a new-covenant community empowered to embody the law of Christ. For full preterists, this event inaugurates the kingdom, shifting the focus from a temple-centered worship to a Spirit-filled community.

With the outpouring of the Holy Spirit, believers embody the new covenant, symbolizing God's law now written on hearts rather than tablets. This event becomes a living testimony that the temple is no longer a physical structure but a community filled with his Spirit, marking a radical shift toward an accessible, intimate relationship with God. The Spirit's presence within believers foretold the soon-to-come judgment upon Jerusalem, solidifying the shift from the old to the new.

Trumpets (Rosh Hashanah)

A time of spiritual preparation, the Feast of Trumpets called Israel to repentance with the blast of the shofar. This festival, for full preterists, is seen in the warnings of impending judgment upon Jerusalem. Jesus's prophetic words, particularly in Matt 24, serve as this "trumpet call," urging repentance and heralding the transition from old-covenant practices. Trumpets thus foreshadow the final crisis for Jerusalem, marking the culmination of one era and the dawn of the new. As with prophetic warnings in Jeremiah and Isaiah, the sound of the trumpet serves as a divine call to awaken Israel to impending judgment. In Matt 24, Jesus's warnings resonate as the final trumpet, announcing a climactic judgment upon Jerusalem and the transition of God's covenant to a broader kingdom community.

Day of Atonement (Yom Kippur)

The most solemn feast day, Yom Kippur, called for national repentance and atonement, a moment when the high priest entered the holy of holies on behalf of Israel. Full preterists see Christ's sacrifice as the ultimate atonement, fulfilling all that Yom Kippur represented. The judgment upon Jerusalem in AD 70 signifies the final atonement for Israel under the old covenant. Through Christ, believers now stand eternally reconciled to God, no longer dependent on an annual ritual for purification.

Tabernacles (Sukkot)

Tabernacles celebrates Israel's wilderness journey and God's provision, with participants dwelling in temporary booths to remember their reliance on him. Full preterists interpret this feast as representing God's permanent "tabernacling" with his people under the new covenant, no longer bound to a physical temple. This feast epitomizes the arrival of the kingdom in its fullness, where God's presence dwells within the community of believers, symbolizing divine fellowship unbound by time or place. God's intention is to permanently "tabernacle" among his people—not in tents or temples. This new dwelling signals the culmination of the covenantal promises, where the separation of sin is erased and God's presence is eternally accessible.

FROM SHADOW TO SUBSTANCE: THE FEASTS IN FULLNESS

Together, these feasts create a tapestry of redemption that reaches its peak in Christ. Each festival anticipated stages of divine fulfillment, fulfilled in his dual missions: his first coming to extend new life and his second in judgment, signaling the covenantal shift from the old to the new (Beale 1999, 1040; Wright 2018, 122). Through this lens, the feasts serve not only as historical remembrances but as divine appointments that reflect God's faithful hand guiding the course of history toward its fulfillment. The Jewish feasts

Feast Fulfillment

offer a profound glimpse into the continuity of God's promises, where the sacrificial system, once bound to temple and ritual, finds its completion in the eternal "tabernacle" of his people.

18

The Age of Harvest

He that observeth the wind shall not sow; and he that regardeth the clouds shall not reap.

—Eccl 11:4

In Matt 13:39, Jesus declares, "The harvest is the end of the age." This statement, rich with eschatological meaning, signifies the culmination of the old covenant and the ushering in of the new. The harvest was an ancient promise, rooted in the prophetic traditions of the Old Testament. Its fulfillment marked the transition from the old covenant, bound to the law and national Israel, to the new covenant, where God's kingdom extends beyond one nation and includes the entire world.

For the harvest to be fulfilled, the old covenant had to be in effect. It follows, then, that the harvest was completed at the close of the old covenant, which ended with the destruction of Jerusalem in AD 70. This event signified the fulfillment of the promises to Israel and the beginning of a new era. The language Jesus used in Matt 28:20 is key here: "I am with you always, even unto the end of the age" (Greek: *aion*), not "world," as often mistranslated (Mounce 1993, 268). In ancient Jewish understanding, *aion* often signifies a defined period, particularly in relation to covenants. The end of the age, therefore, refers to the conclusion of the Mosaic covenant era, fully completed with Jerusalem's fall. This perspective affirms that Jesus's promises about the "end" were specific to Israel's old-covenant age, positioning his kingdom as the enduring reality across all generations.

THE UNIVERSAL PROCLAMATION OF THE GOSPEL

The New Testament makes it clear that the gospel was preached to the whole world during this period. Paul writes in Rom 10:18: "But I say, Have they not heard? Yes verily, their sound went into all the earth, and their words unto the ends of the world."

Similarly, in Col 1:23, Paul affirms that the gospel had been preached to "every creature which is under heaven." This shows that by the time of the destruction of Jerusalem, the message of the kingdom had reached the farthest corners of the known world. The Jewish diaspora, scattered across the Roman Empire, had heard the gospel, and through this proclamation, the elect—those destined for reconciliation—were gathered in, or "harvested," into God's kingdom (Chilton 1987, 346).

This harvest extended beyond Israel. Jesus, though sent primarily to Israel during his earthly ministry (Matt 15:24), was also the light to the gentiles, fulfilling Rom 15:8, which states that he came to confirm the promises made to the patriarchs. The children of God, scattered throughout the world—both Jews and gentiles—were gathered together, fulfilling John 11:51–52: "He prophesied that Jesus should die for that nation; and not for that nation only, but that also he should gather together in one the children of God that were scattered abroad."

Thus, the harvest symbolizes not only the end of Israel's unique covenant status but also the expansion of God's kingdom to encompass all nations. No longer was it one nation under God, but the entire world became his kingdom. This inclusive harvest transformed the concept of Israel's covenant with God, opening it to all who would receive his invitation. No longer bound to ethnic lineage, God's kingdom now embraced both Jews and gentiles as equal heirs, fulfilling the promise that "and in thee shall all families of the earth be blessed" (Gen 12:3).

Section 2: Key Full Preterist Interpretations of Prophecies

THE LAMENT OVER ISRAEL AND THE INVITATION TO OTHERS

Yet, despite this grand harvest, Jesus laments the impenitence of Israel. In Matt 23:37, he mourns over Jerusalem, "O Jerusalem, Jerusalem, thou that killest the prophets, and stonest them which are sent unto thee." Israel, by and large, rejected the call of the kingdom, forsaking their place at the banquet (Matt 22:2–14). Because of their refusal, the invitation was extended to others—gentiles who were once outside the fold. This shift marks the expansion of the harvest beyond national Israel to all the nations, fulfilling the ancient promise that "the kingdoms of this world have become the kingdoms of God and His Christ" (Rev 11:15).

THE END-TIME EXPECTATIONS: A UNIFIED PICTURE

Throughout the New Testament, various end-time expectations are woven together. The harvest, the second appearing of Christ for salvation (Heb 9:28), the coming on the clouds (Mark 13:26), the resurrection (John 11:25), and the reconciliation of all things to God through Christ are not separate events but different aspects of the same reality. These all speak of Christ's authority and the restoration of mankind's relationship with God.

For instance, Matt 24:31 and 2 Thess 2:1 describe the gathering of the elect, a central part of the harvest. This moment of gathering coincides with Christ's return, when he draws all to himself and inaugurates the new-covenant era.

THE IMMINENCE OF JUDGMENT AND THE WINNOWING OF THE WORLD

John the Baptist had already proclaimed the nearness of this judgment. He declared that "the axe is laid unto the root" and that the winnowing fan was already in hand, ready to separate the wheat from the chaff (Matt 3:10, 12). This imagery of imminent destruction and separation speaks directly to the harvest. The time for judgment was upon Israel, and those who rejected the Messiah would be like chaff, burned in the fire of God's judgment. This judgment culminated in the destruction of Jerusalem, the symbolic end of the old-covenant age (Gentry 1998, 327).

Jesus himself emphasizes the nearness of the harvest in John 4:35, saying, "Say not ye, There are yet four months, and then cometh harvest? Behold, I say unto you, Lift up your eyes, and look on the fields; for they are white already to harvest." This underscores the urgency and immediacy of the situation—the harvest was not some distant event but already unfolding before their eyes. This was the time of decision, and the kingdom was at hand.

Jesus's declaration not only invited his disciples to recognize the immediate arrival of God's kingdom but also conveyed an urgent call for decision. Israel's fate was at a turning point, with a limited opportunity to accept the Messiah. The "fields white to harvest" metaphor served as a final appeal for repentance before the impending judgment on the old-covenant order.

In the biblical narrative, harvest is a dual process—gathering the elect as "wheat" while separating and judging the "chaff." The destruction of Jerusalem, then, represented this sorting on a grand scale, where God's faithful were gathered into the kingdom and the rebellious faced judgment. This winnowing process ensured that, through judgment, the reconciliation of all things would take root in the new-covenant era.

THE FULFILLMENT OF PROPHECY

The idea of the harvest was promised long ago. Hosea 6:11 speaks of a harvest appointed for Judah, and this promise was fulfilled in the events surrounding AD 70. Jesus's return, the gathering of the elect, and the establishment of the new covenant were all part of this grand eschatological event.

A crucial point in understanding the fulfillment of these prophecies is the connection between Matt 24:14 and its fulfillment in passages such as Rom 10:18; 16:26; and Col 1:6, 23. In Matt 24:14, Jesus says, "And this gospel of the kingdom shall be preached in all the world for a witness unto all nations; and then shall the end come." Paul's letters confirm that this had indeed occurred by the time of Jerusalem's fall. The Greek word used for "world" (*oikoumene*) in Matt 24:14 refers to the inhabited world, specifically the Roman Empire, which aligns with Paul's description of the gospel reaching all creation under heaven (Wright 2015, 149).

Thus, the promise of the harvest was fulfilled—the old covenant ended, the gospel reached the nations, and God's kingdom was established. The harvest was not merely the end of an age but the beginning of a new

Section 2: Key Full Preterist Interpretations of Prophecies

one, where the reconciliation of all things to God through Christ is made manifest.

The harvest of the end of the age fulfilled centuries of prophecy, bringing God's promises to their fullest expression. The old covenant's dissolution cleared the path for the new covenant to flourish—a kingdom no longer defined by ethnic borders but by faith and reconciliation with God. The eschatological harvest accomplished this transformation, establishing an eternal kingdom that would bear fruit for all generations.

19

The Great White Throne Judgment

And I saw the dead, small and great, stand before God; and the books were opened... and the dead were judged out of those things which were written in the books, according to their works.

—REV 20:12

THE GREAT WHITE THRONE judgment, as described in Rev 20:11–15, presents a scene of final judgment that has captivated theological discourse for centuries. Traditionally interpreted as an eschatological event that will occur at the end of time, this chapter will explore the great white throne judgment from a full preterist perspective, emphasizing its fulfillment in the first century, during the end of the old-covenant era and the destruction of Jerusalem in AD 70.

But before we tie this event into the preterist timeline, we must first understand what the great white throne represents and where this imagery originates. Is it rooted in Jewish thought, Hellenistic influences, or something unique to early Christian apocalypticism?

Section 2: Key Full Preterist Interpretations of Prophecies

WHAT IS THE GREAT WHITE THRONE?

The image of the great white throne in Revelation is one of awe and power. In Rev 20:11–12 we read:

> And I saw a great white throne, and him that sat on it, from whose face the earth and the heaven fled away; and there was found no place for them. And I saw the dead, small and great, stand before God; and the books were opened: and another book was opened, which is the book of life: and the dead were judged out of those things which were written in the books, according to their works.

In biblical symbolism, white often represents purity and holiness. The throne itself, a place of authority and judgment, points to the ultimate seat of God's justice (Beale 1999, 339). The great white throne signifies divine authority, from which there is no escape—earth and heaven flee before the presence of God, showing the magnitude and purity of the judgment.

The great white throne can also be seen as the ultimate seat of covenant judgment, where God addresses Israel's faithfulness to the terms of the covenant. Just as ancient Israel stood accountable to covenantal laws, so here, the judgment at the throne represents the final reckoning for the nation that has rejected its Messiah. This judicial imagery is rooted in Israel's history, evoking scenes where God, as the ultimate Judge, presides over his people's covenant loyalty or disloyalty (Deut 32).

Some scholars suggest that the imagery of a "throne" for judgment draws upon both Jewish and Hellenistic influences. In Jewish apocalyptic literature, such as the book of Daniel, God is depicted as seated on a throne during the final judgment (Dan 7:9–10), presiding over the fate of the world. Daniel's vision of "thrones set in place" and the "Ancient of Days" seated upon a throne of fiery flame establishes a precedent for the apocalyptic throne scene later depicted in Revelation (Collins 1993, 301).

However, Greek and Roman culture also emphasized the throne as a symbol of imperial power and judgment. For instance, the Roman emperors often rendered judgment from their thrones in public spectacles. It is likely that the author of Revelation combined these elements, adapting the throne imagery for early Christian apocalyptic thought, where God's judgment supersedes both Jewish temple authority and Roman imperial power (Beale 1999, 340).

THE GREAT WHITE THRONE JUDGMENT

THEMES OF JUDGMENT IN THE GREAT WHITE THRONE SCENE

The central theme of the great white throne judgment is accountability. In Rev 20:12, the dead, both "small and great," are brought before God, and the books are opened. This judgment is comprehensive: no one is excluded. The opening of the books reflects the ancient custom of recording deeds, a practice also found in Jewish tradition (Dan 7:10; Mal 3:16) where God keeps a record of every person's actions. Additionally, the "book of life" represents those who are granted eternal life, drawing a clear distinction between those who belong to God and those who do not.

THE PRETERIST PERSPECTIVE ON THE GREAT WHITE THRONE JUDGMENT

Within the full preterist framework, the great white throne judgment must be understood as a fulfilled event tied to the first century and the end of the old covenant. Preterism asserts that the imagery in Revelation is not predictive of future events but rather reflective of the climactic judgment that came upon Israel and the old-covenant system in AD 70.

The destruction of Jerusalem by the Roman army, and the temple's obliteration, marked the definitive end of the old-covenant era. Matthew 24:34 states, "Verily I say unto you, This generation shall not pass, till all these things be fulfilled." For preterists, this signals that the judgment Jesus speaks of—often associated with his second coming—was fulfilled within the generation of those alive in the first century (DeMar 1999, 93). The great white throne judgment, therefore, corresponds to the judgment of Israel, where God judged the nation for its rejection of the Messiah.

Matthew 23:36 echoes this same theme of imminent judgment, where Jesus says, "All these things shall come upon this generation," referring to the bloodshed of the prophets and Israel's ultimate guilt. This judgment culminated in the destruction of the temple, symbolizing the old covenant's dissolution. The great white throne, within this context, represents God's final judicial decree against the corrupt temple system and those who rejected the new covenant.

Throughout Israel's history, rejection of God's prophets was met with judgment, as seen in the exile narratives and prophetic warnings (e.g., Jer 25). The great white throne judgment magnifies this principle, with apostate Israel held accountable for rejecting Christ—the ultimate prophet and mediator of the new covenant. This rejection, culminating in Jerusalem's downfall, serves as a final reckoning for the nation that has repeatedly strayed from its divine calling.

Scholar David Chilton argues that the "second death" in Rev 20:14, where death and hell are cast into the lake of fire, symbolizes the spiritual death of those who were outside the new covenant, primarily apostate Israel (1987, 539). The lake of fire is the judgment that awaited those who were not written in the book of life—the final separation between the faithful and the unfaithful, a judgment realized in AD 70.

THE BOOKS AND THE BOOK OF LIFE

The concept of books recording deeds and the "book of life" also fits neatly into the preterist framework. In the first-century Jewish context, the scribes kept detailed records, especially regarding legal matters and covenants. The imagery of books being opened reflects the covenantal framework under which Israel was judged. In the ancient world, written records of covenantal obligations were kept meticulously, with blessings and curses associated with adherence or disobedience to the covenant. The opening of books in Revelation alludes to this practice, symbolizing God's thorough reckoning of Israel's actions. This imagery underscores that judgment was not arbitrary but directly tied to Israel's response to the covenant and, specifically, to their treatment of God's final emissary, Christ (Heb 10:28–29). The faithful, those who accepted Christ's new covenant, were inscribed in the book of life. Those who rejected him faced the consequences of their choice.

Paul writes in Rom 2:6 that God "will render to every man according to his deeds," a statement that reflects the same idea as the books of deeds being opened in Revelation. For preterists, this does not point to a future event but to the comprehensive judgment that occurred in the first century when God rendered judgment on Israel.

FIRST-CENTURY FULFILLMENT OF THE JUDGMENT

A key feature of preterist interpretation is the concept of time indicators. Revelation repeatedly emphasizes the nearness of the events it describes. For example, Rev 1:1 states, "The revelation of Jesus Christ, which God gave unto him, to shew unto his servants things which must shortly come to pass." The use of terms like "shortly" and "soon" throughout Revelation supports the full preterist argument that the great white throne judgment was not a distant eschatological event but was fulfilled in the near future relative to the book's original audience. These time indicators underscore the immediacy of the events in question, aligning with the expectation of the first-century audience. This context strengthens the preterist view that the judgment symbolized Jerusalem's fall and the transition from the old-covenant to the new-covenant age.

The destruction of Jerusalem and the end of the Jewish sacrificial system marked the final judgment against the old covenant, leaving only the new covenant in its place. The great white throne judgment is the judicial moment when God pronounced his final judgment on the old order, ushering in the full realization of his kingdom.

THE FINAL JUDGMENT REALIZED

The great white throne judgment, traditionally viewed as a future event, takes on a different meaning within the preterist framework. By understanding the throne as a symbol of divine authority, rooted in both Jewish and Greco-Roman traditions, and recognizing the comprehensive nature of the judgment scene in Revelation, we can tie this judgment to the first century. The destruction of Jerusalem and the temple fulfilled the old-covenant promises, and the judgment recorded in Revelation reflects God's final dealing with apostate Israel, culminating in the establishment of the new-covenant age.

The great white throne judgment thus represents the end of an era, the closing of the old covenant that stood as Israel's legal and spiritual framework for centuries. With the dissolution of the old-covenant order, the new covenant emerged in its fullness, establishing a kingdom not bound to one nation but encompassing all who enter into faith in Christ. The judgment was the threshold that brought the promises of the new covenant into reality, a transformative moment in redemptive history.

20

The Timing and Nature of the Resurrection

The resurrection is not a return to the former life but a transformation into a higher and purer existence.

—Origen, *De Principiis*

When Jesus raised Lazarus from the dead, he made a profound statement that went beyond physical revival: "I am the resurrection and the life" (John 11:25). Lazarus was not resurrected in the ultimate sense but resuscitated—brought back temporarily to his decaying body. This was no final resurrection but rather a divine interruption in the course of death, meant to lead the onlookers to believe in Christ's power over life and death. "Because of the people who are standing by I said it, that they may believe" (John 11:42). Lazarus would die again, but his raising was a signpost, pointing toward something much greater: the reconciliation between humanity and God, the true meaning of resurrection (Chilton 1987, 540).

The Timing and Nature of the Resurrection

RESURRECTION: NOT JUST BRINGING BACK THE TENT

When Jesus says "I am the resurrection" in John 11:25, he is telling us something far deeper than just physical revival. This resurrection is about life itself—life in its truest, most eternal form. In the Jewish tradition, resurrection often conveyed hope for national restoration, a return to favor with God. Yet in Christ, this expectation is fulfilled and transformed—not in the form of a national revival but in an entirely new-covenantal reality. This resurrection brings believers into a state of eternal life, one that surpasses and replaces the need for an earthly, nationalistic fulfillment (Beale 1999, 1039). It's not the glorification of this "tent" that we inhabit either. No, Paul, a tentmaker by trade, knew all too well the impermanence of tents. In 2 Cor 5:1–4, he draws a sharp distinction between our temporary, earthly bodies and the eternal, heavenly ones awaiting us:

> For we know that if our earthly house of this tabernacle [tent] were dissolved, we have a building of God, a house not made with hands, eternal in the heavens. . . . We that are in this tabernacle do groan, being burdened: not for that we would be unclothed, but clothed upon, that mortality might be swallowed up of life. (2 Cor 5:1–4)

The tent—the earthly body—is destined for decay. But what's waiting for us isn't just a fancier, more permanent tent. Paul wasn't promising a celestial "glamping" experience. He's talking about something radically different: "a house not made with hands"—a divine, otherworldly dwelling that is eternal (DeMar 1999, 211).

If we're imagining the resurrection as simply receiving refreshed or souped-up versions of our physical bodies, we're missing the point. Anything we can conceive of, anything we can touch or feel, ultimately fails the test because "the things which are seen are temporal; but the things which are not seen are eternal" (2 Cor 4:18). That includes even our best mental images of resurrection bodies. Paul makes it clear: "Flesh and blood cannot inherit the kingdom of God" (1 Cor 15:50). What's ahead of us isn't a glorified body made of dust and bone but something far more enduring (Beale 1999, 1039).

LAZARUS AS A SIGNPOST, NOT THE DESTINATION

When Jesus raised Lazarus, it was for one reason: "that they may believe" (John 11:42). Lazarus didn't experience the final resurrection. He was brought back for a time, but his body, like all bodies, would eventually return to dust. Lazarus was a sign—a tangible example to point toward the unseen, eternal truth that Jesus embodies: resurrection is about life, about relationship with God. It's not just about delaying death or reanimating the flesh but about something much deeper, more profound (Wright 2015, 211–12).

Jesus doesn't promise physical immortality to those who believe in him. He promises eternal life. "Though he were dead, yet shall he live" (John 11:25). This isn't physical life that never ends; it's spiritual life—reconciliation with God. Romans 6:23 tells us, "The wages of sin is death, but the gift of God is eternal life through Jesus Christ our Lord." This eternal life is something beyond the physical realm, as Paul emphasizes that the unseen things are eternal (2 Cor 4:18).

THE FUTILITY OF GLORIFYING THE FLESH

Futurist interpretations often see the resurrection as the glorification of the physical body. But Paul emphatically rejects this idea. "Flesh and blood cannot inherit the kingdom of God; neither doth corruption inherit incorruption" (1 Cor 15:50). To insist on the glorification of this "tent" is to miss the point entirely. Paul, ever the tentmaker, would have found this insistence on elevating a temporary structure laughable. The tent, our physical body, is bound for destruction. The one in the tent—our true self—is what's destined for glory (DeMar 1999, 191–92).

Think of it like this: You wouldn't put marble countertops and chandeliers in a collapsing tent. The tent is temporary. No amount of refurbishing will make it last forever. Instead, you look forward to something better, something eternal: "a house not made with hands, eternal in the heavens" (2 Cor 5:1). The glorified body isn't just an upgrade to our current form; it's a completely new, divine reality. This transformation transcends the physical, hinting at the radical shift from the old-covenant world to the new. The "spiritual body" that Paul describes does not imply a physical reconstruction but a life that has fully entered into God's presence and reality. It's not a renewed mortal form but a participation in the divine—eternal and incorruptible. This is the life of the new covenant, one that bypasses fleshly decay entirely and places believers in an unbroken relationship with God (Wright 2015, 149).

To fixate on glorifying the flesh is like trying to patch up a tent during a hurricane—it's futile. What we look forward to is not the renewal of what we can see but the unveiling of what we cannot. "It doth not yet appear what we shall be: but we know that, when he shall appear, we shall be like him" (1 John 3:2). This "likeness" to Christ isn't a carbon copy of the physical body but a participation in the eternal, unseen life of God.

THE RESURRECTION BODY: SPIRITUAL, NOT PHYSICAL

The resurrection body, as Paul describes in 1 Cor 15:44, is "sown a natural body; it is raised a spiritual body." The contrast between the natural (physical) and the spiritual is crucial. The resurrection is not about animating dead flesh but about receiving a body suited for the eternal, unseen reality of God's kingdom. Paul's point is that the resurrection body is imperishable because it's not bound by the same physical limitations as the bodies we now inhabit (Beale 1999, 1040).

Jesus himself exemplified this in his post-resurrection appearances. While he showed his physical wounds to Thomas and the disciples, the body he revealed was still of this world—scarred, damaged, and ultimately not the glorified body of the resurrection (Luke 24:39). This is confirmed in 2 Cor 5:16, where Paul states that "though we have known Christ after the flesh, yet now henceforth know we him no more." Jesus's glorification and resurrection life weren't tied to his physical form but to his restored relationship with the Father, the very thing Adam had lost in Eden (Chilton 1987, 540–41).

THE TIMING OF THE RESURRECTION: FIRST-CENTURY FULFILLMENT

Throughout the New Testament, the resurrection is portrayed as something imminent—set to occur within the lifetime of Jesus's first-century followers. Matthew 16:27–28 declares that some standing with Jesus would not taste death until they saw the Son of Man coming in his kingdom. This ties the resurrection to the events surrounding AD 70, when Jerusalem fell and the old covenant was finally done away with (DeMar 1999, 191–92).

Paul's words in 1 Thess 4:15–17 offer reassurance to the early Christians: those who had died would not be left out of the resurrection. "We who are alive and remain"—Paul includes himself in this expectation—"shall not prevent them which are asleep." The timing of the resurrection was not some distant event but something Paul fully expected to witness (Chilton

1987, 540–41). This imminence is central to the preterist perspective. The early Christians, including Paul, awaited the resurrection in the context of the anticipated judgment on Jerusalem and the culmination of the old-covenant age. As AD 70 approached, the destruction of the temple marked the ultimate judgment, completing the transition to the new-covenant era. The expectation was not a millennia-distant resurrection but an imminent transformation, aligning with Jesus's prediction that "this generation shall not pass, till all these things be fulfilled" (Matt 24:34).

Furthermore, 1 Pet 4:7 reminds readers, "The end of all things is at hand: be ye therefore sober, and watch unto prayer." The apostles were not looking forward to an event millennia in the future; they were preparing for something imminent, something their generation would see (DeMar 1999, 159).

THE FIRST AND SECOND RESURRECTION: COVENANT, NOT CORPSES

Revelation 20 draws a critical distinction between two resurrections. The first (Rev 20:4–6) describes those who reigned with Christ during the symbolic 1000 years—beginning with His enthronement around AD 30 and ending with the Jewish-Roman War in AD 66. This reign includes not only the martyrs but also faithful believers who entered the New Covenant. They are described as *souls* (*psychas*), alive in the Spirit and seated with Christ—not physically raised but spiritually resurrected (Eph 2:5–6; Col 3:1). This was a covenantal resurrection into Kingdom life. "The rest of the dead" lived not again until the end of this period, marking a clear contrast between those within the New Covenant and those outside it.

Jesus anticipates this twofold framework in John 5:24–29. First, He refers to a present resurrection: those who hear and believe "have passed from death to life" (v.24)—a spiritual awakening. Then He speaks of a future resurrection, where "all that are in the graves. . . shall come forth" (v.29), echoing Daniel 12:2, which compresses both outcomes—life and judgment—into one vision. Revelation, however, unfolds them sequentially: first the spiritual resurrection of the saints, then the exposure and judgment of the covenantally dead.

A curious passage often cited in this discussion is Matthew 27:52–53: "many bodies of the saints. . . arose, and came out of the graves. . . and appeared unto many." Though placed in the crucifixion narrative, it occurs

The Timing and Nature of the Resurrection

after Jesus' resurrection. Its placement is puzzling, and its nature—literal or symbolic—is unclear. Notably, it is never referenced again by Paul, the evangelists, or the early church. If it were a literal bodily resurrection, why is it omitted from detailed resurrection texts like 1 Corinthians 15 or 1 Thessalonians 4?

This moment is best approached with interpretive humility. It could be a small, literal "firstfruit" sign of resurrection or a symbolic flourish in the apocalyptic tradition, portraying the spiritual breakthrough that Jesus' death inaugurated. Either way, it does not disrupt the preterist understanding—it enriches it by showing symbolic or literal power breaking into history.

Tension arises when comparing this view with Paul's statement in 1 Thessalonians 4:15–17: "The dead in Christ shall rise first." If the first resurrection includes saints spiritually raised between AD 30–66, does Paul not imply they were still awaiting resurrection?

Here we must recall Paul wrote before AD 70. The faithful dead, though spiritually alive and seated with Christ (Eph 2:6), still awaited public vindication—the full revelation of their status at the judgment of the Old Covenant. Their resurrection was not anatomical but covenantal. Paul's comfort lies not in biological exactitude but in apocalyptic justice: the dead would not be forgotten when the Kingdom was revealed. His language evokes royal and judicial themes, not physical reanimation.

Thus, "the dead rising first" fits Revelation's two-stage vision. The saints were already alive in Christ, yet their vindication—especially in the eyes of a world still clinging to the Old Covenant—awaited a final, public moment. That moment came with the fiery judgment of Jerusalem, when the just were revealed and the covenantally dead judged. The paradox resolves: the dead were alive spiritually, and then revealed to be so through the collapse of the old order.

The second resurrection (Rev 20:12–13) concerns those who did not share in the first—those still bound to the Old Covenant or who rejected Christ's call. This is not a universal "end-of-world" event, but a covenantal reckoning tied to Israel's prophetic guilt (Matt 23:35), fulfilled in AD 70. "Death and Hades" represent the defeat of the Old Age, not literal realms. The martyrs under the altar (Rev 6) were told to wait a "little season" until justice was executed. That season ended with the fall of Jerusalem—not as a global catastrophe, but a climactic covenantal closure.

The second resurrection is not about corpses rising from the dust. It is the moment when the spiritually dead—those outside Christ's covenant—are judged in the light of fulfilled redemption. The righteous are vindicated; the unfaithful exposed. Resurrection, like the Kingdom, was never fundamentally about biology—it was about belonging.

RESURRECTION AS ETERNAL, UNSEEN LIFE

Nicodemus's bewilderment—"How can a man be born when he is old?"—reveals the blindness to spiritual truths that Jesus came to confront. The "born again" experience wasn't about crawling back into a womb but about dying to the old self and rising into a new spiritual life. This is the resurrection, not some Marvel fantasy but a present, radical transformation. Jesus's words cut through materialist expectations, pushing Nicodemus—and us—beyond flesh and bone to embrace a living reality. The resurrection isn't coming; it's here, for those with eyes to see it. The resurrection, therefore, marks entry into the new creation where believers live as new creatures (2 Cor 5:17). This new creation is not a future construct but a present reality realized in the lives of those who are in Christ, those who are reconciled to God through the Spirit. By placing faith in Christ's finished work, believers participate in the resurrection life, embodying the transformation of the new covenant and reflecting the restored relationship that Adam lost in Eden (DeMar 1999, 245).

The resurrection is not about glorifying this fragile tent but about stepping into the eternal, unseen life of God. As Paul says in 2 Cor 4:18, "We look not at the things which are seen, but at the things which are not seen: for the things which are seen are temporal; but the things which are not seen are eternal." The resurrection isn't the transformation of this earthly body but the full realization of our reconciliation with God, the life Adam lost and Christ restored. The resurrection is about stepping into the eternal house not made with hands—the divine reality of God's eternal kingdom (DeMar 1999, 191–92). Thus, the resurrection, as understood within the full preterist framework, is the ultimate realization of covenantal life, a spiritual reality inaugurated through Christ and fully established by the events of AD 70. The new-covenant life is here and now, where believers dwell not in anticipation of a renewed earthly form but in the eternal life already begun—"hid with Christ in God" (Col 3:3) and manifesting the kingdom that endures beyond the physical and temporal.

21

The Return of Our Lord Jesus Christ with His Kingdom

Christ is both the way and the destination, for He comes in His kingdom to those who have awaited Him faithfully, and they shall reign with Him.

—SAINT AUGUSTINE, *CITY OF GOD*

THE CULMINATION OF PROPHECY, the climactic return of Christ with his kingdom, forms the bedrock of full preterist interpretation. This chapter unravels the timeline and nature of this event, exploring how it unfolded in the first century. It delves into themes such as the nature of Christ's kingdom, the wedding feast, the antichrist, and the imminent language used in the New Testament.

CHRIST'S RETURN AND THE KINGDOM THAT DOESN'T COME WITH OBSERVATION

Jesus made it clear that the nature of his kingdom was not one that could be pinpointed with outward signs. "The kingdom of God cometh not with observation: Neither shall they say, Lo here! or, lo there! for, behold, the

Section 2: Key Full Preterist Interpretations of Prophecies

kingdom of God is within you" (Luke 17:20-21). This statement underscores that his kingdom was not a physical realm to be established with fanfare or political conquest, but a spiritual reality—an indwelling of God's presence among his people. This internal kingdom reshapes expectations of messianic triumph. Unlike kingdoms secured by territorial conquest, Christ's reign is characterized by transformation from within, a divine rule not confined by borders or physical boundaries. Jesus's presence among his people inaugurates this kingdom, a realm that operates beyond sight and is experienced by faith. As Wright notes, the kingdom of God functions within the hearts of believers, a reality evident in the early church's transformed lives (2015, 213).

Christ's return with his kingdom was not an event to be observed with the naked eye, nor would people say, "Look here!" or "Look there!" This nonphysical manifestation makes sense of his words in Matt 24:27, "For as the lightning cometh out of the east, and shineth even unto the west; so shall also the coming of the Son of man be." Here, "lightning" does not signify literal bolts from the sky but rather a sudden, unmistakable judgment. The judgment's clarity and inevitability would be as evident as lightning flashing across the sky—seen from one end to the other. This Hebraic hyperbole highlights the indelible nature of God's judgment rather than pointing to a physical, geographical phenomenon (Chilton 1987, 89). In Hebrew Scripture, cosmic signs often denote shifts in divine authority or moments of profound judgment. The lightning in Matt 24:27 draws on this imagery, symbolizing God's unmistakable presence in judgment rather than literal bolts. For the Jewish mind, steeped in prophetic language, such imagery conveyed the sweeping change brought by Christ's rule, confirming his reign without requiring physical spectacle.

Some have speculated that the phrase has Greek undertones, possibly alluding to divine epiphany or manifestations of deities. However, the language is very much rooted in Hebraic poetic tradition, where cosmic imagery was often used to describe the magnitude of divine acts. The return of Christ with his kingdom was not an event of spectacle but of profound spiritual significance, culminating in the judgment upon Jerusalem.

THE ANTICHRIST: NOT A FUTURE FIGURE BUT A PRESENT SPIRIT

The popular conception of the antichrist as a singular, future figure stems from misunderstanding the term's use in the New Testament. In fact, 1 John 4:3 states, "This is that spirit of antichrist, whereof ye have heard that it should come; and even now already is it in the world." The antichrist is described as a spirit that was already active during the apostolic era, restrained but present.

Paul writes in 2 Thess 2:6–7 of a restraining force that held back the "man of lawlessness," indicating that whatever this antichrist spirit was, it existed in the first century and was waiting to be fully unleashed (DeMar 1999, 312). John's writings highlight this antichrist spirit as a pervasive force, already manifest in the first century and defined by its resistance to Christ's authority. The antichrist, then, is not the central villain of some future apocalypse but represents a principle of opposition to Christ that was alive and active during the early church. This understanding demystifies the antichrist as not a distant antagonist but a recurrent mindset and force opposing the gospel within that era's cultural and religious tensions.

THE IMMINENCE OF CHRIST'S RETURN: A FIRST-CENTURY EXPECTATION

Scripture overflows with language that speaks to the imminent return of Christ. Passages such as Matt 16:27–28 and Heb 10:37 highlight the expectation that his return was "at hand."

> For the Son of man shall come in the glory of his Father with his angels; and then he shall reward every man according to his works. Verily I say unto you, There be some standing here, which shall not taste of death, till they see the Son of man coming in his kingdom. (Matt 16:27–28)

Here, Jesus directly tells his listeners that some of them would not die before witnessing his return in the kingdom. This isn't the language of distant prophecy but of an event that was to unfold in their lifetime. Similarly, Heb 10:37 asserts, "For yet a little while, and he that shall come will come, and will not tarry," using the language of urgency and nearness.

Matthew 24:34 reinforces this time frame, as Jesus proclaims, "Verily I say unto you, This generation shall not pass, till all these things be fulfilled." It is difficult to reconcile such statements with a timeline extending thousands of years into the future. These passages make it clear that the apostles expected Christ's return to occur within their own generation (Wright 2015, 210).

Paul's writings also demonstrate this first-century expectation. In 1 Thess 4:15–17, he comforts the church concerning those who had died: "We which are alive and remain unto the coming of the Lord shall not prevent them which are asleep. . . . And the dead in Christ shall rise first."

Paul addresses the living, reassuring them that they would not miss out on the event. The expectation was that it would happen within their lifetimes. James 5:8–9 also echoes this urgency: "The coming of the Lord draweth nigh. . . . Behold, the judge standeth before the door," further emphasizing the immediacy of Christ's return (DeMar 1999, 198).

THE WEDDING FEAST AND THE KINGDOM

The theme of the wedding feast in the New Testament symbolizes the union of Christ and his church. Isaiah 62:1–5 anticipates this union with imagery of joy and marriage: "For as a young man marrieth a virgin, so shall thy sons marry thee: and as the bridegroom rejoiceth over the bride, so shall thy God rejoice over thee" (Isa 62:5).

This Old Testament imagery finds its fulfillment in the New Testament, where Paul works diligently to prepare the church for this imminent event. Second Corinthians 11:2 reflects this preparation: "For I am jealous over you with godly jealousy: for I have espoused you to one husband, that I may present you as a chaste virgin to Christ."

Ephesians 5:32 clarifies that the mystery of marriage between man and woman actually refers to "Christ and the church," marking the anticipated wedding feast as a first-century reality. The culmination occurs in Rev 19:7, "Let us be glad and rejoice, and give honour to him: for the marriage of the Lamb is come, and his wife hath made herself ready." The bridal imagery emphasizes that the church was to prepare for Christ's imminent arrival, signifying the consummation of the kingdom and the establishment of the wedding feast.

The Return of Our Lord Jesus Christ with His Kingdom

ZION AND THE KINGDOM: EXPANSIVE AS AUSTRALIA

The metaphor of Zion and the kingdom is strikingly vast, almost beyond comprehension. If taken literally, it's more than five million square kilometers. This figure is derived from symbolic numbers (length, width, and height of 12,000 stadia and walls 144 cubits thick). Just as Australia spans a massive continent, so does the kingdom encompass not only the spiritual realm but also the entirety of God's dominion. The new Zion isn't a physical plot of land but an expansive reality that embraces all believers who are in Christ. This spiritual Zion defies geographical limitation, symbolizing a universal community bound by faith rather than borders. The vastness of this kingdom transcends any one nation or physical space, encompassing believers across every land.

As Paul writes in Gal 4:26, "But Jerusalem which is above is free, which is the mother of us all," indicating that the new Zion reflects a global, heavenly city that embodies Christ's spiritual reign over his church. As Heb 12:22–23 states, "But ye are come unto mount Sion, and unto the city of the living God, the heavenly Jerusalem," emphasizing a kingdom not limited by geography but boundless in its reach (Beale 1999, 345).

CRITIQUE OF FUTURIST TELEOLOGY: MISALIGNED WITH APOSTOLIC INTENT

The futurist interpretation centers on a distant, future hope of Christ's return, overlooking the immediacy and urgency conveyed in Scripture. The apostles didn't prepare the church for an event thousands of years away. Instead, they spoke with a sense of imminency, constantly encouraging the early believers to be ready for Christ's return in their time. Revelation 1:1 and 22:6 assert that these events would "shortly come to pass," underscoring the urgency with which John wrote.

The futurist teleology, then, misaligns with the textual evidence. It shifts the hope of the apostles into an indefinite future, contradicting the clear expectation set forth by Jesus and the early church.

> But when they persecute you in this city, flee ye into another: for verily I say unto you, Ye shall not have gone over the cities of Israel, till the Son of man be come. (Matt 10:23)

Section 2: Key Full Preterist Interpretations of Prophecies

The Synoptic Gospels of Mark and Luke contain identical statements to Matthew, so we pass over them here and look instead at John: "If I will that he tarry till I come, what is that to thee? Follow thou me" (John 21:22). Here, Jesus specifies that, although Peter would give his life in martyrdom, the apostle John would live until he had come again. History confirms that John lived in Ephesus until the time of Trajan.

FULFILLMENT OF PROPHECY AND THE KINGDOM UNVEILED

This chapter has explored the return of Christ and the establishment of his kingdom as a reality for the early church, grounded in the urgent language of the New Testament. Within a full preterist perspective, the return of Jesus and the consummation of his kingdom marked the completion of prophecy and the ultimate judgment upon Jerusalem. The spiritual nature of this kingdom, a realm within and among the faithful, shifted the expectations of a physical reign to one that transcends visible borders.

By understanding the return of Christ as a first-century event, we align with the apostles' own sense of immediacy and the fulfillment of Jesus's promises. This perspective not only respects the original context of these teachings but underscores a profound reality: Christ's kingdom is present, alive, and accessible to all who seek it. The old covenant has passed; the new covenant and the reign of Christ endure eternally. From a full preterist perspective, the consummation of Christ's kingdom was an assured, realized event within the first-century context. The apostolic church did not look toward a far-off future but lived in expectation of the kingdom's arrival within their generation. The prophetic language fulfilled in AD 70 affirms that Christ's rule was established, his reign is ongoing, and his kingdom—now unbound by time or location—continues as an active, spiritual reality accessible to all who enter into covenant with him.

22

The Dating of Revelation

History is the light of truth, revealing all things in their true order.
—Polybius (ca. 200–118 BCE), Greek historian

THE DATING OF THE book of Revelation has been a contentious topic among scholars, with significant implications for its interpretation. Two primary positions dominate the debate: the early date, suggesting that the book was written before the destruction of the Jerusalem Temple in AD 70, and the late date, which places its composition towards the end of Emperor Domitian's reign in the mid–AD 90s. Understanding when Revelation was written affects how its prophecies and imagery are contextualized—whether as predictive of events leading up to the destruction of Jerusalem or as relating to later Roman persecutions (Aune 1997; Beale 1999). An early date would strongly imply that its apocalyptic warnings were addressing events surrounding the collapse of the Jewish state and temple, reflecting imminent judgment. In contrast, a late date would frame Revelation as anticipating prolonged periods of tribulation and potential Roman persecution, or even prophetic visions extending into future epochs (Yarbro Collins 1984). The evidence surrounding this debate is vast and varied, encompassing external

Section 2: Key Full Preterist Interpretations of Prophecies

testimonies from early church fathers and internal indications within the text itself.

EXTERNAL EVIDENCE FOR DATING

The external evidence regarding the dating of Revelation is drawn from early church writings and historical context. The most commonly cited sources include the testimonies of Irenaeus, Tertullian, and other early church figures, along with historical accounts that depict the conditions under Roman emperors Nero and Domitian (Bauckham 1993, 45). The evidence can be divided into arguments for both early and late dates, with each side presenting its own interpretation of these ancient sources.

IRENAEUS AND THE AMBIGUITY OF HIS TESTIMONY

Irenaeus, a primary source for the late-date theory, claimed Revelation "was seen... towards the end of Domitian's reign" (ca. AD 95–96). However, ambiguity in the original Greek surrounding the verb tense and subject-object relationship raises questions about whether Irenaeus referred to John himself or to his vision (Irenaeus 1885, 558–59). Scholars like Gentry (1998, 67) and Robinson (2000, 89) argue that these linguistic nuances weaken Irenaeus's testimony as definitive evidence, particularly as his information was secondhand, derived from Polycarp's teachings.

Robinson also criticizes the credibility of Irenaeus's testimony due to his other historical inaccuracies, such as the claim that Jesus was fifty years old at the time of his crucifixion (2000, 102). Robinson argues that if Irenaeus is mistaken about significant details, his dating of Revelation may also be questionable. Furthermore, Irenaeus's account is secondhand at best, as he did not personally know the apostle John but relied on the teachings of Polycarp, who had been a disciple of John. The gaps in time and potential distortions over generations raise doubts about the reliability of Irenaeus's assertion (Osborne 2002, 56).

OTHER EARLY WITNESSES: PAPIAS, POLYCARP, AND THE SHEPHERD OF HERMAS

Papias, likely a disciple of John, claimed John died under Jewish authority before Jerusalem's destruction, suggesting an early date (Bauckham 2007, 134). Yet questions about Papias's connection to John and lost original texts limit the reliability of this testimony (Hill 2006, 45).

The Shepherd of Hermas, a popular early Christian text, also factors into the dating discussion. Its similarities with Revelation suggest it may have been influenced by John's writing. Some scholars propose that if the Shepherd was written in the AD 80s or earlier, it would support an early composition date for Revelation, as the text would have needed time to circulate and impact the Shepherd's composition (Aune 1997, 58). However, the lack of direct citations complicates the use of the Shepherd as definitive evidence for an early date (Beale 1999, 115).

NERO VS. DOMITIAN: COMPARING THE PERSECUTION

The historical backdrop of Nero's persecution is far more substantiated than that of Domitian's, providing compelling support for an early dating of Revelation. In the wake of Rome's great fire in AD 64, Nero launched a brutal campaign of systematic executions and torture against Christians (Gentry 1998, 85; Bauckham 1993, 112; Tacitus 1942 15.44). In contrast, Domitian's alleged persecution remains far more ambiguous, with scholars like Wilson noting its contentious nature (2005, 143). Frend (1965, 312) and Jones (1992, 89) even argue that later sources may have amplified Domitian's actions to rival Nero's infamous cruelty. The relentless tribulation depicted in Revelation (2:10; 3:10) resonates more vividly with the dark certainties of Nero's reign than with Domitian's uncertain shadow (Yarbro Collins 1984, 93).

THE SYRIAC WITNESSES AND LATER COMMENTATORS

The Syriac versions of the New Testament and later commentators, such as Arethas of Caesarea (AD 860–939), provide significant support for an early dating of Revelation. The Syriac tradition explicitly states that John was exiled to Patmos under Nero, lending strong credibility to the Neronic date (Roberts et al. 1994, 112). This early dating is further supported by Arethas's

SECTION 2: KEY FULL PRETERIST INTERPRETATIONS OF PROPHECIES

ninth-century commentary, which reflects a tradition that Revelation was written before the destruction of Jerusalem. While Arethas wrote centuries after the events, his commentary demonstrates the persistence of an early dating tradition that may have originated from reliable, early sources (Aune 1997, 78; Bauckham 1993, 112).

The Syriac witnesses play a crucial role in the dating debate because of their relative antiquity and the explicitness with which they tie John's exile to the reign of Nero. Unlike Irenaeus's ambiguous statement, these witnesses offer a more straightforward connection to the earlier date, even though they appear in texts later than Irenaeus's testimony. This persistence of an early dating tradition into the ninth century challenges the view that a late Domitianic date was universally accepted in the early church (Osborne 2002, 12).

THE ROLE OF TERTULLIAN AND CHURCH TRADITION

Tertullian, an early Christian apologist writing in the late second and early third centuries, adds another layer to the external evidence for the dating of Revelation. In *The Prescription Against Heretics*, Tertullian connects John's exile on Patmos to the period of Peter and Paul's martyrdom, traditionally dated under Nero's persecution (Tertullian 1896b 36). While his statement does not explicitly mention Nero, it implies that John's exile occurred contemporaneously with the reign of Nero, which aligns with the early dating view (Aune 1997, 67).

However, Tertullian's testimony, like Irenaeus's, is not without its limitations. Although he offers an indirect connection to Nero's reign, he does not provide concrete chronological details. Yet, when combined with the Syriac tradition and other early testimonies, Tertullian's account contributes to the plausibility of an early date (Bauckham 1993, 127). The church's memory of John's exile seems to associate it more with the persecution under Nero than under Domitian, at least in certain circles.

EVALUATING THE EXTERNAL EVIDENCE

While external evidence for the late date is often seen as dominant due to Irenaeus's testimony, significant ambiguities and contradictions exist. Irenaeus's statement is open to varying interpretations, as noted earlier, and the reliability of his account is questioned due to other historical inaccuracies

(Gentry 1998, 48; Robinson 2000, 221–53). In contrast, early witnesses like the Syriac tradition and Arethas, alongside Tertullian's indirect testimony, favor an early date.

Although external evidence remains inconclusive, the ambiguity in Irenaeus's statement, combined with early testimonies favoring an early date, provides stronger support for an earlier timeline for Revelation's composition. The internal evidence, to which we now turn, further bolsters this early dating hypothesis.

INTERNAL EVIDENCE FOR DATING

The internal evidence found within the text of Revelation itself provides significant clues regarding its date of composition. This includes the atmosphere of persecution described in the book, references to the temple, and various time indicators that suggest an imminent fulfillment of the prophecies. These elements contribute to a strong case for an early dating of Revelation, likely during Nero's reign in the AD 60s, rather than a later date under Domitian.

REFERENCES TO THE TEMPLE

Revelation 11:1–2 contains a key passage where John is instructed to measure the temple, with no indication that it has already been destroyed. The omission of any reference to the destruction of the temple, which occurred in AD 70, strongly suggests that the book was written while the temple was still standing. John's reference to the temple being measured and the Holy City being trampled underfoot points to a time just before the temple's destruction (Gentry 1998, 143–45; Beale 1999, 561–62).

Moreover, the language in Rev 11 closely mirrors Jesus's prophecy in Luke 21:24, where Jesus predicts that Jerusalem will be "trampled by the Gentiles." The similarity between these passages suggests that Revelation is referring to the same imminent events leading up to the destruction of Jerusalem, which would support an early date of composition (Robinson 2000, 240–41).

If Revelation had been written after the temple's destruction, it would be unusual for such a monumental event to go unmentioned, especially in a text so focused on divine judgment and cataclysmic events. The fact that

Section 2: Key Full Preterist Interpretations of Prophecies

the temple is portrayed as still standing strengthens the argument for an early dating of the book, prior to AD 70 (Aune 1997, 586).

EVALUATING THE INTERNAL EVIDENCE

The internal evidence for an early date is compelling. The atmosphere of persecution, the references to the temple, and the urgency of the time indicators all align with a first-century context, particularly during Nero's reign. If Revelation were written during Domitian's reign in the AD 90s, one would expect the text to reflect the destruction of the temple, an event of monumental significance to early Christians. The absence of any reference to this event strongly suggests that the book was written before AD 70.

Moreover, the use of cryptic language, such as the "number of the beast" (666), which scholars frequently link to Nero Caesar, supports the idea that Revelation was addressing immediate concerns for its audience, including the persecution under Nero (Beale 1999, 715; Gentry 1998, 200–201). The characterization of Nero as a "beast" fits the imagery in Revelation. The numerical reference to 666 in Rev 13:18, decoded through gematria, aligns specifically with "Nero Caesar" in Hebrew transliteration, directly pointing to Nero as the "beast." This ciphering technique, well understood in the first century, implies an immediate reference recognizable to contemporary readers, providing internal evidence for Revelation's early composition during or shortly after Nero's reign (Beale 1999, 716–17). The use of apocalyptic language and the focus on imminent judgment also fits the broader literary style of early Jewish and Christian apocalyptic writings, which often emphasized near-term fulfillment (Aune 1997, 58–59).

While proponents of the late date may argue that Revelation's prophecies could apply to Domitian's reign or even later periods, the text's focus on urgency and immediacy makes such interpretations more difficult to sustain. The language of "soon" and "at hand" is difficult to reconcile with a delay of several decades or centuries. As such, the internal evidence overwhelmingly supports an early date for the composition of Revelation, most likely in the late AD 60s, during the reign of Nero.

ANALYSIS OF KEY ARGUMENTS

The debate on the dating of Revelation extends beyond external and internal evidence, encompassing interpretative parallels, theological implications,

The Dating of Revelation

and historical context. Key arguments include the striking similarities between Revelation and contemporary historical events, such as the Jewish War, as well as the theological themes that frame its prophetic tone.

PARALLELS WITH HISTORICAL EVENTS AND JOSEPHUS

One of the strongest arguments for an early date is the remarkable resemblance between the descriptions in Revelation and the historical accounts of the first-century Jewish historian Josephus. In his *Wars of the Jews*, Josephus details the horrors of the First Roman-Jewish War, culminating in the destruction of Jerusalem in AD 70. The imagery in Rev 6, where famine, war, and death ravage the land, closely mirrors Josephus's descriptions of the chaos and suffering in Jerusalem during the siege. Josephus's firsthand accounts of Jerusalem's destruction—including descriptions of factional conflict and Roman onslaught—mirror Revelation's apocalyptic imagery, such as the four horsemen and plagues, suggesting synchronous anticipation (Gentry 1998, 142–44).

Revelation's description of the "great city" being divided into three parts (Rev 16:19) also parallels Josephus's account of the internal strife within Jerusalem, where rival factions divided the city during the Roman siege. These striking similarities suggest that Revelation may have been written in anticipation of these events, or at least during the early stages of the Jewish War, reinforcing the argument for an early date (Gentry 1998, 142–44; Wright 1996, 321–22).

Further, the portrayal of the two witnesses in Rev 11, who are killed and resurrected, could be seen as reflecting the fate of prophets or figures in Jerusalem during the Roman siege, although this remains a more speculative connection. Nevertheless, the vivid parallels between Revelation's apocalyptic imagery and the historical realities described by Josephus strengthen the case that the book was written before these events unfolded, rather than decades later under Domitian (Beale 1999, 561–62; Aune 1997, 586).

THEOLOGICAL IMPLICATIONS AND MARTYR VINDICATION

Revelation's central theme of martyrdom and vindication also lends support to an early date. Throughout the book, there are repeated references to the martyrs who cry out for justice (Rev 6:9–11; 20:4). This theme of divine retribution for the shedding of innocent blood resonates with Jesus's pronouncements of judgment upon first-century Jerusalem, particularly in passages like Matt 23:35–36, where Jesus condemns the generation that killed the prophets and says that "all these things shall come upon this generation" (Robinson 2000, 240; Gentry 1998, 143–45).

The prophetic vindication of the martyrs in Revelation can be understood as part of the divine judgment on Jerusalem, culminating in the destruction of the city in AD 70. This aligns with Old Testament prophecies that depict the "last days" of Israel as a time of reckoning for the nation's unfaithfulness and its persecution of the righteous (Joel 3:19–21; Isa 2:12–19). In this context, Revelation's focus on martyrdom is not an abstract or distant future event but a reflection of the imminent judgment that was to fall on first-century Jerusalem, further supporting the early date (Beale 1999, 561–62; Wright 1996, 321–22).

PROPHETIC TIME INDICATORS AND AUDIENCE RELEVANCE

Revelation's emphasis on imminence ("must shortly come to pass" [Rev 1:1]; "the time is at hand" [Rev 22:6]) supports a first-century date, aimed at an audience facing immediate tribulation. Addressing local challenges—such as persecution under Nero and false teachings—the letters to the seven churches (Rev 2–3) reinforce this urgency. Located along an established Roman mailing route, these churches were positioned to quickly receive and share John's message, further emphasizing its relevance to a contemporary audience facing present trials rather than a distant future (Gentry 1998, 63–64; Osborne 2002, 12).

The apostolic language of imminence aligns with the broader eschatological expectation within early Christianity, which anticipated the fulfillment of significant prophetic events within a generation. Wright and other scholars observe that phrases like "soon" and "at hand" resonate with Jesus's warnings in the gospels about the impending fall of Jerusalem, creating a cohesive framework in which Revelation's prophecies, too, would find fulfillment within the first century (1996, 331–32). This expectation is further evidenced in other New Testament writings, where apostles frequently speak of Christ's return and judgment as events the faithful should expect to see in their lifetime (1 Pet 4:7; Jas 5:8–9).

In addition, Kenneth Gentry highlights that key terms in Revelation—such as the Greek *táchos* (meaning "quickly" or "shortly")—suggest an immediate fulfillment, consistent with other New Testament uses that imply urgency (1998, 144–45). This contrasts with the book of Daniel, where the sealing of the prophecy signaled a long-delayed fulfillment (Dan 12:9). In Revelation, however, John is instructed explicitly not to seal the prophecy "because the time is near" (22:10), further suggesting that its events were expected to unfold soon after its writing, not in a distant epoch (Osborne 2002, 785).

These time indicators, combined with the letters' attention to real first-century issues, strongly support an early dating of Revelation before the destruction of the Jerusalem Temple in AD 70, consistent with its urgency and prophetic relevance for its original audience (Beale 1999, 47–48). The cumulative internal evidence thus underpins an early date for Revelation, framing it as a document crafted for the immediate encouragement and warning of a first-century readership.

THE SEVEN CHURCHES AND HISTORICAL CONTEXT

The historical situation of the seven churches adds further credence to an early date. For instance, the church at Smyrna is warned of an impending tribulation that would last "ten days" (Rev 2:10), a phrase often interpreted as a symbolic reference to a brief period of persecution. This kind of localized persecution fits the context of Nero's reign, during which Christians were sporadically targeted in various regions of the Roman Empire (Frend 1965, 210–11). In contrast, the evidence for widespread persecution under Domitian is weak, and it is unclear whether the churches in Asia were under significant threat during his reign (Jones 1992, 112–13).

Additionally, the message to the church at Laodicea (Rev 3:14–22) contains references to the city's wealth and self-sufficiency, which align with historical records of Laodicea's economic prosperity in the mid-first century. This detail suggests that the letters were written while Laodicea was still thriving, which would fit an early date rather than a later Domitianic context, as the city suffered damage in an earthquake around AD 60 and underwent a period of rebuilding (Osborne 2002, 158–59).

These letters, with their direct addresses to contemporary communities and concerns, further emphasize the book's relevance to the first-century audience, reinforcing the likelihood of an early composition.

Section 2: Key Full Preterist Interpretations of Prophecies

REVELATION 22:11

In Rev 22:11, the language strikes with stark finality: "He that is unjust, let him be unjust still: and he which is filthy, let him be filthy still: and he that is righteous, let him be righteous still: and he that is holy, let him be holy still." This verse carries an unsettling permanence, a declaration that the time for moral change has passed—that people will remain in the state they are in when the moment arrives. The immediacy is palpable, the tone uncompromising, as if judgment is so near that one's moral trajectory can no longer be altered.

To the early audience of Revelation, these words did not invite a prolonged period of self-improvement or moral introspection. Instead, they echoed the imminent collapse of an age, a cataclysm at the door. The tone here suggests that the prophecies spoken by John were on the verge of fulfillment—that the listeners would soon find themselves locked in their spiritual state, with no opportunity for further transformation. The call was not to look toward a distant, undefined future but to prepare for something immediate—something they believed was unfolding within their own lifetime.

Revelation 22:11's stark division between the "unjust" and the "holy" emphasizes that the lines had already been drawn. The early Christians, facing persecution and trials, understood these words not as metaphorical but as a divine announcement that the day of reckoning was upon them. For the righteous, it was a time to persevere; for the unrighteous, a sign that their window for change had closed. The sense of urgency underscores the belief that divine intervention and judgment were not far-off ideas but realities already descending upon the first-century world.

Today, such imminency is difficult to fathom, and Rev 22:11 remains one of the most jarring verses because it defies our modern expectations of endless opportunity for redemption. It reflects a mindset that history was hurtling toward a climactic end—one tied to events the early Christians believed were imminent, like the destruction of Jerusalem in AD 70. For them, time was not an open-ended resource; it was collapsing rapidly, and the world as they knew it was drawing to a close. This verse, then, is a window into how they perceived their reality, as people living on the cusp of divine judgment and finality.

In contrast, our world stretches time infinitely. The moral urgency, once felt so keenly, now dissipates in the belief that "there is always tomorrow." But for John's audience, tomorrow had already arrived.

EVALUATING THE FULL EVIDENCE

The evidence for dating the book of Revelation is complex and multifaceted. While external sources such as Irenaeus and later church tradition lean toward a Domitianic date, significant ambiguities and conflicting testimonies weaken the reliability of these sources (Robinson 2000, 224–25). In contrast, early testimonies from figures like Papias and the Syriac tradition, as well as parallels with Josephus's accounts of the Jewish War, lend strong support to an early date.

The cumulative internal evidence—sense of urgency, temple references, and cryptic allusions to Nero—supports an early date, aligning Revelation within first-century tribulation and providing contextually immediate relevance to its audience. Additionally, the consistent use of time indicators such as "soon" and "at hand" reinforces the idea that the prophecies were meant to be fulfilled in the near future, making a late date less plausible.

Despite arguments for a late date, the cumulative evidence—especially the internal indicators—points compellingly toward an early date. This perspective allows for a coherent interpretation of the book as a prophetic warning about the impending judgment on Jerusalem and the transition from the old covenant to the new. As Gentry argues, understanding Revelation as a text addressed to the immediate concerns of its first-century audience allows us to interpret its apocalyptic imagery within the historical and theological framework of the early Christian church, rather than as a prediction of distant future events (Gentry 1998, 104–5). In sum, the preponderance of evidence—particularly the internal textual indicators of urgency, the temple reference, and the cryptic reference to Nero—favor an early dating of Revelation. While external sources such as Irenaeus have traditionally supported a Domitianic date, interpretive ambiguities and gaps in historical accuracy dilute their conclusiveness. Taken together, the internal and corroborative external evidence strongly supports the composition of Revelation in the AD 60s, firmly grounding it within the context of first-century Jewish and Christian experiences of tribulation, thereby shaping its eschatological relevance for the intended audience.

23

Yes, But . . .

> Our interpretations of signs are as varied as our doubts.
> —Plutarch (ca. AD 46–119), Greek historian

ONE OF THE MOST persistent challenges full preterism faces is the "Yes, but" argument—a tendency among futurists to latch onto isolated passages or specific physical events as evidence that the eschatological narrative is still unfolding. This selective focus often stems from a misunderstanding of the time statements and symbolic language used throughout the prophetic texts. Full preterism, in contrast, understands these events as already realized through a spiritual and symbolic lens, often in direct historical contexts.

REVISITING THE TIME STATEMENTS

The New Testament is filled with time-sensitive statements regarding the fulfillment of prophecy. These phrases leave little room for a long, drawn-out timeline stretching into an indeterminate future. The immediacy of these time-sensitive statements is evident, as seen in John's words in 1 John 2:18: "Little children, it is the last hour: and as ye have heard that antichrist shall come, even now are there many antichrists; whereby we know that it is the last hour." This is not a vague metaphor for a distant end—it speaks of an imminent culmination.

Similarly, Jesus himself declared: "Verily I say unto you, This generation shall not pass, till all these things be fulfilled" (Matt 24:34). He was addressing his contemporaries, clearly pointing to events that would unfold within their lifetimes (France 2007, 940).

These time statements permeate the New Testament, making it clear that the fulfillment of prophecy was not a far-off event but something already underway. In Rev 22:10, John is told, "Seal not the sayings of the prophecy of this book: for the time is at hand." The urgency and immediacy of these declarations leave little room for futurist interpretations that stretch these events into the twenty-first century or beyond (Beale 1999, 48–49).

THE 144,000 AND THE SPIRITUAL NATURE OF PROPHECY

Another frequently debated point is the mention of the 144,000 in Rev 7:4 and 14:1–5. Futurists often argue that this number represents a future, literal group of people. But in full preterism, the 144,000 are understood symbolically, as representative of a faithful remnant of Israel who remained loyal to Christ in the first century (Gentry 2010, 45–46).

The 144,000, like much of Revelation, symbolize spiritual realities rather than a literal count of future believers. This remnant mirrors the concept found in the Old Testament, where a select group is spared as a symbol of God's faithfulness in preserving his people. This remnant had already been sealed, marking the completion of God's redemptive work in the past, not some yet-to-come future fulfillment.

THE "THIEF IN THE NIGHT" AND THE ELEMENT OF SURPRISE

Another argument used in the "Yes, but" line of reasoning is the "thief in the night" imagery. First Thessalonians 5:2 says: "For yourselves know perfectly that the day of the Lord so cometh as a thief in the night." This phrase has been used by futurists to argue that the second coming could happen at any moment, unexpectedly. However, in its first-century context, the "thief in the night" refers to the suddenness of God's judgment on Jerusalem, a

Section 2: Key Full Preterist Interpretations of Prophecies

judgment that came without warning for those who were spiritually unprepared (Ferguson 2018, 89). Jesus used similar language in Matt 24:43 when discussing the impending destruction of the temple.

The element of surprise is not a sign of future delay but a warning of the impending judgment on Jerusalem, which came in AD 70 with the Roman destruction of the city. This fulfillment was both immediate and decisive, catching those unaware who did not heed the prophetic signs (Josephus 1981, 209–10).

PHYSICAL VS. SPIRITUAL FULFILLMENT: THE DRYING UP OF THE EUPHRATES

One of the classic "Yes, but" arguments revolves around Rev 16:12, where it speaks of the Euphrates River drying up to prepare the way for the kings of the East. Many futurists interpret this as a literal prophecy that will be fulfilled through modern events, such as news reports about the river's diminishing water levels. They see this as a sign that the end is near.

However, full preterism approaches this passage from a symbolic perspective. The Euphrates, throughout Scripture, often represents the boundary between God's people and their enemies. Its drying up, therefore, is a metaphor for the removal of obstacles to judgment and the downfall of a great empire (Gentry 2010, 141). In the historical context of Revelation, this symbolizes the collapse of the Roman Empire's dominance, allowing for God's judgment to unfold.

By focusing on the literal river, futurists miss the spiritual and symbolic message embedded in Revelation's imagery. The vision speaks to a specific historical event—the removal of an empire's power in the first century—rather than a modern-day environmental occurrence (Beale 1999, 835).

THE TRAP OF SELECTIVE LITERALISM

Futurists persist with the "Yes, but" approach, often seeking a single unfulfilled prophecy or event to unravel the entire full preterist case. They ask, "Yes, but what about this prophecy?" without engaging with the larger framework of spiritual realization. For example, they might cite modern political events or natural phenomena as evidence that the final judgment is still ahead. But this narrow focus on isolated, literal details misses the bigger picture.

The drying up of rivers, the darkening of the sun, and the stars falling from the sky are all examples of apocalyptic language used throughout the Bible to communicate significant spiritual truths. These images point to covenantal transitions, divine judgments, and the end of specific historical eras, not literal future events (France 2007, 935).

NEVER SATISFIED: THE FUTURIST'S UNENDING SEARCH

A key challenge in addressing these "Yes, but" arguments is that those who subscribe to futurist interpretations are often never satisfied with the fulfillment already achieved in the first century. This mirrors the warning given in Matt 6:23: "But if thine eye be evil, thy whole body shall be full of darkness. If therefore the light that is in thee be darkness, how great is that darkness!"

Futurists, in their continual search for physical signs and literal fulfillments, can become blinded by the very darkness they seek to avoid.

The focus on literalism blinds them to the profound spiritual realities that have already taken place. The drying of the Euphrates or the stars falling from the heavens were not meant to be literal signs but symbolic events that signified spiritual judgment and fulfillment.

REAFFIRMING THE SPIRITUAL NATURE OF PROPHECY

The nature of prophecy, particularly in Revelation, is not about ticking off future, isolated events but about revealing spiritual truths that have already been realized. Revelation and other prophetic texts describe God's redemptive work in history, centered around the first-century destruction of Jerusalem, the end of the old covenant, and the full establishment of the kingdom of God (Gentry 2010, 202).

The "Yes, but" arguments often fail because they cling to a literalistic reading of Scripture that was never intended by the biblical authors. The richness of biblical prophecy reveals profound spiritual realities fulfilled in the first century, rather than predictors of millennia-spanning geopolitical events.

SECTION 3

Implications and "What's Next" for Full Preterism

Now, standing in the light of a world where the kingdom has already dawned, we find ourselves with a new map to navigate, a fresh cartography with clearer lines, leading us into uncharted territory. The Christian life within this realized kingdom requires orientation within a landscape transformed; it is not a map of waiting but of presence. Here, in this new charted terrain, the long-held questions arise with new significance: If Christ has already returned, how are we to understand a world that is still fraught with difficulty? What of the expectations we once held, and how do we make sense of the loss and disorientation that lingers? This section provides a refined compass for navigating a faith that no longer anticipates but instead embodies the present kingdom. For believers, this shift redefines life in profound ways, including a potential glimpse into eternity, an orientation toward life beyond biological experience. The journey is both practical and existential, calling us to live with a new awareness and resilience, rooted in a faith that is grounded not in waiting for an end but in walking within the already-established kingdom. Through this new map, we gain a redefined purpose and a clarity that urges us to embrace the "now" of the faith journey, discovering what it means to live as citizens in a kingdom that has indeed arrived.

24

The Void and Reorientation

Do not conform any longer to the pattern of this world, but be transformed by the renewing of your mind.

—Rom 12:2

Embracing full preterism can stir a deep sense of bitterness or loss. The lingering echoes of the futurist perspective may taunt, whispering: "Is this all there is?" or "Are we left with nothing but hopelessness?" Yet, these words hold no true power. They are the final faint scribbles of a spent quill, drawn from the cracked and drying ink of a fading futurist narrative.

THE SENSE OF LOSS

Futurism handed you a piece of fruit that would never ripen. You knew there was bitterness in the bite, but you never thought you'd have to experience that acrid taste, having been told it would ripen in time. You were assured that if you didn't taste its sweetness, your children or grandchildren would. Discarding it feels painful because you invested so much into that fruit, perhaps even structured your entire life around it—your work, your relationships, your dreams, all intertwined with this elusive hope.

Section 3: Implications and "What's Next" for Full Preterism

For years, you nurtured the expectation of a sweet bite, waiting for the green to turn ruddy. Yet now, under the light of full preterism, you realize that the season of waiting has passed. The true fruit has already come, though the experience of its ripeness feels bitter. The sweetness you anticipated seems lost. The grand finale you once awaited—a climactic, material fulfillment—is not forthcoming. Instead, the end has already occurred, leaving a yearning for what was once promised. This lingering desire clings to what could never mature, much like the ash of the Herodian Temple after AD 70, when old hopes crumbled into dust. That fruit, once held so dearly, is now only a shadow of the reality that was fulfilled.

Yet within this yearning lies the seed of true fulfillment—a call to lift our gaze from shadows to substance.

It means that the promises once anticipated are not lost but transformed—translated from earthly expectations to heavenly fulfillments. In the light of Christ's victory, we are not left in despair but in realization. The kingdom has come, not in the distant future but here and now, filling the space of each moment with the presence of God. The physicalist longing is replaced by something deeper, truer, and, ultimately, more profound: the nearness of God himself.

The ache of loss, then, is not the end. Instead, it's the beginning of a reorientation, an invitation to lift our gaze from the world's definition of victory and embrace the eternal kingdom, woven into the very fabric of our lives. It means moving beyond the shadows of past expectations and stepping fully into the living reality of Christ's fulfilled promise.

This is not the loss of hope but the realization that hope has already found us, calling us forward, not to wait, but to live.

Our Lord endowed us with confidence, assuring us of his victory when he declared that the days of vengeance in the first century were those in which "all things which are written may be fulfilled" (Luke 21:22). With this understanding, we no longer wait passively. Instead, we are called to action, living out the kingdom that is already present.

METAPHOR OF THE MAP

Our journey now is not a cautious stalking through uncertainty but a confident stride empowered by fulfillment. We aren't merely reading the map differently; we're holding an entirely new one. In the same way that a seismic shift reshapes landscapes, the destruction of the temple in AD 70 marked the start of a new spiritual terrain. Our old map no longer matches the territory, and with this reorientation, we move from a focus on expectations of the future to the richness of a present reality. Rather than searching for landmarks of a coming kingdom, we now recognize signs of a kingdom that already surrounds us, ready to be explored and understood. Each step forward, rather than a hesitant look to the horizon, becomes an engagement with a world we inhabit here and now.

Imagine a coronal mass ejection, where instead of plasma, the radiance of God's presence and his Messiah burst forth, lighting up the dark skies of deferred futurist hopes. Like the Northern Lights, this aurora—God's reconciliation with mankind—dances in vibrant colors, reminding us of his ever-present kingdom. We live now with the beauty of this reconciliation, no longer awaiting it. The ministry of reconciliation is complete (2 Cor 5:18–19).

This new orientation, like an aurora in the heavens, signals the divine presence in the here and now. Where our old orientation was fixed on distant, future milestones, this new reality invites us to navigate a living kingdom, unfolding moment by moment. No longer do we interpret the world by what we think should happen. Instead, we are guided radically by truth, no matter where it leads. The map has changed because our understanding has changed; we are no longer travelers seeking a far-off destination but residents uncovering the beauty of a kingdom already at hand. This fearless allegiance to truth cuts through the self-limiting beliefs that once held us captive.

Our compass no longer points to some distant tomorrow. It points at us, asking, "What of today?"

PRACTICAL REORIENTATION

This reorientation is rooted in truth and love, the hallmarks of those who dwell within the kingdom. Our internal compass points inward now because the kingdom of heaven is within us (Luke 17:21). It is not an external reality waiting to break through the clouds but an internal state that we manifest through our actions. This does not mean we are always happy or immune to sorrow; after all, "Jesus wept" (John 11:35). But it does grant us resilience, knowing that the kingdom is within and around us.

A friend of mine once described the Holy Spirit's influence as a "divine impulse" within us, revealing God through faith rather than intellectual speculation. This divine impulse is the inner prompting by which believers experience the presence of Christ, activating within us a deeper spiritual awareness. Ultimately, it is not through theology, creeds, or the ornate trappings of religion that we commend ourselves to God. Rather, it is through the actions, behaviors, and attitudes shaped by the spirit and truth within us. This—living out his will—is the worship we offer now.

Through this inward prompting, we are called to live out the truth. In the same way that light, once hidden, is meant to be uncovered, our inner transformation ignites Christ's nature within us (Luke 11:33). This is the kingdom made manifest—not in waiting for a distant future but in our very lives today.

THE STORY OF THE PRODIGAL SON: AN EXAMPLE OF REORIENTATION

In this context, the parable of the prodigal son (Luke 15:11–32) offers a powerful illustration of reorientation. The younger son, after squandering his inheritance, finds himself in a void—a place of spiritual and material loss. In his moment of despair, he reorients himself, realizing that even his father's servants live better than he does. This shift in perspective prompts his return to the father, who welcomes him with open arms, signifying reconciliation and restoration. Like the son, we, too, are called to reorient ourselves, not toward a distant hope but toward the truth that the Father has already reconciled us through Christ.

25

God's Will in a New Era

God is love; and he that dwelleth in love dwelleth in God, and God in him.
—1 John 4:16

The petition "Your will be done on earth as it is in heaven" (Matt 6:10) from the Lord's Prayer is not a passive request but a clarion call for the transformative power of God's will to reshape the very reality we experience here on earth. It's an appeal for divine order and intention to pervade the here and now, to realign the human heart and community in ways that reflect heaven's purity, justice, and love.

THE INTERNAL REALITY OF THE KINGDOM

Jesus's words in Matt 7:21 bring the sharp reality of this call into focus: "Not everyone that saith unto me, Lord, Lord, shall enter into the kingdom of heaven; but he that doeth the will of my Father which is in heaven." The kingdom is not accessed through empty words or performative religiosity. The mere proclamation of "Lord, Lord" holds no currency in this divine economy. Why? Because the kingdom of God, as Jesus teaches in Luke 17:20–21, "cometh not with observation: neither shall they say, Lo here! or, lo there! for, behold, the kingdom of God is within you." This is a profound statement—it tells us that the kingdom is not some external, geographic domain waiting to be established; it is the internal reality of God's reign within. The kingdom's presence is a lived experience of God's will, a transformation of the heart that is invisible to those who seek only outward signs.

The internal nature of the kingdom requires that this transformation manifests outwardly, bearing fruit in our relationships, actions, and attitudes. Jesus taught in the Sermon on the Mount that the kingdom's citizens are recognized by their mercy, humility, and love—a reflection of God's own nature. The kingdom's reality unfolds not in grand displays of power but in the quiet, steady presence of lives transformed by his love and truth.

Thus, Matt 7:21 isn't merely about compliance with divine commandments; it speaks to the disposition of the heart. Entry into the kingdom isn't about a magic phrase or theological formula—it's about the deep work of embodying God's will in one's life. It's an internal reality of submission to the Spirit, allowing God's love and truth to reign in all things.

THE WILL OF GOD IS RELATIONAL

To fully grasp this, we must return to Jesus in the garden of Gethsemane. As he prays, "O my Father, if it be possible, let this cup pass from me: nevertheless not as I will, but as thou wilt" (Matt 26:39), we witness the ultimate example of submitting to God's will. Just as Jesus trusted God's purpose in Gethsemane, even in the face of suffering, we, too, are called to a trust that transcends our immediate comfort. Our own "Gethsemane moments" may come when we are faced with choices that demand surrender to God's greater plan, accepting that his ways, though often mysterious, lead us into deeper communion with him and alignment with his will. In his humanity, Jesus experiences dread and anguish at the path ahead, but he acknowledges that God's will transcends his discomfort. This isn't about two wills in conflict but a profound trust in the divine plan, despite the bitter cup.

Similarly, in John 4:34, Jesus describes his sustenance in terms of God's will: "My meat is to do the will of him that sent me, and to finish his work." Here, we see the will of God framed as both vocation and fulfillment. It is not something abstract or distant but the very essence of life itself. To do God's will is to live in divine purpose, in step with the rhythms of heaven, just as Jesus demonstrated throughout his ministry (Augustine 1888 13.1–2).

THE FAMILY OF GOD

Moreover, Jesus redefines spiritual kinship in Matt 12:50, stating, "For whosoever shall do the will of my Father which is in heaven, the same is my brother, and sister, and mother." In this, we see that participation in God's will creates an unbreakable spiritual bond. To obey God is to be part of his family, to share in the intimate reality of divine relationship. This family, united in purpose and love, transcends biological ties and religious affiliation.

GOD'S WILL IS RESTORATIVE, NOT PUNITIVE

While Jesus did use strong language of condemnation, particularly toward those who resisted or misrepresented God's message, his intent was primarily corrective, offering paths to repentance and reconciliation. Revelation's imagery of the "second death" speaks to a final judgment on those who fully reject God's love. Many interpret this not as an endless punishment but as a representation of profound separation from God, underscoring the seriousness of rejecting the transformative power of grace. This perspective keeps in view the justice and mercy in God's will, balancing accountability with an enduring invitation to redemption. If Jesus wanted to reveal a God of vengeance, he could have easily done so. Instead, he healed, restored, and uplifted.

Acts 10:38 reminds us "how God anointed Jesus of Nazareth with the Holy Ghost and with power: who went about doing good, and healing all that were oppressed of the devil; for God was with him." The consistent theme of Jesus's life is the redemptive will of God, not retribution (Aquinas 1920, q. 19, a. 6). Consider Jesus's healings and compassion as examples of this restorative will. From the leper to the Samaritan woman, each encounter was a revelation of God's intent to restore, not merely to heal the body but to reconcile the soul. Every act of compassion was a reminder that God's will is to draw humanity back to himself in love, healing every kind of brokenness. First John 1:5 declares, "God is light, and in him is no darkness at all." God's nature, as revealed through Christ, is one of healing and renewal, not destruction. James 1:17 affirms that "every good gift and every perfect gift is from above," showing that God's will is not to afflict but to bless and restore. In this, we are called to reevaluate our understanding of God's character and will. Paul calls us in Rom 12:2 to be "transformed by the renewing of your mind, that ye may prove what is that good, and acceptable, and perfect will of God."

PEACEMAKERS AND THE KINGDOM

Jesus pronounces, "Blessed are the peacemakers: for they shall be called the children of God" (Matt 5:9). The will of God is not aligned with conflict or division but with peace and reconciliation. It is those who embody peace, who seek to restore and heal rather than tear down, who truly reflect God's nature and inherit the kingdom. The full preterist understanding of the kingdom is deeply tied to this call: the kingdom is now, and the sons and daughters of God—those who live in peace, justice, and love—are its true citizens.

This dovetails with Rom 8:19, where Paul writes, "For the earnest expectation of the creature waiteth for the manifestation of the sons of God." The whole of creation yearns for the revelation of those who live out God's will, whose lives are testimonies to the peace and restoration that the kingdom brings.

REJECTING FUTURIST DESPAIR

For too long, many Christians have been taught to view the world through a lens of impending doom, anticipating its decline as a necessary prelude to Christ's return. This worldview sees humanity as irredeemably corrupt, the earth as disposable, and divine love as conditional. But this is a betrayal of the gospel's true hope. The kingdom of God is not about abandoning the earth for some celestial escape; it is about the restoration of all things. Jesus didn't come to condemn the world but to save it (John 3:16–17). Full preterism invites us to rest in the completed work of Christ, freeing us from the burden of waiting for external signs of his coming. Instead, it challenges us to perceive God's kingdom in the small, daily expressions of faith, love, and justice we bring to the world around us. With this perspective, we can live in joyful certainty, knowing that the kingdom is not something we anticipate but something we actively participate in each day.

C. S. Lewis captures this perfectly, reflecting on two kinds of people: those who say to God, "Thy will be done," and those to whom God says, in the end, "All right, have it your way" (Lewis 1945, 75). Futurism, with its fixation on materialism and physicalism, is an "all right, have it your way" theology—forever striving for a kingdom that can be seen only with the eyes, not the heart. It leads to frustration and ultimately despair. In contrast, full preterism invites us to embrace the will of God, which has already brought the kingdom into our midst, if we have the eyes to see it.

THE WILL OF GOD REVEALED THROUGH LOVE

Aquinas reminds us that "the will of God is the first cause of all things and impossible for anything to happen contrary to this will" (1920, q. 19, a. 6). What this means for the full preterist is that God's will has already played out in history—his promises have been fulfilled, and the kingdom is now. We are living in the new era of God's reign. Calvin's caution against overspeculating about God's will is also important, but let us not forget that Jesus is the Word of God, and the Scriptures testify of him (Calvin 2008). The will of God is not a mystery locked in theological doctrines but is revealed through the life and teachings of Christ.

THE DIVINE WILL AS RESTORATIVE

God's will is not an impenetrable screenplay that we must decode. It is a dynamic, living reality we engage with daily. It's relational, not rigid. It's a fluid movement of love, not confined to church routines or even Scripture study, although it is present in those places. God's will is love in action, and that love is vividly captured in 1 Cor 13:4-8, where love is described as patient, kind, and enduring. This love in action is the essence of God's will. It is a call to live out love's qualities, to be patient, to show kindness, and to bear with one another as we seek to manifest his kingdom. Paul reminds us that love is the greatest commandment, and by embodying it, we fulfill the law. In this, we experience God's kingdom not only as a theological reality but as a lived truth that transforms us and our communities. In this, we see the will of God most clearly—God is love (1 John 4:16), and it is through love that his kingdom manifests.

26

Spiritual Rebirth and Nicodemus

Behold, I make all things new.

—REV 21:5

THE ENCOUNTER BETWEEN NICODEMUS and Jesus in John 3:1–21 offers a profound metaphor for the radical transformation required to enter the kingdom of God. Nicodemus, whose name means "victory of the people" (from the Greek *nikē* and *dēmos*), reflects a worldview rooted in material success, lineage, and social status. He approaches Jesus from a perspective focused on human achievement and physical birth. However, Jesus—whose name means "God is salvation"—offers an entirely different understanding of victory: one achieved through spiritual rebirth. Jesus declares that to enter God's kingdom, one must be "born of water and the Spirit" (John 3:5), signaling that true victory transcends the material world and is realized in spiritual transformation.

This rebirth places believers in God's kingdom now, not in a distant future. Nicodemus, representing those grounded in social and religious hierarchies, grapples with this new paradigm. His journey illustrates the challenge faced by anyone tethered to material assurances when confronted with the call to spiritual depth. Jesus's call to be "born again" disrupts the notion that status or lineage grants entry into the kingdom. Instead, it demands an inward renewal, a breaking of ties with inherited assumptions and a reorientation toward the divine reality now accessible.

PNEUMATIC HERMENEUTICS AND PAUL'S USE OF OLD TESTAMENT SCRIPTURE

In early Christian tradition, particularly in the teachings of Jesus and Paul, Scripture was interpreted through pneumatic hermeneutics—a dynamic, Spirit-led reading that sought to uncover Christ in every passage. Unlike modern biblical scholarship, which often focuses on original languages and historical context, pneumatic hermeneutics moves beyond the literal text to reveal deeper spiritual truths.

For instance, Jesus reinterpreted Old Testament imagery to point to himself as the true manna from heaven (John 6:50) and the new temple (John 2:19–22). Similarly, during his walk with the disciples on the road to Emmaus, Jesus opened their eyes to the fact that all of Scripture pointed to him (Luke 24:26–27, 31–32). In these examples, Christ reorients Old Testament symbols to reveal their ultimate fulfillment in him.

Paul's approach was no different. In Rom 9:25–26, he cites Hos 2:23 and 1:10, originally prophecies about the restoration of Israel, and reinterprets them to include the gentiles. By doing so, Paul expands the promises of God beyond Israel, demonstrating that gentiles, once considered "not my people," are now included in the covenant through Christ. This pneumatic exegesis illustrates the expansive nature of God's salvation, using Scripture in a fluid, Christ-centered way to unveil its fulfillment in the church.

Paul's method highlights the limitations of rigid literalism. A literal, surface-level reading of Scripture can miss the life-giving truths embedded in the text. It is through the Holy Spirit's guidance that the deeper meanings of Scripture are revealed, allowing us to engage in a dynamic, relational experience with God. This Spirit-led hermeneutic remains just as vital today, where literalism can still confine us to surface meanings, while pneumatic interpretation allows Scripture to resonate within our lives, revealing layers of relevance and divine truth. Through this approach, Scripture becomes a living text—active, transformative, and consistently pointing us back to Christ. When we read through the Spirit's lens, we encounter a relational God, who meets us within our contexts, experiences, and spiritual journey.

Section 3: Implications and "What's Next" for Full Preterism

FORGIVENESS AND LUTHER'S HERMENEUTIC SHIFT

One of the essential aspects of spiritual rebirth is cultivating a forgiving and grace-filled heart. Without this disposition, engagement with Scripture and spiritual growth can become rigid and lifeless. Martin Luther's theological journey provides a cautionary example of this transformation. Early in his career, Luther practiced a pneumatic and allegorical interpretation of Scripture, often finding Christ in Old Testament passages (Wood 1963, 155). This flexible, Spirit-guided approach allowed Luther to uncover deeper spiritual truths.

However, as Luther faced growing opposition during the Peasants' War, his disputes with the Anabaptists, and his increasingly hostile stance toward Jews, his interpretive method shifted. What had once been an expansive, Christ-centered reading of Scripture became a *sensus literalis*—a rigid, literalist approach that focused on the plain meaning of the text. This shift reflected Luther's frustration with rebellion and conflict, and his literalist readings increasingly justified severe actions against those he deemed heretical (Whitford 2016, 3–5).

Luther's departure from a pneumatic approach to Scripture led to a more rigid, uncompromising theology. As his interpretations became more literal, his writings supported violent measures, revealing how literalism can be used to justify hostility and persecution. This shift also highlights how abandoning a Spirit-led interpretation can lead to an exclusive and inflexible faith, one that stifles compassion in favor of strict adherence to text. When disconnected from the Spirit, even Scripture's life-giving truths risk becoming instruments of division. Luther's journey serves as a powerful reminder of the need to ground our faith in the Spirit's transformative power, lest we fall into the rigidity that stifles love and grace. This transformation illustrates the dangers of losing sight of the Holy Spirit's guidance in interpretation. Second Corinthians 3:6 provides a stark reminder: "The letter kills, but the Spirit gives life." Luther's later theological stance serves as a cautionary tale about the consequences of departing from a relational, Spirit-filled engagement with Scripture.

SCRIPTURA SUI IPSIUS INTERPRES AND LUTHER'S CHALLENGE TO THE CATHOLIC CHURCH

Luther's doctrine of *scriptura sui ipsius interpres*—the idea that "Scripture is its own interpreter"—was a direct response to the Roman Catholic Church's view that Scripture required ecclesiastical mediation, particularly from the pope, to be fully understood. The Catholic tradition, drawing on thinkers like Erasmus, argued that the Bible was a "dark book," inherently obscure and inaccessible to the common believer. Thus, the church's teaching office was seen as necessary to interpret Scripture (A. McGrath 1993, 85).

Luther challenged this by asserting the Bible's clarity and transparency. For him, Scripture was not obscure; it was accessible to all believers through the guidance of the Holy Spirit. This belief tied into Luther's broader Reformation principle of the "priesthood of all believers," which held that Christians did not need intermediaries to interpret God's word. Instead, Scripture could be understood directly by individuals, with the Holy Spirit providing insight (Preus 1974, 374).

While this idea was revolutionary in its time, *scriptura sui ipsius interpres* has faced significant criticism. Critics argue that Scripture is not inherently self-interpreting in a straightforward way. The Bible is a collection of diverse texts written in various historical and cultural contexts, and without a guiding framework—whether through tradition or church authority—interpretation can become fragmented. This has been especially evident in the many Protestant denominations that emerged post-Reformation, each with differing interpretations of Scripture (Pelikan 1996, 45). While Luther's challenge to the church may have freed Scripture from ecclesiastical control, it also introduced the challenge of interpretive chaos, demonstrating the difficulty of relying solely on individual interpretation.

HOW TO BE SAVED

To ask how one is saved is to step into a vast theological terrain—one layered with legal metaphors, mystical union, and ultimately, covenantal transformation. Traditionally, salvation has been framed as a threefold path: a legal declaration (justification), a moral transformation (sanctification), and a final eschatological fulfillment (glorification). These categories, especially in the Pauline corpus, helped early believers understand their standing with God amidst a world of temple ordinances and sacrificial systems. And yet, while these terms are valid within their covenantal context, they belong to what Paul called a shadow—the law economy, a mythopoetic scaffold through which God communicated His unfolding drama of redemption (Hebrews 8:13). But we are no longer under the law. Christ has fulfilled it. We are not waiting for access to the Most Holy Place—we are the temples now. The gospel is not a deal we negotiate, but a reality we awaken to. In this awakening we bring ourselves into alignment and obedience.

Salvation, in this light, is not merely legal rescue from punishment. It is the unveiling of what always was: that we were made to dwell in God, and He in us (John 17:21). The Cross was not the start of a contract but the revelation of a mystery hidden from the ages—that humanity is called into union, into Theosis, into love itself (2 Peter 1:4). If we follow the arc from justification to glorification, and beyond into union, we see that salvation is not transaction but transformation. It is not fear-based rhetoric about eternal destinations, but a call to alignment—to walk in the Spirit, to rest in the Father's embrace, to let the Kingdom within emerge (Luke 17:21). The old question "What must I do to be saved?" shifts in this fulfilled context to a deeper one: "What must I see to be free?" And the answer is: see what God has already done. See who you already are in Him.

LEAVING BEHIND THE PRIMITIVE: SPIRITUAL GROWTH AND REBIRTH

Spiritual rebirth, as Jesus explained to Nicodemus, involves moving beyond the primitive desires and worldly attachments that dominate human life—the "victory of the people"—and embracing a life rooted in God's salvation. True spiritual rebirth challenges us to leave behind the ego-driven desires that bind us to the world, allowing us to reorient toward God's eternal purposes. These worldly attachments, embodied by the dark traits of self-centeredness, keep us from realizing the freedom and dignity we have in Christ.

In psychological terms, the darker traits associated with the dark tetrad—narcissism, Machiavellianism, psychopathy, and sadism—represent the self-centered and materialistic desires that hinder spiritual growth. To experience true spiritual rebirth, believers must identify and release these destructive tendencies. As Paul urges in Eph 4:22, "Put off your old self, which belongs to your former manner of life and is corrupt through deceitful desires." It is only through this shedding of the old self that one can step into the fullness of God's salvation.

Spiritual Rebirth and Nicodemus

Charlotte Brontë's *Jane Eyre* beautifully illustrates this inner conflict between worldly limitations and spiritual freedom. Jane's assertion of her spiritual dignity captures the essence of spiritual rebirth:

> Do you think I am an automaton?—a machine without feelings? and can bear to have my morsel of bread snatched from my lips, and my drop of living water dashed from my cup? Do you think, because I am poor, obscure, plain, and little, I am soulless and heartless? You think wrong!—I have as much soul as you,—and full as much heart! And if God had gifted me with some beauty and much wealth, I should have made it as hard for you to leave me, as it is now for me to leave you. I am not talking to you now through the medium of custom, conventionalities, nor even of mortal flesh:—it is my spirit that addresses your spirit; just as if both had passed through the grave, and we stood at God's feet, equal,—as we are! I am a free human being with an independent will, which I now exert to leave you. (Brontë 1847, 369)

Brontë's words resonate with the idea of spiritual rebirth—the recognition of one's dignity before God and the freedom to live according to divine will. In the same way, Jesus calls us to be born again, and Paul reminds us to let go of the old self. Spiritual rebirth requires a relinquishing of our worldly expectations and an embrace of the present kingdom of God.

Furthermore, a pneumatic approach to Scripture—one that embraces the Spirit's guidance—enables believers to enter into a dynamic, relational experience with God. This approach does not limit Scripture to rigid literalism but rather opens the way for divine promptings to shape both our understanding of Scripture and our daily living. When we allow the Spirit to breathe life into our reading of Scripture and our actions in the world, we cultivate a richer, more intimate relationship with God, marked by ongoing transformation, relational depth, and spiritual clarity.

Luther's journey demonstrates the consequences of departing from such an approach. As Luther shifted away from a Spirit-guided hermeneutic toward a rigid literalism, his theology grew more severe, justifying violence and persecution. In contrast, a pneumatic embrace of Scripture fosters a dynamic and relational encounter with God, which is essential for interpreting the divine promptings of the Spirit and for living a spiritually renewed life. Ultimately, spiritual rebirth is not a one-time event but an ongoing transformation in which we participate daily, guided by the Spirit's whisper. Each encounter with Scripture, each moment of prayer, is an invitation to deepen our understanding of God's will and to embody the

Section 3: Implications and "What's Next" for Full Preterism

kingdom here and now. In this relational journey, we are not only readers or hearers of the word but active participants in a divine narrative, allowing God's Spirit to shape and renew us continuously

27

Sin and Evil in Society

Wherever there is a human being, there is an opportunity for kindness.
—Seneca, *Letters to Lucilius*

In addressing sin and evil within a realized eschatological framework, one naturally asks: Is sin still active, and does the devil continue to wield influence over human society? Despite the kingdom of God being spiritually realized, sin and evil clearly manifest in the physical and societal realms. From corporate greed to foreign policy and identity politics, sin infiltrates the structures we live within. These are the complexities of a world still contending with the shadows of the old age, despite the promises of the new.

THE DYSFUNCTION OF MAN

The human condition often carries an overwhelming burden of guilt. We see this acutely in the life of Martin Luther, who tortured himself with endless penance and self-flagellation, haunted by the question: "Will I ever know I've done enough to satiate the judgment of God?" It is natural to question what kind of God we are worshipping when this anxiety overwhelms us.

Section 3: Implications and "What's Next" for Full Preterism

It is understandable how the God of Moses might inspire such fear—presented as a divine warrior who demands holiness and instills awe. But that portrayal, conditioned by the environment and experiences of the ancient peoples, was not the full picture. Despite God's constant effort to reveal himself, the human medium through which divine revelation passed often filtered that truth through the broken ceramic of their context. The result is a mosaic—a fragmented image of God shaped by the ink of the ancient world's culture.

In contrast, Christ offers us the highest resolution of God's character. The stark differences between Old and New Testament depictions invite comparison. Consider the contrast between Old Testament verses like "God hates his enemies" (Ps 5:5) and Christ's command to "love your enemies" (Matt 5:44). Or where Isa 45:7 says God creates "darkness and evil," whereas the New Testament describes him as the "Father of lights, in whom there is no darkness" (Jas 1:17). These contrasts do not reflect a change in God's nature but rather the evolving clarity of human understanding. Christ reveals God's true nature in its most complete form, not contradicting but fulfilling the incomplete depictions that preceded him.

God remains a constant source of love; the issue lies in our interaction with God and the human medium through which he communicates. Just as trauma and cynicism can color our perceptions of the divine, so too does the collective consciousness of an ancient people under oppression shape their prophetic voices. When rage and vengeance grip the human heart, we find ourselves removed from the divine counsel of peace that Christ embodies. As my Scottish grandfather used to say, "Keep the heid," urging a calm mind amid life's storms. This wisdom mirrors Christ's spirit, calling us to resist the neurochemical triggers—like cortisol and adrenaline—that stoke our fear and aggression.

These biochemical forces (dopamine, norepinephrine, etc.) hijack our reasoning, constraining us with reactive impulses that offer no long-term vision of the kingdom. Yet, Paul's admonishment to "pray without ceasing" and give thanks (1 Thess 5:16–18) aligns with modern psychology. Studies show that gratitude reshapes the brain through neuroplasticity, allowing us to break free from stress cycles and live with the vibrant palette of a "happy mind" (Kabat-Zinn 1990, 298).

THE POWER OF FORGIVENESS

Take, for example, the abolition of slavery by William Wilberforce and his British contemporaries. Their fight against the world's oldest trade culminated in Britain waging war to end slavery, petitioning African kings to cease trading their people, and paying reparations—debts that were only finally settled in the early 2000s (Walvin 2013, 156). This tremendous moral victory, however, is often viewed with cynical disdain, as though the clear moral advances of history are diminished by the darkness of the times from which they emerged. This attitude, blind to human progress, negates the "stars" in the sky because their light does not fully vanquish the night.

Forgiveness, both individually and collectively, acts as a balm to the deep wounds inflicted by centuries of systemic injustice. When societies, like individuals, embrace forgiveness, they not only mend fractured relationships but open pathways for social healing. This forgiving stance doesn't overlook injustice but creates the space to address it with grace, propelling society toward a vision of peace and unity.

NATURAL EVIL

Natural evil, as we call it, is less the embodiment of moral wickedness and more a reflection of the inherent volatility in the fabric of creation. Earthquakes, famines, and tsunamis—all these calamities reflect not the hand of divine retribution or satanic malice but the reality of a world imbued with chaos, complexity, and limitation. This volatility is built into the world as a feature, not a bug. If the natural order were sterile, if the human experience were devoid of rough edges, we might find ourselves suspended in some kind of blissful nutrient goo, hooked up to perpetual pleasure machines—a grotesque parody of existence. But this is not our reality, nor should it be. In navigating the coarseness in reality, our human response becomes vital. Natural calamities, though seemingly indifferent, present opportunities for profound acts of compassion and resilience. Just as storms test the strength of a tree, so these events challenge our collective spirit, calling forth the divine image within us to respond with empathy, courage, and solidarity. To be human is to feel the sting of futility, to wrestle with the edges of existence, and to face the limitations of our physical world.

We live not in a utopia but in a dynamic universe where change is constant, often violent, and frequently indifferent. Whether the mechanisms that govern these cataclysms will always operate as they do is a question for another chapter. But it is clear that these natural occurrences are not the result of divine punishment or cosmic rebellion. They simply are. And our response to them, our ability to navigate these tragedies, reveals something profound about human nature. We are not only resilient; we are determined, emotively driven creatures. The beauty of humanity lies in its ability to face natural disasters with raw, unyielding courage—a reflection of our divine inheritance as children of God.

IS SIN STILL ALIVE?

James, ever practical, warns us: "Let no man say when he is tempted, I am tempted of God: for God cannot be tempted with evil, neither tempteth he any man: But every man is tempted, when he is drawn away of his own lust, and enticed. Then when lust hath conceived, it bringeth forth sin: and sin, when it is finished, bringeth forth death" (Jas 1:13–15).

Here, we encounter the delineation between natural evil and moral evil—the latter being the province of sentient beings. Humans, both vulnerable and complex, are prone to manipulation both from within and without. James, with sharp insight, holds up the mirror: sin is born in the heart of each individual. It is not imposed by some external force—neither demon nor devil can be blamed. This internal reckoning places responsibility firmly on our own lusts, our desires ungoverned by reason, that lead to sin and, ultimately, to death.

Yet Jesus introduces another dimension: "Woe unto the world because of offences! for it must needs be that offences come; but woe to that man by whom the offence cometh!" (Matt 18:7). This warning addresses a larger scale. Where James speaks of the micro-level—individual responsibility—Jesus turns to the macro-level. The ripple effects of our inner sins spill into the broader world, contaminating others. Like a noxious neurochemical, our unchecked impulses spread, influencing and corrupting those around us. These sins grow, manifesting as complex social systems of exploitation, criminal networks, and moral decay. This is the shadow kingdom—the antichrist order—that runs parallel to the kingdom of light.

In the grander theological narrative, the corporate sin of old-covenant Israel was dealt with, its eschatological weight lifted. The ritual atonements, the blood of bulls and goats, no longer hold sway. Yet the individual reality of sin persists. As beings who continually miss the mark—a phrase that speaks to the etymology of sin in both Hebrew and Greek—humans still require forgiveness. Though we are reconciled to God, the ability to sin remains a human constant. And forgiveness, when rightly embraced, offers not only spiritual peace but psychological and physiological freedom. Unforgiveness traps us, pressing stress hormones into overdrive and leaving us vulnerable to the weaknesses of the flesh (Toussaint et al. 2015, 91–106). Studies affirm that our quality of life is significantly enhanced when we live within the pattern of forgiveness.

DEMONIC ACTIVITY

While sin originates within, there are those whose deeds transcend the scope of everyday wickedness, plunging into depths we scarcely comprehend. The atrocities committed by certain gang members, hidden in the dark corners of our cities, defy the limits of human imagination. We live among psychopaths—1 in every 100 people (Hare, 1999). To stigmatize them would be to misunderstand their nature. They are not monsters but humans, occupying a necessary role in the human experience—one that confronts us with the tension between justice and mercy. Yet, when culture and circumstance steer these individuals into committing vicious evil, it becomes difficult to maintain composure.

At such moments, we might rightly describe their actions as *demonic*. Not necessarily in the folkloric sense of possession, but in the sense that their cruelty seems to tap into something far deeper—something older. Biblically and apocryphally, the category of the demonic is not monolithic. In fact, ancient Jewish thought presents three main kinds of supernatural evil:

Fallen Angels

Figures such as Azazel or Shemihazah (1 Enoch) were believed to be angelic beings who rebelled, descended to earth, and transgressed divine boundaries. Their punishment was to be bound in chains until the day of judgment, but their legacy continued in the corruption they instigated—particularly through their offspring, the Nephilim. These angels represent rebellion at the cosmic level, the original spiritual insurgents.

Section 3: Implications and "What's Next" for Full Preterism

Territorial Spirits

These beings were believed to govern regions or nations, influencing empires and ideologies. The "Prince of Persia" in Daniel 10 is one such entity, delaying angelic messengers. Asmodeus, in Tobit 3:8, is another example—depicted as a malevolent spirit afflicting individuals across generations. Paul's reference to "principalities and powers" (Colossians 2:15) likely echoes this tradition, viewing oppressive spiritual forces as embedded in the structures of earthly dominion.

The Restless Dead

Arguably the most unsettling category. In *1 Enoch 15:8–12*, demons are described as the disembodied spirits of the Nephilim—hybrid offspring of angels and humans destroyed in the flood. Cut off from heaven and unfit for Sheol, they were condemned to wander the earth without rest. This idea became deeply embedded in Second Temple Judaism, where demons were widely believed to be restless dead—not fallen angels per se, but disembodied spirits of violent or lawless beings. Some traditions expanded this even further, associating demons with the spirits of wicked humans who had died in alienation from God. In this view, demons are not merely alien intruders, but broken remnants of humanity—what remains when image-bearers are utterly cut off from the Source of life. When Jesus cast out unclean spirits, His contemporaries would have understood them as precisely these entities: ghosts of a corrupted lineage or tormented human souls, spiritually ruined and desperate for embodiment.

Some might find this classification speculative or unsettling, but it reveals something profound about how ancient minds interpreted the intersection of spiritual evil and human suffering. These categories were not meant to be clinical definitions—they were narrative frameworks for understanding chaos, cruelty, and corruption in the world. And whether one sees them as literal beings or mythic personifications, their influence remains relevant. Because ultimately, the demonic was never just about them—it was about us.

This ancient schema does not offer us a Hollywood demonology, but something more disturbing: a vision of evil that is systemic, personal, and tragically human. Evil does not come only from outside us—it emerges from within us, and from what we as a species have collectively become.

Jesus' confrontation with *Legion*—a man tormented by many spirits—reveals just how entangled psychological trauma, social alienation, and spiritual disorder can be. Were those demons literal beings? Disembodied memories? Territorial echoes? The Gospels don't say. But they do say Christ had authority over them.

Some traditions, such as the Christadelphians, dismiss demons as figurative language for mental illness or spiritual distress. And while the Bible certainly uses metaphor and imprecise categories at times, it also affirms that the spiritual world is not empty. Paul's words in Colossians 2:15 describe Christ's triumph over principalities and powers—whatever they are—as part of the cross's cosmic victory. These principalities, whether angelic, ideological, or human, represent the forces Christ defeated. But the nature of those forces remains mysterious.

Ultimately, the Bible gives us no encyclopedia of evil. It gestures at it, names it in passing, confronts it directly in Christ—but rarely categorizes it neatly. Perhaps that's because evil itself is disintegrated, fragmented, and illegible. Even if such entities exist, Scripture does not clearly detail their origin or fate. We are left with glimpses: chained angels, wandering spirits, and a realm of "outer darkness" where there is weeping and gnashing of teeth (Matt 8:12). Perhaps those who persist in evil become disembodied themselves—souls unmoored from the light of God, drifting in spiritual exile. If demons are real, they are not merely supernatural—they are theological artefacts of covenantal failure, the echoes of a humanity that has forgotten its name.

IS THE DEVIL STILL ALIVE?

It has been said, "The greatest trick the devil ever played was convincing the world he never existed." In the modern world, evil motivations swirl beneath the surface, often masquerading behind individuals or even entire organizations. These forces are the living satanic entities of our time. Jesus, ever perceptive, rebuked Peter with the words "Get behind me, Satan!" not because Peter was possessed but because his words carried the influence of satanic thought. Christ, with his perfect clarity, could discern the spiritual forces at work behind human actions.

The character of Satan evolves throughout Scripture—from a member of God's council in Job, to a figure of immense power in Matt 4, capable of offering dominion over the world, to a fallen power and, finally, a defeated foe. Revelation 20:10 presents the clearest image of his fate: "And the devil that deceived them was cast into the lake of fire . . . and shall be tormented day and night for ever and ever."

And then comes the death of death itself. In Rev 20:14–15, death and Hades are cast into the lake of fire—the second death. The symbolic meaning here is vast, with centuries of debate surrounding this mysterious "second death." Some view it as an eternal separation from God; others see it as annihilation, a final obliteration of the soul. Yet the metaphor of the "second death" invites us to consider a broader spiritual reality—one where the ultimate separation or "death" is from our fallen self, our ties to sin, and the dark impulses that once held us. In this sense, the "second death" may not be a literal annihilation but a purification, burning away the remnants of the old world to usher in a new creation. This interpretive openness allows believers to see the lake of fire as both judgment and renewal, a purging flame that solidifies the kingdom's triumph over all forms of death. From a full preterist perspective, this moment symbolizes the end of the old-covenant system of sin and death. The lake of fire marks the point where death, once a looming power, is rendered powerless and the new-covenant era begins, free from the grip of sin's eschatological shadow.

So, is the devil still alive? In the preterist understanding, no—not in the apocalyptic sense Scripture portrays. The devil as a covenantal adversary, as the accuser under the Law, has been judged and cast down. His role within the drama of redemptive history has ended. What lingers today are not literal horns and pitchforks, but systems, ideologies, and human choices that echo his legacy. The spirit of accusation, deception, and domination lives on—not as a surviving personified being, but as the residue of a world once enslaved to sin and law. Though the strong man was long ago bound and cast down, the echo of his voice lives on in the systems and choices of a world still learning to walk free. The call of the gospel, then, is not to fear a devil in the shadows, but to walk in the Spirit, resisting the lingering patterns of a world already overcome.

EMBRACING THE KINGDOM'S LIGHT

In examining the interplay of sin, evil, and the complexities of both natural and moral catastrophes, we are drawn into the heart of the human experience—an experience fraught with struggle, yet laden with divine potential. Sin, though no longer the covenantal weight it once was, persists in the undercurrents of human nature. It ripples outward, influencing societies and shaping the structures of power. But just as evil manifests in dark networks of human and spiritual influence, so too does the light of redemption continue to shine through, illuminating paths toward forgiveness, restoration, and ultimately, reconciliation with God.

The presence of evil in the world is often raised as an objection to the idea that Christ is already reigning. If the Kingdom has come, why do suffering, corruption, and injustice persist? But this assumes that Christ's reign must function like a top-down dictatorship, rather than a spiritual reality animated by free will, love, and participation. In truth, evil is not a failure of God's reign—it is a consequence of incarnation itself.

To enter creation—to take on flesh and dwell among us—is to enter a space where choice, temptation, and even rebellion exist. God's rule does not override agency; it dignifies it. The Kingdom advances not through coercion, but through invitation. Just as Eden contained both communion and the possibility of exile, the New Covenant world holds both Spirit and resistance. Evil still exists not because Christ is not reigning, but because His reign allows for relationship—and relationship, by nature, allows for rejection.

In this light, evil is not proof of Christ's delay, but of humanity's ongoing freedom to align or resist the Spirit. The "loosing of Satan" for a little season (Rev 20:3) affirms this further: the end of the Old Covenant didn't eliminate all opposition, but exposed and judged its systems, allowing the age of the Spirit to emerge in fullness. The battle is no longer cosmic but personal—no longer eschatological but ethical.

Natural evil, for all its destructive force, reflects the chaotic beauty of a world in flux, one in which we learn, grow, and face the harsh realities of existence. Moral evil, whether spawned in the depths of the human heart or in the intricate designs of larger systems, reminds us of the fragile tension between our fallen nature and our divine calling. And as for the devil, whether he lurks in the shadows or has been rendered powerless by the cross, his fate is sealed in the eschatological fire of judgment.

The darkness may surround us, but it is not final. The Kingdom is ever at hand, and in moving toward the light of God, we cast out the shadow of sin. This journey toward light is both personal and cosmic. Each act of kindness, every choice to forgive, and each instance of resisting darkness contributes to a larger tapestry of redemption. We do not wage this battle alone; we are part of a divine mission, empowered by the Spirit to manifest

Section 3: Implications and "What's Next" for Full Preterism

the Kingdom's light. In embracing this role, we participate in the very renewal that Christ initiated, becoming vessels of the Kingdom's love in a world desperate for restoration. What we now live is the process of realization—of divine truth, of personal responsibility, and of a future where evil and death are no more. We are, as ever, the stewards of this ongoing transformation, charged with wielding the light in a world still learning to escape the night.

28

The Christian Worldview vs. Ideology

But seek ye first the kingdom of God, and his righteousness; and all these things shall be added unto you.

—MATT 6:33

THROUGHOUT HISTORY, COMMUNITIES OF faith have struggled with forces that stifle inquiry, foster division, and overshadow the transformative essence of their beliefs. In Christianity, this often takes the form of rigid institutional frameworks—ecclesiocracy, clericalism, Phariseeism, legalism, and creedalism—that prioritize conformity over spiritual renewal. These systems cast a shadow over the church's ability to embrace diversity in theological thought, creating an oppressive atmosphere where honest questions are met with suspicion and condemnation.

This oppressive dynamic could be described as a moral pall—a figurative cloud that hangs over sincere inquiry and exploration of faith, discouraging the pursuit of truth. It is under this pall that full preterists, for their eschatological convictions, are often dismissed as heretical. This dismissal reflects not a genuine engagement with Christ's teachings but an overreliance on ideological frameworks that obscure the relational faith Christ exemplified.

Section 3: Implications and "What's Next" for Full Preterism

WORLDVIEW VS. IDEOLOGY IN CHRISTIANITY

To understand the tension between full preterists and mainstream Christianity, we must distinguish between worldview and ideology. A Christian worldview reflects the lived faith of Christ, rooted in unity with God, love for neighbor, and the fulfillment of divine promises. It is dynamic, spiritual, and relational, focusing on transformation over mere compliance. Christian ideology, by contrast, calcifies faith into rigid structures like creeds and institutional authority. It prioritizes adherence to doctrinal formulations, creating barriers to spiritual growth and fostering exclusion.

This ideological impulse mirrors the Phariseeism critiqued by Jesus—a focus on outward conformity and rule following at the expense of the heart's transformation. It also reflects clericalism, where clergy and institutional power are elevated to an undue status, placing human authority above the Spirit-led discernment of the individual believer. Full preterists, by emphasizing the fulfilled promises of God and the present reality of his kingdom, align with Christ's worldview but diverge from the creedalism, legalism, and clericalism often associated with mainstream Christianity.

THE REFRAMING OF CHRISTIAN VALUES

The institutional church, operating as an ecclesiocracy, often reframes Christian values as ideological markers, much like the totalizing ideologies of secular universalism. This shift creates several tensions:

Rigid Doctrines vs. Living Faith

Just as Phariseeism emphasized rule following over the spirit of the law, Christian creedalism risks reducing faith to adherence to fixed propositions. Full preterists challenge this by focusing on the lived reality of God's fulfilled promises.

Exclusion Through Clericalism and Legalism

Clericalism and legalism marginalize those who do not conform to prescribed norms, even when they embody the principles of Christ. By elevating institutional authority and rigid rule following over the Spirit, these frameworks suppress diversity in theological interpretation. Full preterists, though ideologically distinct, live out the Christian worldview through love, reconciliation, and spiritual renewal.

The Totalizing Nature of Ideology

Ideology, whether secular or religious, demands a utopian "arrival." In eschatology, this takes the form of a yet-future apocalypse. Full preterists challenge this by asserting that the kingdom of God is not a distant promise but a present reality requiring ongoing participation.

THE MORAL PALL OF ECCLESIOCRACY, CLERICALISM, AND LEGALISM

The moral pall over full preterism reflects the dangers of a faith dominated by ecclesiocracy, clericalism, and legalism. When institutional power and rigid rule following overshadow the relational faith Christ taught, the church risks repeating the errors of the Pharisees. Consider Christ's rebuke in Matt 23:23: "Woe to you, scribes and Pharisees, hypocrites! For you tithe mint and dill and cumin, and have neglected the weightier matters of the law: justice and mercy and faithfulness."

Just as the Pharisees substituted legal adherence for true faithfulness, modern clericalism elevates human authority above the Spirit, and creedalism risks reducing Christianity to a checklist of beliefs. This approach dismisses full preterists as heretical for rejecting future eschatological expectations, despite their alignment with the worldview of Christ.

RECLAIMING A CHRISTIAN WORLDVIEW

To dispel this moral pall, the church must reject ecclesiocracy, clericalism, legalism, and creedalism as ultimate measures of faith. Instead, it should embrace the transformative worldview of Christ, rooted in love, fulfillment, and the lived reality of God's kingdom. This requires:

Section 3: Implications and "What's Next" for Full Preterism

Rejecting Ecclesiocracy and Clericalism for Relational Faith

The institutional church must recognize that authority flows not from rigid structures or clergy but from the Spirit of God, who empowers believers to live in alignment with his promises.

Moving Beyond Legalism

Faith cannot be reduced to rule following. Full preterists, in their focus on the fulfillment of God's promises, embody the freedom and renewal Christ offers.

Challenging Creedalism as a Barrier

While creeds have value in preserving theological truth, they must not become gatekeeping mechanisms that marginalize those who interpret Scripture differently. Full preterists' emphasis on the present reality of the kingdom exemplifies the spirit of Christian faith, even if it challenges traditional formulations.

BEYOND THE PALL

The tension between worldview and ideology offers a lens through which to understand the church's treatment of full preterists. When ecclesiocracy, clericalism, Phariseeism, legalism, and creedalism dominate, the church risks perpetuating a moral pall that obscures the light of Christ.

Full preterists, far from heretical, live out the worldview of Christ—rooted in love, fulfillment, and unity with God. To move beyond the pall, the church must embrace this alignment, recognizing that Christian values are not bound by institutional frameworks but by the transformative power of God's kingdom, here and now.

29

A Critique of Israel-Only Theology

For mine house shall be called an house of prayer for all people.
—Isa 56:7

THE THEOLOGICAL FRAMEWORK OF Israel-only (IO) theology asserts that God's covenantal dealings were exclusively with Israel, to the exclusion of all other nations and peoples. While this perspective attempts to highlight the centrality of Israel in the biblical narrative, it ultimately falls short of addressing the broader, universal dimensions of God's engagement with humanity. However, IO theology raises significant questions that are frequently discussed in preterist circles, particularly about the scope of God's redemptive plan and the relationship between Israel and the nations. Addressing these questions is not only worthwhile but also essential for better informing the full preterist position. This chapter challenges the IO perspective by presenting robust biblical evidence and theological arguments that emphasize God's universal sovereignty, justice, and redemptive purposes.

Section 3: Implications and "What's Next" for Full Preterism

THE DEFINITION OF "GENTILE": RHETORICAL AND PRESUPPOSITIONAL CHALLENGES

The term "gentile" is central to the IO argument, yet its definition and usage in Scripture undermine their exclusivist framework. Derived from the Latin *gentilis*, meaning "of a nation," the term corresponds to the Hebrew *goyim* and the Greek *ethnos*, both commonly translated as "nations." Throughout the Bible, "gentile" consistently refers to peoples and nations outside the covenant community of Israel.

BIBLICAL CONTEXT AND CLARITY

Old Testament Usage

The Hebrew term *goyim* appears frequently in the Old Testament to designate nations distinct from Israel:

a. "When the Lord thy God shall bring thee into the land . . . and shall cast out many nations (*goyim*) before thee: the Hittites, and the Girgashites, and the Amorites. . ." (Duet. 7:1). This verse names the nations being driven out, there can be no mistaking them for Israelites.

b. "For the nation [*goy*] and kingdom that will not serve thee shall perish; yea, those nations shall be utterly wasted" (Isa 60:12). In this prophetic vision, *goyim* explicitly refers to non-Israelite nations subject to divine judgment.

New Testament Usage

The Greek *ethnos* in the New Testament maintains this distinction:

a. "For salvation is of the Jews. But the hour is coming, and is now here, when the true worshipers will worship the Father in spirit and truth" (John 4:22–23). Jesus differentiates Jews from the broader nations, illustrating that salvation is offered universally.

b. "Here there is not Greek and Jew, circumcised and uncircumcised, barbarian, Scythian, slave, free; but Christ is all, and in all" (Col 3:11). Paul explicitly includes "barbarians" and "Scythians"—groups definitively outside the covenant community of Israel—as part of the new covenant through Christ.

A Critique of Israel-Only Theology

ISRAEL ONLY'S REDEFINITION OF "GENTILE"

The IO perspective presuppositionally redefines "gentile" as synonymous with "scattered Israelites." However, this interpretation imposes a theological framework onto the text, rather than allowing the text to define its terms. This rhetorical sleight of hand erases references to non-Israelites by conflating distinct categories, as demonstrated in their interpretation of Eph 2:12: "That at that time ye were without Christ, being aliens from the commonwealth of Israel, and strangers from the covenants of promise, having no hope, and without God in the world."

Israel-only theology insists that "aliens from the commonwealth of Israel" refers to Israelites who lost their heritage. However, the plain reading of the text identifies a group entirely outside the covenant—a description that fits gentiles as non-Israelites.

RHETORICAL IMPOSITION AND PRACTICAL ILLOGIC

The IO redefinition of "gentile" is not supported by the linguistic or contextual use of *goyim* or *ethnos* in Scripture. Instead, it serves as a rhetorical imposition designed to sustain the exclusivist narrative. This approach is both practically illogical and inconsistent with the broader biblical message:

Practical Illogic

If gentiles are scattered Israelites, Paul's distinction between Jew and gentile in Rom 3:29—"Is He the God of Jews only? Is he not also of Gentiles also? Yes, of Gentiles also"—becomes redundant. The distinction collapses, rendering Paul's argument nonsensical.

Eisegetical Approach

By redefining gentiles presuppositionally, IO theology engages in eisegesis, reading its framework into the text rather than drawing meaning from the text itself. This undermines the integrity of the biblical narrative, which consistently emphasizes the inclusion of non-Israelites in God's redemptive plan.

Section 3: Implications and "What's Next" for Full Preterism

BIBLE EVIDENCE FOR UNIVERSAL INVOLVEMENT

Judgment on Non-Israelite Nations

The Bible explicitly records God's dealings with nations beyond Israel, demonstrating his concern for universal morality and justice. Consider the following examples:

> Behold, this was the iniquity of thy sister Sodom, pride, fulness of bread, and abundance of idleness was in her and in her daughters, neither did she strengthen the hand of the poor and needy. And they were haughty, and committed abomination before me: therefore I took them away as I saw good. (Ezek 16:49–50)

> Arise, go to Nineveh, that great city, and cry against it; for their wickedness is come up before me. (Jonah 1:2)

> Defile not ye yourselves in any of these things: for in all these the nations are defiled which I cast out before you: And the land is defiled: therefore I do visit the iniquity thereof upon it, and the land itself vomiteth out her inhabitants. (Lev 18:24–25)

> We have heard of the pride of Moab; he is very proud: even of his haughtiness, and his pride, and his wrath: but his lies shall not be so. (Isa 16:6)

> For the indignation of the Lord is upon all nations, and his fury upon all their armies: he hath utterly destroyed them, he hath delivered them to the slaughter. (Isa 34:2)

These verses collectively dismantle the notion that God's judgments were confined to Israel or hinged solely on their interactions with Israel. They highlight God's universal concern for justice and righteousness.

God's Sovereignty over All Nations

God's actions with figures like Melchizedek, Cyrus, and the city of Nineveh underscore his engagement with non-Israelite entities:

> Melchizedek: Described as a priest of the Most High God, Melchizedek blessed Abraham (Gen 14:18), demonstrating that the worship of the true God existed outside the covenant with Israel.

A Critique of Israel-Only Theology

Cyrus the Great: Referred to as God's "anointed" (Isa 45:1), Cyrus was instrumental in fulfilling God's purposes, even though he was a Persian king.

Nineveh: The repentance of Nineveh under Jonah's reluctant preaching (Jonah 3) highlights God's mercy and justice toward non-Israelite nations.

These examples affirm that God's redemptive and judicial actions transcend the boundaries of Israel.

Universal Promises

From the Abrahamic covenant onward, the Bible emphasizes God's intent to bless all nations:

> In thee shall all families of the earth be blessed. (Gen 12:3)

> And the scripture, foreseeing that God would justify the heathen through faith, preached before the gospel unto Abraham, saying, In thee shall all nations be blessed. (Gal 3:8)

> Where there is neither Greek nor Jew, circumcision nor uncircumcision, Barbarian, Scythian, bond nor free: but Christ is all, and in all. (Col 3:11)

> Also the sons of the stranger, that join themselves to the Lord, to serve him, and to love the name of the Lord, to be his servants, every one that keepeth the sabbath from polluting it, and taketh hold of my covenant;
> Even them will I bring to my holy mountain, and make them joyful in my house of prayer: their burnt offerings and their sacrifices shall be accepted upon mine altar; for mine house shall be called an house of prayer for all people. (Isa 56:6–7)

These promises extend beyond Israel, pointing to a universal plan of redemption.

Section 3: Implications and "What's Next" for Full Preterism

THEOLOGICAL CHALLENGES TO ISRAEL ONLY

Metaphysical Theodicy and the Scope of Redemption

Israel-only theology falters when examined through the lens of metaphysical theodicy. If God's purposes are restricted to Israel, what is his relationship to the broader creation? How does IO account for the universal experience of sin, suffering, and moral accountability?

Paul addresses this in Rom 5:12: "Wherefore, as by one man sin entered into the world, and death by sin; and so death passed upon all men, for that all have sinned." This verse underscores the universality of sin's impact, tracing it back to Adam, the representative of all humanity. Similarly, Rom 8:20–22 describes creation itself groaning for redemption, emphasizing the cosmic scope of Christ's work.

By narrowing God's purposes to Israel, IO theology fails to provide a coherent framework for understanding God's justice and providence on a universal scale. If God's dealings are limited to Israel, what of the rest of humanity and creation?

Inconsistencies in Interpretation

Israel-only proponents often rely on circular reasoning and selective interpretations to support their claims. For example:

Ephesians 2:12 describes gentiles as "aliens from the commonwealth of Israel, and strangers from the covenants of promise, having no hope, and without God in the world." If this referred to scattered Israelites, it would contradict the prophetic assurances of their inclusion in God's covenantal promises (e.g., Ezek 37:21–22). Romans 2:14–15 speaks of gentiles who, without the law, are a law unto themselves, with their consciences bearing witness. This universal moral accountability undermines the IO claim that sin and salvation are exclusive to Israel.

Jesus's Ministry and the Inclusion of Non-Israelites

Jesus's interactions with non-Israelites, such as the Roman centurion (Matt 8:10) and the Canaanite woman (Matt 15:21–28), illustrate the universal reach of God's kingdom. Mark 7:26 explicitly states the Canaanite woman was "a Greek, a Syrophoenician by nation." This description clearly places her outside the covenant community of Israel. If you believe she was an Israelite, I'd be interested to see any evidence supporting a more detailed biography of this woman that identifies her as such.

The gospel writers seem to go out of their way to emphasize her non-Israelite identity—calling her a Canaanite in Matt 15:22 and specifying her Greek and Syrophoenician origins in Mark. These descriptions are not incidental; they serve a theological purpose, contrasting her faith with the unbelief often seen among Israelites. Claiming she was an Israelite adopting Canaanite culture feels like an ideological overlay that runs counter to the text. The writers' consistent portrayal of her as a gentile challenges exclusivist interpretations, illustrating that faith, not ethnicity, grants access to God's blessings.

The Great Commission and Paul's Ministry

The Great Commission explicitly calls for making disciples of all nations (Matt 28:19). Similarly, Paul's ministry extended to non-Israelites, as seen in his address to the Athenians in Acts 17 and his declaration in Rom 11:13: "I am an apostle to the Gentiles."

THE UNIVERSAL NEED FOR SALVATION: ADDRESSING THE ISRAEL-ONLY CHALLENGE

The question "What does a non-Israelite need saving from?" arises frequently in discussions with proponents of IO theology. At its core, this question reveals a misunderstanding of both the biblical portrayal of sin and the scope of salvation offered through Christ.

SIN AS A UNIVERSAL PROBLEM

Sin is not limited to Israel. The Bible consistently portrays sin as a universal issue, affecting all of humanity since the fall of Adam. Romans 5:12 states, "Wherefore, as by one man sin entered into the world, and death by sin; and so death passed upon all men, for that all have sinned." This verse does not restrict sin or its consequences to Israel; it ties the entire human race to Adam's disobedience. If sin is a universal inheritance, then salvation must also address this universal condition.

Paul further reinforces this in Rom 3:23: "For all have sinned, and come short of the glory of God." Here, "all" includes both Jews and gentiles, showing that the need for redemption transcends ethnic boundaries.

CONSCIENCE AND ACCOUNTABILITY

Romans 2:14–15 explains that even those without the Mosaic law—gentiles—are still accountable for their actions because God has written his law on their hearts: "For when the Gentiles, which have not the law, do by nature the things contained in the law, these, having not the law, are a law unto themselves: Which shew the work of the law written in their hearts, their conscience also bearing witness, and their thoughts the mean while accusing or else excusing one another." This passage highlights the universality of moral accountability. Every person, regardless of their lineage, is judged by their conscience and their adherence to God's moral standards.

BIBLICAL EXAMPLES OF NON-ISRAELITE ACCOUNTABILITY

The Bible repeatedly shows God holding non-Israelite nations accountable for their sins, independent of their relationship to Israel:

> Sodom and Gomorrah: "Behold, this was the guilt of your sister Sodom: she and her daughters had pride, excess of food, and prosperous ease, but did not aid the poor and needy" (Ezek 16:49–50).
>
> Nineveh: "Arise, go to Nineveh, that great city, and call out against it, for their evil has come up before me" (Jonah 1:2).
>
> The flood: Humanity as a whole was judged for its wickedness, long before the establishment of Israel (Gen 6:5–7).

These examples dismantle the IO claim that sin and judgment are limited to Israel.

SALVATION BEYOND THE MOSAIC COVENANT

While it is true that the Mosaic law was given specifically to Israel, salvation is not confined to that covenant. The New Testament expands on this by presenting Jesus as the savior of the entire world. John 3:16 declares, "For God so loved the world, that he gave his only begotten Son, that whosoever believeth in him should not perish, but have everlasting life." This promise is not restricted to Israel but extended to "whoever believes."

In Col 3:11, Paul writes, "Where there is neither Greek nor Jew, circumcision nor uncircumcision, Barbarian, Scythian, bond nor free: but Christ is all, and in all." The inclusion of "Barbarian" and "Scythian"—terms used to describe non-Israelite peoples—emphasizes the universality of Christ's redemptive work.

THE UNIVERSAL MISSION OF CHRIST

Jesus's ministry consistently pointed to a broader audience than Israel alone. His interactions with the Roman centurion (Matt 8:10), the Samaritan woman (John 4:7-26), and the Canaanite woman (Matt 15:21-28) illustrate the inclusivity of God's kingdom. In the case of the Canaanite woman, Jesus commended her faith and granted her request, despite her non-Israelite identity. This demonstrates that salvation is not contingent on ethnic lineage but on faith.

A UNIVERSAL GOD

Israel-only theology falters not just in its narrow scope but in its failure to appreciate the universal character of God as revealed in Scripture. The God of the Bible is not limited to tribal boundaries or national identities. As Jesus declares in John 17:3, YHWH is "the only true God," the Creator and Sustainer of all things, whose authority extends across every nation and people group. This truth is foundational to understanding the entire biblical narrative and dismantles the IO claim that God is exclusively concerned with Israel.

The apostle Paul's speech in Acts 17 exemplifies this universality. By reinterpreting the Greek poet Aratus's reference to Zeus, Paul points beyond pagan misunderstandings to the only true God. This inclusivity shows that all human striving toward the divine, no matter how flawed, ultimately finds its answer in YHWH. Similarly, biblical accounts—from the fall of humanity in Genesis to moral judgments on nations like Sodom and Nineveh—demonstrate God's engagement with all people, not just Israel. Even Israel's covenantal election was never for exclusivity but illumination;

Section 3: Implications and "What's Next" for Full Preterism

they were chosen to serve as a light to the nations (Isa 49:6), not to hoard the knowledge of God.

Psalm 24:1 proclaims, "The earth is the Lord's, and everything in it, the world, and all who live in it." This declaration, echoed in Isa 45:5–7 and Col 1:16–17, affirms the scope of God's authority and creative power. The Babel narrative in Gen 11 further challenges IO theology, as it highlights humanity's collective rebellion and God's intentional dispersion of people. If the sons of Adam are all Israelites, as IO contends, this story makes little sense. Why would God scatter and judge nations if his focus were exclusively on Israel?

Israel-only theology misinterprets Israel's covenantal role, seeing it as an end in itself rather than a means to reveal God's redemptive purposes. Israel's identity as God's inheritance is covenantal language, reflecting their role in the unfolding divine plan, not God's exclusion of other nations. The inclusion of gentiles like Rahab and Ruth in Israel's story, as well as the ministry of figures like Daniel in foreign courts, underscores this truth. These accounts reflect a God deeply invested in humanity as a whole, not bound by ethnic or geographical limits.

By confining God's concern to Israel alone, IO theology diminishes the grandeur of God's character and the scope of the gospel. YHWH is not merely the God of Israel but of all creation. As Paul writes in Rom 3:29, "Is He the God of the Jews only? Is He not also of the Gentiles? Yes, of the Gentiles also." This declaration encapsulates the message of Scripture: God's covenant with Israel was a vehicle for his broader purpose—to reconcile the world to himself through Christ.

Ultimately, IO theology's narrow lens obscures the expansive beauty of the biblical narrative. From Genesis to Revelation, the consistent message is that YHWH's story is for the redemption of all humanity. Israel's set-apartness was not for exclusivity but to reflect God's holiness and reveal his love to the world. To confine God's purpose to one nation is to misunderstand both his nature and his mission, which encompasses all peoples, nations, and languages for his glory.

30

Our Eternal Story

And this is the promise that he hath promised us, even eternal life.

—1 John 2:25

THIS IS THE FINAL chapter of our journey, but in many ways, it feels like the beginning of a much greater story. Picture the end of a bright, radiant day, not fading into night but into an even more brilliant dawn—the warm glow of a new morning stretching across the horizon, illuminating everything with a deeper, richer clarity. As the sky shifts from gold into the lighter hues of blue, we step into the next stage of our eternal existence. It is this moment—this dawning of realization—that we find ourselves living in the present reality of God's fulfilled promises, with eternity spread before us like an open field.

We have already explored the foundations of history, from the early church fathers to the cultural forces that shaped Christian thought. We have unpacked the prophetic Scriptures, which, from a full preterist perspective, have already reached their divine fulfillment. And we have asked ourselves how to live in light of this truth—a truth that not only changes our understanding of the past but reorients our entire existence. Now, we turn our attention to the eternal trajectory of the human soul.

Section 3: Implications and "What's Next" for Full Preterism

We have, through the course of this book, unpacked the foundations of our faith. We've explored the vast sweep of church history, the cultural and theological forces that shaped early Christian thought, and the nuances of prophecy now fulfilled. We've uncovered how to live in light of the truth we've embraced—a truth that, like the soft hues of a sunset, subtly transforms everything it touches. But there remains the ultimate question that tugs at the heart of every believer: What is next? What is the eternal state of the human being?

RESURRECTION LIFE: LIVING IN THE REALITY OF THE FULFILLED PROMISES

The resurrection life, as traditionally understood in much of Christianity, is something to be awaited—a climactic moment of transformation where believers are raised from the dead to live eternally with God. But from the lens of full preterism, this resurrection life is already a present reality. The resurrection was not only a future hope for the early believers but a reality they could experience in their present spiritual life through Christ.

In this view, resurrection life is not something to come in the distant future but something we now live out. As Paul wrote to the Colossians, "If ye then be risen with Christ, seek those things which are above" (Col 3:1). This is not a distant hope; it is an instruction for the present, where our spiritual resurrection allows us to walk in newness of life. The resurrection, having occurred in Christ's own victory over death, is now shared by believers. We are part of this new creation, and this realization changes everything about how we live and view the world.

UNIVERSAL RECONCILIATION: THE GRAND RESTORATION

A central theme in the full preterist perspective is universal reconciliation. From this vantage point, reconciliation with God is not a matter of some future apocalypse or second coming; it is a reality that has already been accomplished. When Christ completed his redemptive work and the final judgment took place with the destruction of Jerusalem in AD 70, the entire cosmos was reconciled to God.

This universal reconciliation calls us not only into personal response but into a communal journey—a shared life of reflecting God's love to one another and to the world. In living out this reconciled existence, we manifest God's kingdom in our collective actions and relationships, becoming ambassadors of his grace within our communities. This communal expression of faith echoes Paul's vision of the body of Christ, unified in purpose, each member contributing to the fullness of the divine tapestry.

Paul's declaration in 2 Cor 5:19—"God was in Christ, reconciling the world unto himself"—captures the essence of this cosmic reconciliation. The world, broken and separated from God through sin, has now been brought back into alignment with its Creator. But this reconciliation isn't simply an abstract theological concept; it is the very fabric of the new-covenant reality we live in. The dividing wall between God and humanity has been obliterated, and all things have been restored.

In this dispositional sense, universal reconciliation is God's enduring stance toward humanity. There is no longer wrath, condemnation, or judgment awaiting the nations. God's heart is eternally inclined toward grace, forgiveness, and restoration. The work of Christ has forever changed the nature of the relationship between the divine and the human, and this reconciliation is universal. It applies to every person, every soul, regardless of nationality, creed, or moral standing.

HUMAN AUTONOMY AND THE RESPONSE TO GRACE

But while reconciliation has been objectively accomplished, it is not something that happens automatically to every individual. Humanity, endowed with free will and autonomy, must respond to the reality of this reconciliation. God's grace is extended to all, but it requires a personal response. Each person must decide whether to accept this divine offer or resist it.

In this tension between divine sovereignty and human responsibility lies one of the most profound mysteries of the Christian faith. The reconciliation of the world is not something God forces upon us. Rather, it is an invitation—an invitation to step into the fullness of what has already been accomplished on our behalf. As we choose to respond to God's grace, we begin to experience the subjective reality of that reconciliation. We begin to live in the truth that, from God's perspective, we have already been brought near.

And while some may resist this invitation for a time, full preterism suggests that, eventually, all will respond. Whether in this life or the next, every knee will bow and every tongue will confess the truth of Christ's lordship (Phil 2:10–11). This is not a forced submission but the natural outcome of encountering divine love. In the end, the beauty of God's grace will draw all souls into reconciliation, and the victory of Christ over sin and death will be complete.

LIVING IN THE NEW HEAVEN AND NEW EARTH: A PRESENT REALITY

One of the most transformative aspects of this theology is the understanding that we are already living in the new heaven and new earth. This is not some future state to be realized after death or at the end of time. Instead, it is a present reality—a spiritual dimension in which we currently reside. This new life in the new heaven and new earth invites us into an active, ongoing participation in the divine unfolding of creation's redemption. Each step, every choice, reflects the kingdom's values and furthers the work of divine love and restoration in the world. As co-creators with God, we build on the foundation laid by Christ, working out the implications of his reconciliation in every sphere of life—personal, relational, and societal.

The *Olam haBa*, the age to come, is not awaiting us in some distant realm; it is the air we breathe now. In a very real sense, we have already transitioned into this new creation, and our task is to live out this reality in our everyday lives. This is why Paul instructs us to "walk in newness of life" (Rom 6:4). We are not awaiting our spiritual transformation; we are actively participating in it.

This new way of living reorients us from expectation to realization. We no longer live with the tension of waiting for God's promises to be fulfilled. Instead, we live in the confident assurance that all things have already been fulfilled. We occupy the space of the new heaven and new earth, not just as a promise but as a lived experience. The cosmic drama has already been resolved, and we now play our part in the unfolding story of eternity.

EARLY UNIVERSALIST THOUGHT: THE REDEMPTION OF ALL THINGS

This new creation brings with it a profound rethinking of some of the most fundamental theological concepts, particularly the nature of hell and the scope of God's redemption.

One of the striking features of early Christian eschatology is its apparent alignment with universalist views. Inscribed in the early Christian catacombs are expressions of faith that reflect not a belief in eternal punishment but rather in the eventual restoration of all things (Hanson 1899, 104–5). This would have made little sense if early Christians thought of the afterlife as a realm where the fate of each soul was eternally fixed. Such inscriptions are evidence that, at least in certain Christian circles, the final destiny of souls was seen as open ended, with prayers for the dead commonly practiced, reinforcing the idea that postmortem change was not only possible but expected.

The theologians Clement of Alexandria and Origen, writing in the second and third centuries, championed a view of salvation that was universal in scope. Clement argued that salvation was intended for all, and Origen went further, teaching that the torments of the damned were not eternal but corrective, serving as divine chastisement to purify souls (Origen 1885b 4.6). Origen's vision of hell was more akin to a fiery furnace of refinement than an eternal dungeon, a place where souls could be purified and restored to divine communion. His view of a universal restoration (or *apocatastasis*) was grounded in the belief that God's mercy ultimately triumphs over judgment.

The dominance of universal salvation was further aided by the linguistic milieu of the early church. While Greek remained the dominant language of Christian theology, universalist thought flourished. However, as Latin began to replace Greek in the theological discourse of the Western Church, the transition brought with it misunderstandings that hardened into a more punitive eschatology. Figures like Tertullian and Augustine, steeped in Roman legalism and perhaps influenced by the pagan background of their philosophical training, misconstrued key Greek terms, promoting eternal punishment as a more fitting divine response to human sin (Hanson 1899, 120–22).

Section 3: Implications and "What's Next" for Full Preterism

THE EVOLUTION OF HELL

The Greek word *aionios*, often translated as "eternal" in modern texts, is key to understanding the theological transition that took place. Contrary to the modern understanding of eternal as "never ending," *aionios* more accurately refers to an age or an indefinite period. The term, which parallels the Hebrew word *olam*, suggests long-lasting, but not necessarily endless, periods of time (Morgan 1994, 45). In many instances in Scripture, *aionios* refers to a time that has a beginning and an end, reinforcing the idea that hell's fires are purgatorial rather than punitive (Vincent 1887, 59–60).

Prominent scholars echo the caution that should be taken when translating such terms. Morgan, for example, warns against assuming a rigid, timeless quality to the concept of eternity in Scripture (1994, 47). As he notes, the biblical vocabulary for time does not neatly align with the modern notion of eternity as endlessness. Vincent similarly points out that neither the noun *aion* nor the adjective *aionios* intrinsically means "forever" in the sense we often assume (1887, 59). Rather, these words tend to denote long durations or indeterminate periods, which may have an end point—an idea that radically alters how we view phrases like "eternal punishment."

A better understanding of these terms reveals that the early Christian vision of hell was not monolithic. Origen, Gregory of Nyssa, and others saw hell not as a final destination but as a temporary state of purification. Gregory of Nyssa famously extended Origen's ideas, arguing that all souls, even the most sinful, would eventually be reconciled to God through divine goodness (Gregory of Nyssa 1893, 5:439). Hell, in this view, was a place of transformation, not endless torment.

This perspective is reinforced by other scriptural passages that describe fire in symbolic, rather than literal, terms. Isaiah's description of Edom's burning as an "eternal fire" that would consume the land "forever and ever" is clearly symbolic, as the fire represents destruction, not perpetual existence (Isa 34:9–10). Boyd notes that such imagery is often misunderstood, leading to a more punitive interpretation of biblical texts than was likely intended (2014).

Universalism vs. Eternal Punishment

It is important to note that universalism was not a fringe doctrine in the early church. For the first five hundred years of Christianity, no official creed endorsed eternal punishment, and universalist thought was widespread. Even Origen's ideas, which were later condemned, were not considered heretical during his lifetime. It was only after the rise of Augustine and the shift towards a more rigid, Roman-influenced theology that universalism began to fall out of favor (Hanson 1899, 135–37). Augustine's background in Roman legal thought, combined with his asceticism, led him to advocate for an eternal hell as a necessary element of divine justice, though even he admitted that many Christians of his day rejected the idea of endless torment (Augustine 1996, 111–12).

The eventual condemnation of universalism, particularly during the reign of Emperor Justinian, marked a shift in Christian eschatology. However, despite efforts to quash it, universalism never entirely disappeared. Figures like Gregory of Nyssa continued to teach the doctrine, and it re-emerged in various forms throughout Christian history, often in opposition to the more punitive models that came to dominate the Western Church.

One of the key factors in this theological shift was Augustine's influence, which led to a darker and more legalistic view of the afterlife. As Latin became the dominant language of the Western Church, many of the nuances of Greek thought were lost or mistranslated, leading to a more rigid and punitive conception of divine justice. Augustine's teachings on eternal punishment laid the groundwork for future violence in the name of Christianity, justifying persecution as a means of saving souls from hell (Hart 2010a, 154).

Yet, even in the face of this shift, the seeds of universalism persisted. Scholars like N. T. Wright have highlighted the Jewish understanding of *aion* in terms of two ages: the present age and the age to come (2013, 141). In this framework, phrases like "life" or "eternal punishment" are more accurately understood as referring to life or judgment "in the age to come," rather than endless states. This Jewish context helps us to better understand the biblical vision of judgment and restoration, where God's purifying fire is not an eternal sentence but a means of refining creation.

THE REORIENTATION TOWARD RESTORATION

In many ways, the shift from universalism to eternal punishment represents a theological narrowing of God's mercy. Where early Christian thinkers like Origen and Gregory saw hell as a place of divine correction—a temporary purging process designed to restore souls to communion with God—later theologians like Augustine saw it as a place of eternal retribution, with no hope of reprieve. This reorientation has had profound consequences for how Christians understand sin, judgment, and salvation.

By revisiting the roots of universalist thought, we can recover a more hopeful vision of the afterlife—one that aligns with the biblical themes of restoration and divine mercy. As scholars have shown, the language of eternity in Scripture is far more flexible than we often assume, and many of the key terms related to judgment and punishment are better understood as referring to long periods, not endless states. This rereading of Scripture allows for a reimagining of hell as a place of refinement, not retribution—a crucible where the dross of sin is burned away, leaving behind a purified soul.

In the end, the doctrine of universalism challenges us to rethink the nature of divine justice. Is God's love not powerful enough to overcome even the most hardened sinner? Or must some souls be consigned to eternal separation? The early church, it seems, leaned towards the former. And perhaps, in our time, we can once again find hope in the idea that God's mercy truly endures forever.

A REVELATION IN THE DARKNESS: ENCOUNTERING THE EDGE OF JUSTICE

It was early 2014, during a period where my faith, though pious, was accompanied by an unsettling anxiety. Life, at that point, was relentless. I had just lost my father, and my grandmother—the family's matriarch—was on her deathbed. These two pillars of my life, the king and queen of our household, were slipping away. It was as if the solar system had lost both its sun and its moon, casting a shadow over everything. This mirrored the biblical imagery of the sun, moon, and stars no longer giving their light (Matt 24:29).

Compounding this grief, my older brother's struggles with mental health loomed large in my mind. Fear gripped me, yet, deep within, I carried an irreducible core of optimism—a fire that refused to die out no matter how dark things became. This optimism, like a red-hot ember, flickered in defiance of the gathering gloom, sustained by either divine grace or some resilient spark of human hope. But the demands on it were heavy, draining whatever reserves I had left.

That night, exhausted by these burdens and wrestling with simmering anger, I finally fell asleep, cradled by my faithful, comforting pillows. In my slumber, I found myself standing on the surface of a frozen lake, gazing at a sky framed by soft clouds, through which a portal of blue sky appeared in the shape of a love heart. I turned to someone beside me in the dream, wanting to say, "I bet heaven is like that," captivated by the serenity.

But, as if the universe sought to dispel that moment of peace, an ominous red-orange glow emerged from beneath the ice, heralding the approach of flames. Nightmares were no stranger to me, and by then, I had grown weary of these relentless tauntings. Resigned to the fire, I did not resist. Then, the most extraordinary event of my life unfolded.

Before the flames could break through the ice, the scene abruptly vanished into darkness. My eyes were closed, but I was no longer asleep. In this black void, I experienced something that transcended anything I had known before. It was as if a thought was directly placed into my mind—telepathy, perhaps, though that term seems insufficient. It was communication without sound, comprehension without words, like a thought resonating powerfully, not just heard but impressed upon me, "Not the danger of justice."

I opened my eyes, utterly still. I felt a sensation cascade down my body, like sparkling, effervescent energy, but only down my torso—not my arms or legs. After this strange, electrifying experience, I was able to move again.

In retrospect, it's easy to attribute such moments to sleep paralysis, especially considering the stress I was under. But this was different. I've experienced sleep paralysis since, and none of those episodes mirrored this occurrence. The clarity and vividness of the mental phenomenon—the "thought" impressed upon me—was unlike any mental self-talk or subconscious intuition.

"Not the danger of justice." It's an odd phrase, one that I wouldn't naturally use, yet it was unmistakably the message I received. The emphasis was on the "danger" and the concept of "justice." What was it trying to tell me? Given the hellish imagery in the dream—the flames under the ice—it seemed that the message was addressing the fear of divine punishment. Was I being told that hell, as I understood it, was not the danger of divine justice?

Perhaps. What struck me most was how my nightmare, so rooted in fear, was transformed into something sublime and revelatory. It felt as if my own incomplete thoughts had met with divine inspiration to bring about a deeper understanding. The message was one of profound peace, a reassurance that the justice of God is not about the fires of condemnation but something far more mysterious and transcendent.

Section 3: Implications and "What's Next" for Full Preterism

HUMAN CONSCIOUSNESS AND THE AFTERLIFE: A CONTINUED STORY

As we approach the concept of the afterlife, it becomes clear that the traditional understanding of heaven and hell as fixed, eternal destinations is far too limited. Instead, the afterlife is better understood as a continued life—a progression of the soul into deeper communion with God, where our consciousness, freed from the limitations of the physical body, experiences the fullness of what it means to be one with the divine.

THE FUTURE OF CONSCIOUSNESS AND THE AFTERLIFE: A NEW WAY OF BEING

One of the most profound developments in the field of consciousness studies, particularly concerning life after death, comes from the work of Dr. Jim Tucker and Dr. Bruce Greyson at the Division of Perceptual Studies at the University of Virginia. These scholars have explored near-death experiences (NDEs) and reincarnation cases, providing a scientific framework for understanding consciousness beyond the limitations of the physical body.

What their work suggests is that consciousness is not simply a by-product of the brain but may, in fact, be a fundamental aspect of reality itself. This aligns with a growing body of research that points to the idea that the brain may not generate consciousness but rather filters or mediates it. In this view, death is not the cessation of existence but a transition into a different mode of being, where consciousness continues in some form (Dossey et al. 2011).

Dr. Bruce Greyson, in particular, has documented numerous cases of individuals who, during NDEs, reported experiences of heightened awareness, even during periods when their brains showed no detectable signs of activity. This raises compelling questions about the nature of human identity and the continuity of the self beyond physical death.

Dr. Jim Tucker's work with children who report past-life memories also provides fascinating evidence that consciousness may not be confined to a single lifetime. His rigorous, methodical investigations into these cases, while leaving theological implications aside, suggest that there is much we do not yet understand about the nature of consciousness and its relationship to the physical body.

These findings resonate with the spiritual understanding that death is not the end of life but merely a transition into a fuller realization of our eternal identity. As believers, this aligns with the biblical teaching that in the afterlife, we are not transformed into something new but rather awaken to the fullness of who we already are in relation to God. As Paul writes, "For now we see through a glass, darkly; but then face to face: now I know in part; but then shall I know even as also I am known" (1 Cor 13:12). This awakening allows us to see with spiritual clarity, understanding ourselves not as mere mortals but as eternal beings already partaking in divine life.

KNOW THYSELF: THE JOURNEY WITHIN

As we move toward the conclusion of this eternal story, it is important to remember that this journey is not just about cosmic realities or abstract theological concepts—it is also a deeply personal journey. The call to know thyself, a central theme in both Christian and philosophical traditions, takes on new meaning in light of full preterism. Knowing ourselves means understanding our place in the divine story, recognizing that we are not merely passive observers but active participants in the unfolding of God's eternal plan.

This call to self-knowledge is also a call to live authentically in the reality of who we are. We are not waiting for some future event to validate our existence; we are already living in the fullness of God's reconciliation. The veil has been lifted, the barriers have been removed, and we are free to walk in the light of God's love. But this requires introspection, a willingness to face the truth of who we are and who God has created us to be.

To know thyself in the context of full preterism is to embrace the truth of reconciliation—that we are already in right standing with God, that the work of Christ has been accomplished, and that our task now is to live out this reality in our everyday lives. This is the ultimate calling of the believer: to walk in the light of the new heaven and new earth, to live in the fullness of God's grace, and to participate in the ongoing work of reconciliation and restoration.

SPIRIT AND TRUTH: THE TEXTURE OF REVELATION

Life, in many ways, is an exercise in moderating information. We are all engaged in pattern recognition—constantly weaving observations, experiences, and insights into the fabric of our relationships. Some patterns resonate with others and are built upon; others are dismissed, reshaped, or left unspoken. This dynamic, this conversational rhythm, is how we learn to refine our understanding of the world.

Even comedians, at their best, function as prophets of the absurd. They expose truths so raw and universal that they provoke laughter—not from amusement alone, but from recognition. A well-crafted joke is not just entertainment; it's a flash of insight, a moment of shared clarity about the strange coherence behind life's contradictions. But truth isn't always welcome. It can be unsettling, confrontational, even socially hazardous. That's why most of us self-censor, dilute our convictions, and hesitate to name the patterns we see too clearly.

Yet truth alone is not sufficient. Raw description is not enough, and neither is crude provocation. A sharp word may be factual, but if it lacks spirit, it can cut rather than heal. Revelation, in the highest sense, is not about lobbing facts like stones. It's about discerning something transcendent and translating it through love, wisdom, and timing. *Truth must be gathered with Spirit, or it becomes just noise.*

It's like the fog nets used in the Atacama Desert—one of the driest places on Earth. The atmosphere is saturated with moisture, but without the right instruments, it evaporates unseen. These nets, delicately woven and positioned, capture the invisible mist. The moisture condenses on the fine threads, drop by drop, until water gathers and flows. Without the net, the air remains full but barren.

So it is with divine truth. The world may be thick with revelation—God's Spirit poured out—but without the careful threads of discernment, humility, and love, it goes uncaught. Spirit and Truth are not two sides of a coin; they are the weave and weft of the same tapestry. The former gives form, the latter gives depth. Together, they create a space where what is true can also be trusted—where what is said may finally be heard.

THE ETERNAL DAWN OF GOD'S LOVE

As we draw this chapter to a close, it is important to reflect on the journey we have taken together. In the first section of this book, we explored the historical context of full preterism, examining why it was not fully embraced by the early church and how cultural influences such as Hellenism and the Enlightenment shaped theological thought. In the second section, we delved into the interpretation of prophecy, unpacking the spiritual and eschatological implications of a fulfilled view of biblical prophecy. And now, in this final section, we have turned our attention to the eternal trajectory of the human soul, exploring what it means to live in the new heaven and new earth.

But this is not the end of the story. In many ways, it is just the beginning. The eternal dawn of God's love continues to break over the horizon, calling us into deeper communion with him. We are not waiting for a future kingdom to come; we are already living in it. We are not waiting for reconciliation; we are already reconciled. And we are not waiting for eternal life to begin; it has already begun.

Our journey in the kingdom is not solely about realizing personal redemption; it is equally about building a collective life that mirrors the reality of God's love. This is the ongoing dawn of God's kingdom—a light we carry into the world, bearing the flame of love, justice, and unity as we walk alongside one another in the eternal morning of his grace. This is our eternal story. It is a story of love, reconciliation, and restoration, a story that stretches beyond time and space, inviting us to participate in the grand narrative of God's redemptive work. And as we live in this reality, we are called to walk in the light of the new day, with hearts open to the infinite possibilities of God's grace.

Appendix A

101 Statements of Imminency

1. "Repent ye: for the kingdom of heaven is at hand." (Matt 3:2)
2. "O generation of vipers, who hath warned you to flee from the wrath to come?" (Matt 3:7)
3. "And now also the axe is laid unto the root of the trees." (Matt 3:10)
4. "Whose fan is in his hand, and he will thoroughly purge his floor." (Matt 3:12)
5. "Repent: for the kingdom of heaven is at hand." (Matt 4:17)
6. "The kingdom of heaven is at hand." (Matt 10:7)
7. "Ye shall not have gone over the cities of Israel, till the Son of man be come." (Matt 10:23)
8. "Neither in this world, neither in the world to come." (Matt 12:32)
9. "For the Son of man shall come in the glory of his Father with his angels; and then he shall reward every man according to his works." (Matt 16:27)
10. "Verily I say unto you, There be some standing here, which shall not taste of death, till they see the Son of man coming in his kingdom." (Matt 16:28; see also Mark 9:1; Luke 9:27)

Appendix A

11. "When the lord therefore of the vineyard cometh, what will he do unto those husbandmen? . . . He will miserably destroy those wicked men." (Matt 21:40–41)

12. "Verily I say unto you, This generation shall not pass, till all these things be fulfilled." (Matt 24:34)

13. "Hereafter shall ye see the Son of man sitting on the right hand of power, and coming in the clouds of heaven." (Matt 26:64)

14. "The time is fulfilled, and the kingdom of God is at hand." (Mark 1:15)

15. "What shall therefore the lord of the vineyard do? He will come and destroy the husbandmen." (Mark 12:9)

16. "Verily I say unto you, that this generation shall not pass, till all these things be done." (Mark 13:30)

17. "O generation of vipers, who hath warned you to flee from the wrath to come?" (Luke 3:7)

18. "And now also the axe is laid unto the root of the trees." (Luke 3:9)

19. "Whose fan is in his hand, and he will thoroughly purge his floor." (Luke 3:17)

20. "The kingdom of God is come nigh unto you." (Luke 10:9)

21. "Be ye sure of this, that the kingdom of God is come nigh unto you." (Luke 10:11)

22. "He shall come and destroy these husbandmen, and shall give the vineyard to others." (Luke 20:16)

23. "For these be the days of vengeance, that all things which are written may be fulfilled." (Luke 21:22)

24. "Verily I say unto you, This generation shall not pass away, till all be fulfilled." (Luke 21:32)

25. "Then shall they begin to say to the mountains, Fall on us; and to the hills, Cover us." (Luke 23:30)

26. "And beside all this, today is the third day since these things were done." (Luke 24:21)

27. "I will not leave you comfortless: I will come to you." (John 14:18)

28. "If I will that he tarry till I come, what is that to thee?" (John 21:22)

101 Statements of Imminency

29. "But this is that which was spoken by the prophet Joel; And it shall come to pass in the last days, saith God." (Acts 2:16–17)

30. "He hath appointed a day, in the which he will judge the world in righteousness." (Acts 17:31)

31. "And have hope toward God . . . that there shall be a resurrection of the dead, both of the just and unjust." (Acts 24:15)

32. "Reasoned of righteousness, temperance, and judgment to come." (Acts 24:25)

33. "But for us also, to whom it shall be imputed, if we believe on him that raised up Jesus our Lord from the dead." (Rom 4:24)

34. "For if ye live after the flesh, ye shall die." (Rom 8:13)

35. "For I reckon that the sufferings of this present time are not worthy to be compared with the glory which shall be revealed in us." (Rom 8:18)

36. "For now is our salvation nearer than when we believed. The night is far spent, the day is at hand." (Rom 13:11–12)

37. "And the God of peace shall bruise Satan under your feet shortly." (Rom 16:20)

38. "The time is short." (1 Cor 7:29)

39. "For the fashion of this world passeth away." (1 Cor 7:31)

40. "Upon whom the ends of the world are come." (1 Cor 10:11)

41. "We shall not all sleep, but we shall all be changed, In a moment, in the twinkling of an eye, at the last trump." (1 Cor 15:51–52)

42. "If any man love not the Lord Jesus Christ, let him be Anathema Maranatha." (1 Cor 16:22)

43. "Not only in this world, but also in that which is to come." (Eph 1:21)

44. "Let your moderation be known unto all men. The Lord is at hand." (Phil 4:5)

45. "Which was preached to every creature which is under heaven." (Col 1:23)

46. "Which are a shadow of things to come." (Col 2:17)

47. "We which are alive and remain unto the coming of the Lord." (1 Thess 4:15)

48. "Your whole spirit and soul and body be preserved blameless unto the coming of our Lord Jesus Christ." (1 Thess 5:23)

49. "When the Lord Jesus shall be revealed from heaven with his mighty angels." (2 Thess 1:7)

50. "Having promise of the life that now is, and of that which is to come." (1 Tim 4:8)

51. "Keep this commandment without spot, unrebukeable, until the appearing of our Lord Jesus Christ." (1 Tim 6:14)

52. "Laying up in store for themselves a good foundation against the time to come." (1 Tim 6:19)

53. "This know also, that in the last days perilous times shall come." (2 Tim 3:1)

54. "I charge thee therefore before God, and the Lord Jesus Christ, who shall judge the quick and the dead at his appearing and his kingdom." (2 Tim 4:1)

55. "Hath in these last days spoken unto us by his Son." (Heb 1:2)

56. "Are they not all ministering spirits, sent forth to minister for them who shall be heirs of salvation?" (Heb 1:14)

57. "For unto the angels hath he not put in subjection the world to come." (Heb 2:5)

58. "And the powers of the world to come." (Heb 6:5)

59. "It is nigh unto cursing; whose end is to be burned." (Heb 6:8)

60. "In that he saith, A new covenant, he hath made the first old. Now that which decayeth and waxeth old is ready to vanish away." (Heb 8:13)

61. "Which was a figure for the time then present." (Heb 9:9)

62. "A high priest of good things to come." (Heb 9:11)

63. "But now once in the end of the world hath he appeared to put away sin by the sacrifice of himself." (Heb 9:26)

64. "A shadow of good things to come." (Heb 10:1)

65. "So much the more, as ye see the day approaching." (Heb 10:25)

66. "A certain fearful looking for of judgment and fiery indignation." (Heb 10:27)

67. "For yet a little while, and he that shall come will come, and will not tarry." (Heb 10:37)
68. "We seek one to come." (Heb 13:14)
69. "As they that shall be judged by the law of liberty." (Jas 2:12)
70. "Go to now, ye rich men, weep and howl for your miseries that shall come upon you." (Jas 5:1)
71. "Be patient therefore, brethren, unto the coming of the Lord." (Jas 5:7)
72. "Be ye also patient; stablish your hearts: for the coming of the Lord draweth nigh." (Jas 5:8)
73. "Ready to be revealed in the last time." (1 Pet 1:5)
74. "Who verily was foreordained before the foundation of the world, but was manifest in these last times for you." (1 Pet 1:20)
75. "Who shall give account to him that is ready to judge the quick and the dead." (1 Pet 4:5)
76. "But the end of all things is at hand: be ye therefore sober, and watch unto prayer." (1 Pet 4:7)
77. "For the time is come that judgment must begin at the house of God." (1 Pet 4:17)
78. "And also a partaker of the glory that shall be revealed." (1 Pet 5:1)
79. "Until the day dawn, and the day star arise in your hearts." (2 Pet 1:19)
80. "Their damnation slumbereth not." (2 Pet 2:3)
81. "There shall come in the last days scoffers." (2 Pet 3:3)
82. "But the day of the Lord will come as a thief in the night; in the which the heavens shall pass away with a great noise." (2 Pet 3:10)
83. "The darkness is past, and the true light now shineth." (1 John 2:8)
84. "The world passeth away, and the lust thereof." (1 John 2:17)
85. "It is the last time." (1 John 2:18)
86. "Even now are there many antichrists; whereby we know that it is the last time." (1 John 2:18)
87. "This is that spirit of antichrist, whereof ye have heard that it should come; and even now already is it in the world." (1 John 4:3)

Appendix A

88. "The Lord cometh with ten thousands of his saints, To execute judgment upon all." (Jude 1:14–15)

89. "There should be mockers in the last time, who should walk after their own ungodly lusts." (Jude 1:18)

90. "To shew unto his servants things which must shortly come to pass." (Rev 1:1)

91. "For the time is at hand." (Rev 1:3)

92. "Hold fast till I come." (Rev 2:25)

93. "I also will keep thee from the hour of temptation, which shall come upon all the world." (Rev 3:10)

94. "Behold, I come quickly: hold that fast which thou hast." (Rev 3:11)

95. "Who was to rule all nations with a rod of iron." (Rev 12:5)

96. "In her was found the blood of prophets, and of saints, and of all that were slain upon the earth." (Rev 18:24)

97. "To shew unto his servants the things which must shortly be done." (Rev 22:6)

98. "Behold, I come quickly: blessed is he that keepeth the sayings of the prophecy of this book." (Rev 22:7)

99. "For the time is at hand." (Rev 22:10)

100. "And, behold, I come quickly." (Rev 22:12)

101. "Surely I come quickly." (Rev 22:20)

Appendix B

The Lukewarm Legacy

- **Persecution of Christians by Christians (1st–4th centuries)**—Early schisms led to internal persecution of various Christian sects.
- **Persecution of pagans by Constantine (4th century)**—Pagans were persecuted under Constantine's rule after Christianity became the state religion.
- **The Council of Elvira (Canon 50) (4th century)**—Laws forbidding Christians from eating with Jews and pagans, fostering exclusion and hostility
- **The Donatist Persecution (4th century)**—The church's crackdown on Donatist Christians in North Africa, involving violence and exclusion
- **The Edict of Thessalonica (AD 380)**—Theodosius I declared Christianity the state religion, persecuting other religions and Christian sects.
- **The execution of Priscillian (AD 385)**—First known execution of a Christian heretic by the church for his gnostic teachings
- **The murder of Hypatia (AD 415)**—The church's role in inciting the brutal murder of the philosopher Hypatia by a Christian mob in Alexandria

Appendix B

- **Augustine's justification of religious persecution (5th century)**—The development of theological justification for the persecution of heretics
- **The repression of paganism (4th–6th centuries)**—Violent suppression of pagan religions throughout the Roman Empire
- **The destruction of pagan temples (4th–6th centuries)**—Churches encouraged the destruction of non-Christian religious sites throughout the Roman Empire.
- **The Codex Theodosianus (AD 438)**—Legal framework under Christian emperors that instituted persecution of non-Christians and heretics
- **The Cadaver Synod (AD 897)**—The posthumous trial and desecration of Pope Formosus, whose body was exhumed and condemned
- **Persecution of Jews during the Crusades (11th–14th centuries)**—Repeated massacres and forced conversions of Jewish communities in Europe
- **Pope Urban II's call for the First Crusade (1095)**—Led to widespread massacres of Jews and Muslims in Europe and the Holy Land
- **The People's Crusade Massacre (1096)**—Massacres of Jews across Europe by unruly crusader mobs on their way to the Holy Land
- **The Crusades (1096–1270)**—Series of religious wars, including the massacres of Jews, Muslims, and Eastern Christians in the Holy Land
- **The sack of Jerusalem (1099)**—During the First Crusade, crusaders massacred tens of thousands of Muslims and Jews in Jerusalem.
- **The suppression of the Waldensians (12th century)**—Persecution and mass killings of Waldensian Christians considered heretical
- **The Northern Crusades (12th–13th centuries)**—Christianization campaigns against pagans in the Baltic region, resulting in mass slaughter
- **The Inquisition (12th–19th centuries)**—A series of institutions and trials aimed at rooting out heresy, leading to torture and executions
- **The blood libel accusations (12th–20th centuries)**—Endorsement of false accusations that Jews murdered Christian children for rituals

- **The Albigensian Crusade (1209-29)**—Campaign against Cathar heretics in southern France, culminating in massacres such as the one at Béziers where it was said, "Kill them all, let God sort them out."
- **The siege of Béziers (1209)**—"Kill them all, let God decide," spoken by a papal legate before slaughtering twenty thousand people, Cathars and Catholics alike
- **The Children's Crusade (1212)**—Thousands of children were led to their deaths or sold into slavery during this disastrous event.
- **The massacre at Montségur (1244)**—The final defeat of the Cathars, with hundreds burned alive
- **The host desecration Trials (13th-17th centuries)**—False accusations against Jews for desecrating the Eucharist, leading to executions
- **The suppression of the Knights Templar (14th century)**—Arrest and execution of the Templars, partly motivated by church politics and greed
- **The crusade against the Serbs (13th-14th centuries)**—Violent campaigns to subdue Orthodox Christians in the Balkans
- **The burning of John Wycliffe's bones (1428)**—English theologian posthumously exhumed and burned as a heretic
- **Persecution of the Lollards (14th-15th centuries)**—Violent suppression of followers of John Wycliffe, many of whom were executed for heresy
- **The Western schism (1378-1417)**—A political and ecclesiastical crisis where two popes vied for power, resulting in violence and confusion
- **The Council of Constance (1414-18)**—Condemnation and execution of Reformers such as Jan Hus
- **The burning of Jan Hus (1415)**—Czech Reformer executed for heresy, leading to the Hussite Wars
- **The Hussite Wars (1419-34)**—Religious wars sparked by the execution of Jan Hus, with brutal suppression of his followers
- **The burning of Joan of Arc (1431)**—French peasant girl and visionary burned at the stake for heresy and witchcraft

APPENDIX B

- **The doctrine of discovery (15th century)**—Papal bulls that justified the colonization and exploitation of non-Christian lands
- **The Waldensian massacres (15th century)**—Violent suppression of the Waldensians, with many burned alive or executed
- **The witch hunts in early modern Europe (15th–18th centuries)**—The church's role in encouraging witch hunts, leading to tens of thousands of executions
- **The Spanish conquest of the Americas (15th–16th centuries)**—Mass killings and forced conversions of Indigenous peoples under the guise of Christian evangelism
- **The Alhambra Decree (1492)**—Forced expulsion of Jews from Spain after centuries of religious persecution
- **The Spanish Inquisition (1478–1834)**—Infamous for its brutal methods, including the torture and execution of thousands of Jews, Muslims, and heretics
- **The scandal of indulgences (16th century)**—The church's practice of selling indulgences, which led to the Protestant Reformation
- **The encomienda system (16th century)**—Forced labor of Native Americans in the Spanish colonies, justified by the church as part of Christianization
- **The persecution of Anabaptists (16th century)**—Thousands of Anabaptists executed by Catholics and Protestants alike for their religious beliefs
- **The smashing of icons during the Reformation (16th century)**—Iconoclastic violence by Protestants who destroyed religious artworks and symbols
- **The Scottish witch trials (16th–17th centuries)**—Hundreds of alleged witches were tortured and executed, often with church involvement.
- **The Wars of Religion (16th–17th centuries)**—A series of conflicts between Catholics and Protestants across Europe, especially in France
- **The Huguenot persecutions (16th–17th centuries)**—Violent persecution of French Protestants, including massacres and forced conversions

The Lukewarm Legacy

- **The auto-da-fé (16th–17th centuries)**—Public executions and burnings of heretics during the Spanish and Portuguese Inquisitions
- **The involvement in the African slave trade (16th–19th centuries)**—The church's tacit approval and occasional involvement in the transatlantic slave trade
- **The affair of the Placards (1534)**—French Protestants were persecuted and executed after a protest against the Mass
- **The siege of Münster (1534–35)**—Violent repression of Anabaptists in the German city of Münster by both Catholic and Protestant forces
- **The execution of William Tyndale (1536)**—English scholar executed for translating the Bible into English
- **The *Index Librorum Prohibitorum* (1559–1966)**—The church's list of banned books, suppressing scientific and philosophical works
- **The execution of Michael Servetus (1553)**—Theologian burned at the stake in Geneva for heresy, denounced by John Calvin
- **The massacre of St. Bartholomew's Day (1572)**—A series of Catholic mob killings of French Huguenots, with thousands massacred
- **The burning of Giordano Bruno (1600)**—Philosopher executed by the Roman Inquisition for heresy and advocating the infinity of the universe
- **The Thirty Years' War (1618–48)**—A brutal war between Catholic and Protestant states in Europe, with millions killed
- **The persecution of Galileo Galilei (1633)**—Tried by the Inquisition for supporting heliocentrism, forced to recant, and placed under house arrest
- **The Conventicle Act (1664)**—An English law prohibiting non-Anglican religious gatherings, leading to the persecution of dissenters
- **The affair of the poisons (1679–82)**—Scandals involving French clergy in witchcraft and poisonings, leading to executions
- **The Irish penal laws (17th–18th centuries)**—Laws restricting the rights of Irish Catholics, leading to widespread oppression and suffering
- **The Puritan witch trials (17th century)**—Witch trials in the American colonies, culminating in the infamous Salem witch trials

Appendix B

- **The Decree of Infallibility (1870)**—The First Vatican Council declared papal infallibility, a move seen as suppressing dissent and critical thought
- **The Kulturkampf (1871–78)**—Church resistance to Bismarck's attempts to reduce Catholic influence in Germany, contributing to social conflict
- **The Magdalene laundries (18th–20th centuries)**—Institutions in Ireland where women were forced into labor under the guise of rehabilitation, often abused
- **The Concordat of 1801**—Agreement between Napoleon and the church that repressed religious freedom in favor of state control
- **The anti-Protestant riots in France (19th century)**—Catholic mobs attacked Protestant communities, killing many.
- **The affair of the Ne Temere Decree (1907)**—The Catholic Church's decree on mixed marriages that caused social unrest, particularly in Ireland
- **The massacre of the Peking missionaries (1900)**—The role of missionaries in inciting violence during the Boxer Rebellion
- **Involvement in the extermination of Herero people (1904)**—Church missions' complicity in the German genocide of the Herero in Africa
- **Church involvement in the Belgian Congo atrocities (19th century)**—Allegations of missionaries' involvement in colonial violence under King Leopold II
- **The Dreyfus affair (1894)**—The church's role in supporting anti-Semitic conspiracies against Jewish officer Alfred Dreyfus in France
- **The Vatican's complicity in the ratlines (1940s)**—Church involvement in helping Nazi war criminals escape Europe after World War II
- **The concordat with Nazi Germany (1933)**—An agreement between the Vatican and Hitler's regime, giving legitimacy to Nazi rule
- **The Vatican's concordat with Fascist Italy (1929)**—Agreement between the Vatican and Mussolini's regime, lending legitimacy to the fascist government

- **The persecution of Jehovah's Witnesses in Spain (20th century)**—Religious repression under Franco's regime, with church approval
- **The Franco dictatorship (1939–75)**—The church's support of Francisco Franco's brutal regime in Spain
- **Pope Pius XII's silence during the Holocaust (1940s)**—Criticized for not speaking out more forcefully against the Nazi genocide of Jews
- **Support for European fascism (20th century)**—The church's alliances with fascist regimes, particularly in Italy, Spain, and Croatia
- **The church's silence during the Argentine Dirty War (1976–83)**—Allegations of church complicity in the repression and disappearances under Argentina's military regime
- **Involvement in the Ugandan genocide (1980s)**—Some members of the church were implicated in the violence of the Obote and Amin regimes.
- **The genocide in Rwanda (1994)**—Some church members were complicit in the genocide, with priests and nuns participating in the slaughter.
- **The cover-up of Marcial Maciel (20th–21st centuries)**—Founder of the Legion of Christ, accused of widespread sexual abuse, covered up by high-ranking officials
- **The clerical abuse scandal (20th–21st centuries)**—Widespread sexual abuse of children by clergy and subsequent cover-ups by church authorities
- **The residential schools in Canada (19th–20th centuries)**—The church's role in the forced assimilation of Indigenous children, resulting in abuse and deaths
- **Opposition to women's rights and ordination (20th–21st centuries)**—The church's resistance to women's rights, particularly in leadership and ordination

References

Aquinas, Thomas. *Summa Theologica: Part I.* Translated by Fathers of the English Dominican Province. 2nd ed. New York: Benziger Brothers, 1920.
Augustine. "Homilies on the First Epistle of John." New Advent, n.d. Translated by H. Browne. From *Nicene and Post-Nicene Fathers*, 1st ser., edited by Philip Schaff, 7:455–83 (Buffalo, NY: Christian Literature, 1888). Revised and edited for New Advent by Kevin Knight. https://www.newadvent.org/fathers/1702.htm.
———. *Enchiridion on Faith, Hope, and Love.* Translated by J. F. Shaw. Lanham, MD: Gateway Editions, 1996.
———. *The City of God.* Translated by Henry Bettenson. Penguin Classics. London: Penguin, 2003.
Aune, David E. *Revelation 1–5.* WBC 52A. Nashville: Nelson, 1997.
———. *Revelation 17–22.* WBC 52C. Nashville: Nelson, 1998.
Balthasar, Hans Urs von. *Origen: Spirit and Fire: A Thematic Anthology of His Writings.* Washington, DC: Catholic University of America Press, 2001.
Barclay, William. *The Revelation of John.* Edinburgh: Saint Andrew, 1976.
Barnard, Leslie W. *Justin Martyr: His Life and Thought.* Cambridge: Cambridge University Press, 1967.
Bauckham, Richard. *The Climax of Prophecy: Studies on the Book of Revelation.* Edinburgh: T&T Clark, 1993.
———. *The Testimony of the Beloved Disciple: Narrative, History, and Theology in the Gospel of John.* Grand Rapids: Baker Academic, 2007.
Beale, G. K. *The Book of Revelation: A Commentary on the Greek Text.* NIGTC. Grand Rapids: Eerdmans, 1999.
Berlin, Isaiah. *The Roots of Romanticism.* Edited by Henry Hardy. Bollingen Series. A. W. Mellon Lectures in the Fine Arts. Princeton, NJ: Princeton University Press, 1999.
Beyer, Bryan. "'For on Him We Depend: Considerations of Philology and Motif in Acts 17:28.'" *NovT* 66 (2024) 446–61. https://doi.org/10.1163/15685365-bja10080.
Biguzzi, Giancarlo. "Is the Babylon of Revelation Rome or Jerusalem?" *Bib* 87 (2006) 371–86. https://doi.org/10.2143/BIB.87.3.3189053.
Boyd, Gregory A. *Satan and the Problem of Evil: Constructing a Trinitarian Warfare Theodicy.* Downers Grove, IL: IVP Academic, 2001.

References

———. "Is Hell Eternal?" ReKnew, Dec. 1, 2014. https://reknew.org/2014/12/hell-and-eternal-punishment/.

Brighton, Louis A. *Revelation*. ConcC. Saint Louis: Concordia, 1999.

Brontë, Charlotte. *Jane Eyre*. London: Smith, Elder & Co., 1847.

Brown, Peter. *Augustine of Hippo: A Biography*. Rev. ed. Berkeley: University of California Press, 2000.

Bruce, F. F. *The Canon of Scripture*. Edinburgh: T&T Clark, 1985.

———. *The Epistle to the Hebrews*. Rev. ed. NICNT. Grand Rapids: Eerdmans, 1990.

Brewer, Marilynn B. "The Psychology of Prejudice: Ingroup Love and Outgroup Hate?" *Journal of Social Issues* 55 (1999) 429–44.

Bruner, Jerome. *Acts of Meaning: Four Lectures on Mind and Culture*. Cambridge, MA: Harvard University Press, 1990.

Calvin, John. *Institutes of the Christian Religion*. Translated by Henry Beveridge. Repr., Peabody, MA: Hendrickson, 2008.

Carrington, Philip. *The Meaning of the Revelation*. Eugene, OR: Wipf and Stock, 2008.

Carson, D. A. *The Gospel According to John*. Pillar New Testament Commentary. Grand Rapids: Eerdmans, 1991.

Carvalho, J. C. "The Nations Between the Angel and the Beast in the Book of Revelation." *Didaskalia* 47 (2017) 43–62.

Chilton, David. *The Days of Vengeance: An Exposition of the Book of Revelation*. Tyler, TX: Dominion, 1987.

Collins, John J. *Daniel: A Commentary on the Book of Daniel*. Hermeneia. Minneapolis: Fortress, 1993.

———. *The Apocalyptic Imagination: An Introduction to Jewish Apocalyptic Literature*. 2nd ed. Biblical Resource. Grand Rapids: Eerdmans, 1998.

———. "From Prophecy to Apocalypticism: The Expectation of the End." In *The Origins of Apocalypticism in Judaism and Christianity*, edited by John J. Collins, 129–61. Vol. 1 of *The Encyclopedia of Apocalypticism*. Grand Rapids: Eerdmans, 2000.

———. *The Apocalyptic Imagination: An Introduction to Jewish Apocalyptic Literature*. 3rd ed. Grand Rapids: Eerdmans, 2016.

Commodianus. "Instructions." Translated by S. Thelwall. In *The Ante-Nicene Fathers*, edited by Alexander Roberts et al., 4:203–23. Buffalo, NY: Christian Literature, 1885.

Corbett, Andrew. "How Will Every Eye See Him?" Andrew Corbett, n.d. https://www.andrewcorbett.net/articles/book-of-revelation/every-eye-will-see-him/.

Chrysostom, John. "Homily IV." In *Nicene and Post-Nicene Fathers*, edited by Philip Schaff, 1st ser., 8:394–97. Buffalo, NY: Christian Literature, 1889.

Daley, Brian E. *The Hope of the Early Church: A Handbook of Patristic Eschatology*. Cambridge: Cambridge University Press, 2002.

Davies, Philip R. *The Origins of Biblical Apocalyptic*. London: Continuum, 2004.

Dawkins, Richard. *The Selfish Gene*. Oxford: Oxford University Press, 1976.

DeMar, Gary. *Last Days Madness: Obsession of the Modern Church*. Powder Springs, GA: American Vision, 1999.

Descartes, René. *Meditations on First Philosophy*. Paris: Soly, 1641.

De Waal, Kayle B. "The Two Witnesses and the Land Beast in the Book of Revelation." *Andrews University Seminary Studies* 53 (2015) 9–28.

Dossey, Larry, et al. "Consciousness—What Is It?" *Journal of Cosmology* 14 (2011) 4697–711.

References

Drake, H. A. *Constantine and the Bishops: The Politics of Intolerance.* Ancient Society and History. Baltimore: Johns Hopkins University Press, 2002.
Duchesne, Ricardo. *The Uniqueness of Western Civilization.* Studies in Critical Social Sciences 28. Vancouver: Brill, 2011.
Dunn, James D. G. *The Theology of Paul the Apostle.* Grand Rapids: Eerdmans, 1998.
Ehrman, Bart D. *Lost Christianities: The Battles for Scripture and the Faiths We Never Knew.* Oxford: Oxford University Press, 2005.
Elkind, David. "Egocentrism in Adolescence." *Child Development* 38 (1967) 1025–34. https://doi.org/10.2307/1127100.
Engberg-Pedersen, Troels. *Paul and the Stoics.* Edinburgh: T&T Clark, 2000.
Evans, Craig A. *Jesus and His Contemporaries: Comparative Studies.* AGJU 25. Leiden: Brill, 2001.
Eusebius. *Demonstratio Evangelica.* Translated by W. J. Ferrar. London: SPCK, 1920.
———. *Preparation for the Gospel.* Translated by E. H. Gifford. Grand Rapids: Baker, 2002.
Eusebius of Caesarea. *Praeparatio Evangelica (Preparation for the Gospel).* Tertullian, 1903. Translated by E. H. Gifford. https://www.tertullian.org/fathers/eusebius_pe_11_book11.htm.
Faraoanu, C. I. "The Unity of God's People: The Two Witnesses in Revelation 11:3–14." *European Journal of Science and Theology* 11 (2015) 95–105.
Ferber, Michael. *Romanticism: A Very Short Introduction.* Very Short Introductions. Oxford: Oxford University Press, 2010.
Ferguson, Everett. *Backgrounds of Early Christianity.* 4th ed. Grand Rapids: Eerdmans, 2018.
Fisher, Christopher. *The Hellenization of Christianity Part I: The Pre-Christian Era.* God Is Open 5. Self-published, 2024.
Ford, J. Massyngberde. *Revelation.* Garden City, NY: Doubleday, 1975.
France, R. T. *The Gospel of Matthew.* NICNT. Grand Rapids: Eerdmans, 2007.
Frend, W. H. C. *Martyrdom and Persecution in the Early Church: A Study of a Conflict from the Maccabees to Donatus.* Oxford: Basil Blackwell, 1965.
Fugett, Eric. *A Personal Revelation.* N.p.: Today's Theophilus, 2003.
Gentry, Kenneth L. *Before Jerusalem Fell: Dating the Book of Revelation.* Atlanta: American Vision, 1998.
———. *The Beast of Revelation: Identified.* 2nd ed. Powder Springs, GA: American Vision, 2010.
Goldingay, John E. *Daniel.* WBC 30. Dallas: Word, 1989.
Gregg, Steve, ed. *Revelation: Four Views; A Parallel Commentary.* Nashville: Nelson, 1997.
Gregory of Nyssa. "Tract in Dictum Apostoli." In *Select Writings and Letters of Gregory, Bishop of Nyssa,* edited by H. Austin Wilson, in *Nicene and Post-Nicene Fathers,* edited by Philip Schaff and Henry Wace, 2nd ser., 5:439–68. Buffalo, NY: Christian Literature, 1893.
Gumerlock, Francis X. "Nero Antichrist: Patristic Evidence for the Use of Nero's Naming in Calculating the Number of the Beast (Rev 13:18)." *WTJ* 68 (2006) 347–60.
Hanson, J. W. *Universalism: The Prevailing Doctrine of the Christian Church During Its First Five Hundred Years.* Boston: Universalist, 1899.
Hare, Robert D. *Without Conscience: The Disturbing World of the Psychopaths Among Us.* New York: Guilford, 1999.

References

Hart, David Bentley. *Atheist Delusions: The Christian Revolution and Its Fashionable Enemies.* New Haven, CT: Yale University Press, 2010.

———. "God, Creation, and Evil: The Moral Meaning of *Creatio Ex Nihilo.*" *Radical Orthodoxy: Theology, Philosophy, Politics* 2 (2010) 1–17.

Hays, J. Daniel. *The Message of the Prophets: A Survey of the Prophetic and Apocalyptic Books of the Old Testament.* Edited by Tremper Longman III. Grand Rapids: Zondervan, 2016.

Hays, Richard B. *The Moral Vision of the New Testament: A Contemporary Introduction to New Testament Ethics.* New York: HarperCollins, 1996.

Hill, Charles E. *The Johannine Corpus in the Early Church.* Oxford: Oxford University Press, 2006.

Hitchcock, Mark L. "A Critique of the Preterist View of Revelation 13 and Nero." *BSac* 164 (2007) 341–56.

Holden, Janice Miner, et al., eds. *The Handbook of Near-Death Experiences: Thirty Years of Investigation.* Santa Barbara, CA: Praeger, 2009.

Hume, David. *An Enquiry Concerning Human Understanding.* London: Millar, 1748.

Irenaeus. *Against Heresies.* Translated by Alexander Roberts and William H. Rambaut. In *The Ante-Nicene Fathers*, edited by Alexander Roberts et al., 1:315–567. Buffalo, NY: Christian Literature, 1885.

Isaac, Gordon. "Martin Luther—Lesson 8: Luther's Approach to Scripture." Biblical Training, n.d. https://www.biblicaltraining.org/learn/institute/ch643-martin-luther/ch643-08-luthers-approach-to-scripture.

Jacobs, Stephen. "A Life in Balance: Sattvic Food and the Art of Living Foundation." *Religions* 10 (2018) 2. https://doi.org/10.3390/rel10010002.

John Jay College of Criminal Justice. *The Nature and Scope of Sexual Abuse of Minors by Catholic Priests and Deacons in the United States, 1950–2002.* Washington, DC: United States Conference of Catholic Bishops, 2004.

Jones, Brian W. *The Emperor Domitian.* London: Routledge, 1992.

Josephus, Flavius. *The Jewish War.* Translated by G. A. Williamson. Penguin Classics. New York: Penguin Classics, 1981.

———. *The Wars of the Jews.* Translated by William Whiston. Cambridge, MA: Harvard University Press, 1987.

Jevons, Frank B. "Hellenism and Christianity." *HTR* 1 (1908) 169–88. https://doi.org/10.1017/S0017816000003588.

Kabat-Zinn, Jon. *Full Catastrophe Living: Using the Wisdom of Your Body and Mind to Face Stress, Pain, and Illness.* New York: Delacorte, 1990.

Keener, Craig S. *A Commentary on the Gospel of Matthew.* Grand Rapids: Eerdmans, 1999.

———. *Christobiography: Memories, History, and the Reliability of the Gospels.* Grand Rapids: Eerdmans, 2020.

Kierkegaard, Søren. *Works of Love.* Translated by Howard V. Hong and Edna H. Hong. Kierkegaard's Writings. Princeton, NJ: Princeton University Press, 1995.

Klein, Isaac. *A Guide to Jewish Religious Practice.* New York: Ktav, 1989.

Koester, Craig R. "The Image of the Beast from the Land (Rev 13:11–18) A Study in Incongruity." In *New Perspectives on the Book of Revelation*, edited by Adela Yarbro Collins, 333–52. BETL 291. Leuven: Peeters, 2017.

Ladd, George Eldon. *The Presence of the Future.* Grand Rapids: Eerdmans, 1974.

Lampe, Peter. *From Paul to Valentinus: Christians at Rome in the First Two Centuries.* Minneapolis: Fortress, 2003.

References

Lane, Melissa S. *Plato's Progeny: How Socrates and Plato Still Captivate the Modern Mind.* Classical Inter/Faces. London: Bloomsbury, 2012.
Lapidge, Michael. "Stoic Cosmology." In *The Stoics*, edited by John M. Rist, 183–204. Berkeley: University of California Press, 1978.
Lewis, C. S. *The Great Divorce.* London: Bles, 1945.
———. *"The Weight of Glory" and Other Addresses.* London: Bles, 1949.
———. *"The World's Last Night" and Other Essays.* London: Bles, 1952.
Locke, John. *An Essay Concerning Human Understanding.* London: Bassett, 1689.
Long, A. A. *Epictetus: A Stoic and Socratic Guide to Life.* Oxford: Clarendon, 2002.
Marshall, I. Howard. *The Acts of the Apostles.* Leicester: Inter-Varsity, 1978.
Martens, Peter W. "Embodiment, Heresy, and the Hellenization of Christianity: The Descent of the Soul in Plato and Origen." *HTR* 108 (2015) 594–620. https://doi.org/10.1017/S0017816015000432.
McGilchrist, Iain. *The Master and His Emissary: The Divided Brain and the Making of the Western World.* New Haven, CT: Yale University Press, 2009.
McGrath, Alister. *Reformation Thought: An Introduction.* Oxford: Blackwell, 1993.
McGrath, James F. "Every Eye Shall See Him, Even Those Who Pierced Him." Patheos, Apr. 20, 2012. https://www.patheos.com/blogs/religionprof/2012/04/every-eye-shall-see-him-even-those-who-pierced-him.html.
Moody, Raymond A. *Life After Life: The Investigation of a Phenomenon—Survival of Bodily Death.* New York: Bantam, 1975.
Morgan, G. Campbell. *The Bible and the Cross.* G. Campbell Morgan Reprint Series. Eugene, OR: Wipf & Stock, 1994.
Motyer, J. Alec. *The Prophecy of Isaiah: An Introduction and Commentary.* Downers Grove, IL: IVP Academic, 1993.
Mounce, Robert H. *The Book of Revelation.* Grand Rapids: Eerdmans, 1977.
———. *Matthew.* NIBCNT 1. Peabody, MA: Hendrickson, 1993.
Muller, Ekkehardt. "The Two Witnesses of Revelation 11." *Journal of the Adventist Theological Society* 13 (2002) 1–22.
———. "The Beast of Revelation 17: A Suggestion (Part II)." *Journal of Asia Adventist Seminary* 10 (2007) 153–76.
Newton, John. *Olney Hymns.* London: Oliver, 1779.
Nickerson, Raymond S. "Confirmation Bias: A Ubiquitous Phenomenon in Many Guises." *Review of General Psychology* 2 (1998) 175–220.
Ogden, Arthur M. *The Avenging of the Apostles and Prophets: Commentary on Revelation.* 3rd ed. Pinson, AL: Ogden, 2006.
Origen. "Contra Celsus." In *The Ante-Nicene Fathers*, edited by Alexander Roberts et al., 4:395–669. Edinburgh: T&T Clark, 1885.
———. "De Principiis." In *The Ante-Nicene Fathers*, edited by Alexander Roberts et al., 4:239–382. Edinburgh: T&T Clark, 1885.
Osborne, Grant R. *Revelation.* BECNT. Grand Rapids: Baker Academic, 2002.
Pascal, Blaise. *Pensées.* Translated by A. J. Krailsheimer. Penguin Classics. New York: Penguin Classics, 1995.
Pelikan, Jaroslav. *Whose Bible Is It? A History of the Scriptures Through the Ages.* New York: Viking Penguin, 1996.
Peters, Ken. "I Saw the Tribulation (Full Version)." YouTube, May 1, 2015. From *Prophecy Club*, 2000. https://www.youtube.com/watch?v=EHtSCWCSe2Q.

References

Plutarch. "Superstition." In *Moralia*, translated by Frank Cole Babbitt, 2:493–555. LCL 222. Cambridge, MA: Harvard University Press, 1928.
Polybius. *The Histories*. Translated by W. R. Paton. London: Heinemann, 1979.
Preston, Don K. *Who Is This Babylon?* Ardmore, OK: JaDon, 2006.
———. *We Shall Meet Him in the Air: The Wedding of the King of Kings*. Ardmore, OK: JaDon, 2008.
Preus, James Samuel. *From Shadow to Promise: Old Testament Interpretation from Augustine to the Young Luther*. Cambridge, MA: Harvard University Press, 1974.
Prigent, Pierre. *L'Apocalypse de Saint Jean*. CNT 14. Paris: Delachaux et Niestlé, 1981.
Proust, Marcel. *À la recherche du temps perdu*. Paris: Gallimard, 1927.
Rankin, David. *Tertullian and the Church*. Cambridge: Cambridge University Press, 1995.
Reydams-Schils, Gretchen. *The Roman Stoics: Self, Responsibility, and Affection*. Chicago: University of Chicago Press, 2003.
Reynolds, Edward E. "The Seven-Headed Beast of Revelation 17." *Journal of Asia Adventist Seminary* 6 (2003) 93–109.
Roberts, Alexander, et al., eds. *The Ante-Nicene Fathers*. Vol. 4. Repr., Peabody, MA: Hendrickson, 1994.
Robinson, John A. T. *Redating the New Testament*. Eugene, OR: Wipf and Stock, 2000.
Russell, J. Stuart. *The Parousia: A Critical Inquiry into the New Testament Doctrine of Our Lord's Second Coming*. Grand Rapids: Baker, 1878.
———. *The Parousia: The New Testament Doctrine of Our Lord's Second Coming*. Grand Rapids: Baker, 1983.
Schaff-Herzog, J. J. *The New Schaff-Herzog Encyclopedia of Religious Knowledge*. Grand Rapids: Baker, 1911.
Schejbal, Maciej. "The Mystery of the Woman and the Beast: Rhetorical-Narrative Analysis of Revelation 17:1–18." Master's thesis, Charles University, Prague, 2018. https://dspace.cuni.cz/handle/20.500.11956/102969.
Scroggs, Robin. "The Last Adam: A Study in Pauline Anthropology." *HTR* 62 (1968) 271–88.
Seneca. *Ad Lucilium: Epistulae Moralis* [Letters to Lucilius: Moral epistles]. Translated by Richard M. Gummere. London: Heinemann, 1917.
Sider, David. *The Epigrams of Aratus*. Oxford: Oxford University Press, 2005.
Smith, Adam. *The Wealth of Nations*. London: Strahan and Cadell, 1776.
Spinoza, Baruch. *Ethics*. Amsterdam: Rieuwertsz, 1677.
Sproul, R. C. *The Last Days According to Jesus*. Grand Rapids: Baker, 1998.
Steenberg, M. C. *Irenaeus on Creation: The Cosmic Christ and the Saga of Redemption*. VCSup 91. Leiden: Brill, 2008.
Strand, Kenneth A. "The Two Witnesses of Revelation 11." *Andrews University Seminary Studies* 19 (1981) 127–35.
Sulpicius Severus. "Sacred History." In *The Ante-Nicene Fathers*, edited by Alexander Roberts et al., 7:283–309. Repr., Peabody, MA: Hendrickson, 1994.
Swete, Henry Barclay. *The Apocalypse of St. John*. London: Macmillan, 1911.
Tacitus. *The Annals of Tacitus*. Edited and translated by Alfred John Church and William Jackson Brodribb. Modern Library. New York: Modern Library, 1942.
Taylor, Charles. *Sources of the Self: The Making of the Modern Identity*. Cambridge: Harvard University Press, 1989.

References

Tertullian. "Concerning the Resurrection of the Flesh." Translated by Peter Holmes. In *The Ante-Nicene Fathers*, edited by Alexander Roberts et al., 3:545–95. Edinburgh: T&T Clark, 1869.

———. "The Prescription Against Heretics." Translated by Peter Holmes. In *The Ante-Nicene Fathers*, edited by Alexander Roberts et al., 3:245–73. Edinburgh: T&T Clark, 1869.

Thomas à Kempis. *The Imitation of Christ*. Edited by H. Houghton. Translated by A. Wright. London: Kegan Paul, Trench, Trübner & Co., 1905.

Thomas, Robert L. *Revelation 8–22: An Exegetical Commentary*. Wycliffe Exegetical Commentary. Chicago: Moody, 1995.

Toussaint, Loren L., et al., eds. *Forgiveness and Health: Scientific Evidence and Theories Relating Forgiveness to Better Health*. New York: Springer, 2015.

Tucker, J. B. *Return to Life: Extraordinary Cases of Children Who Remember Past Lives*. New York: St. Martin's, 2013.

Van Iersel, Bastiaan M. F. "The Sun, Moon, and Stars of Mark 13:24–25 in a Greco-Roman Reading." *Bib* 77 (1996) 84–92. https://doi.org/10.2143/BIB.77.1.3212124.

Van Kooten, George, et al. "How Greek Was Paul's Eschatology?" *NTS* 61 (2015) 239–53.

Victorinus. "Commentary on the Apocalypse." In *The Ante-Nicene Fathers*, edited by Alexander Roberts et al., 7:341–61. Repr., Peabody, MA: Hendrickson, 1994.

Vincent, Marvin R. *Word Studies in the New Testament*. New York: Scribner's Sons, 1887.

Voltaire. *Candide*. Paris: Sirène, 1759.

Walvin, James. *Crossing the Seas: Britain and the Abolition of the Slave Trade*. London: Reaktion, 2013.

Walvoord, John F. *The Revelation of Jesus Christ: A Commentary*. Chicago: Moody, 1997.

Watt, W. C. "666." *Semiotica* 77 (1989) 369–92. https://doi.org/10.1515/semi.1989.77.4.369.

Watts, Rikk E. "Creation, Covenant and Salvation in the Old Testament." *Journal of Biblical Studies* 27 (2000) 15–30.

Whitford, David M. "Religious Violence, Martyrdom, and Martin Luther." *Oxford Research Encyclopedia of Religion*, Dec. 22, 2016. https://doi.org/10.1093/acrefore/9780199340378.013.279.

Wilken, Robert Louis. *The Spirit of Early Christian Thought: Seeking the Face of God*. New Haven, CT: Yale University Press, 2003.

Willy, T. "Heretical, Evil, and Unbiblical: Is Full Preterism JUDGED?!" YouTube, Aug. 11, 2024. https://www.youtube.com/watch?v=Uka5iaq-zgQ.

Wilson, Mark W. "The Early Christians in Ephesus and the Date of Revelation, Again." *Neot* 39 (2005) 163–93.

Witała, Maciej. "Proposition of a Modern Theological Interpretation of Death as a Consequence of Sin." *Poznańskie Studia Teologiczne* 39 (2021) 25–47.

Witherington, Ben, III. *The Acts of the Apostles: A Socio-Rhetorical Commentary*. Grand Rapids: Eerdmans, 1998.

Wood, A. Skevington. *Luther's Principles of Biblical Interpretation*. London: Tyndale, 1963.

Wright, N. T. *Jesus and the Victory of God*. London: SPCK, 1996.

———. *John for Everyone, Part 1: Chapters 1–10*. New Testament for Everyone. Louisville: Westminster John Knox, 2004.

———. *Surprised by Hope: Rethinking Heaven, the Resurrection, and the Mission of the Church*. New York: HarperOne, 2008.

———. *Revelation for Everyone*. Louisville: Westminster John Knox, 2011.

References

———. *How God Became King: The Forgotten Story of the Gospels*. New York: HarperOne, 2012.

———. *Paul and the Faithfulness of God*. Vol. 4 of *Christian Origins and the Question of God*. Minneapolis: Fortress, 2013.

———. *The Day the Revolution Began: Reconsidering the Meaning of Jesus' Crucifixion*. New York: HarperOne, 2015.

———. *Paul: A Biography*. San Francisco: HarperOne, 2018.

———. *History and Eschatology: Jesus and the Promise of Natural Theology*. Waco: Baylor University Press, 2019.

Yarbro Collins, Adela. *Crisis and Catharsis: The Power of the Apocalypse*. Philadelphia: Westminster, 1984.

Yarmolinsky, Avrahm, ed. *Popular Poetry in Soviet Russia*. Berkeley: University of California Press, 1929.

www.ingramcontent.com/pod-product-compliance
Lightning Source LLC
Chambersburg PA
CBHW050846230426
43667CB00012B/2167